1996

GLOBAL HABIT

Paul B. Stares

GLOBAL HABIT

The Drug Problem in a Borderless World

Brookings Institution
Washington, D.C.

Copyright © 1996 by
THE BROOKINGS INSTITUTION
1775 Massachusetts Avenue, N.W., Washington, D.C. 20036

Library of Congress Cataloging-in-Publication data:

Stares, Paul B.
    Global habit : the drug problem in a borderless world / Paul B. Stares.
        p.   cm.
    Includes bibliographical references and index.
    ISBN 0-8157-8140-7 (cloth).
    1. Drug abuse. 2. Drug abuse—Prevention.   3. Substance
abuse.   4. Narcotics, Control of.   I. Title.
HV5801.S75   1996
362.29'17—dc20   95-41815
                                                                                          CIP

9 8 7 6 5 4 3 2 1

The paper used in this publication meets the minimum requirements of the
American National Standard for Information Sciences—Permanence of Paper
for Printed Library Materials, ANSI Z39.48-1984.

Typeset in Sabon with Frutiger display type

Composition by Harlowe Typography, Inc., Cottage City, Maryland

Printed by R. R. Donnelley and Sons, Co., Harrisonburg, Virginia

For Sonni

Foreword

HARDLY A WEEK GOES by without a major drug-related story in the news. Whether it is a report of a record-breaking drug seizure at the border, the arrest of a high-level trafficker, or news of yet another tragedy involving illicit drugs, there is a depressing repetition to the stories. They all reflect a problem that may wax and wane in intensity but ultimately does not go away. In recent years, moreover, it has become increasingly apparent that many more countries around the world are experiencing the same kinds of drug-related problems to which Americans have grown accustomed. The drug problem is becoming global.

Our appreciation and understanding of this transformation have nevertheless been slow. Americans are understandably more interested in what is happening in their neighborhoods than in other countries. To the extent that there is any foreign focus, it is typically directed at the sources of supply. As a consequence, the proverbial "big picture" and its inherent policy implications have gone largely unnoticed and, more important, unassessed. Even less attention has been paid to the potential evolution of the global drug phenomenon and its possible consequences.

This study by Paul B. Stares, a senior fellow in the Brookings Foreign Policy Studies program, represents the first in-depth attempt to understand the complex forces propelling and shaping the global market for drugs and to assess its likely development. His conclusions are disquieting. The situation could deteriorate considerably in the coming years, especially in many postcommunist and developing countries. In an increasingly interconnected world, we cannot remain unconcerned about the harm that a burgeoning drug trade can do to the social, political, and economic development of these countries, in addition to the challenge it presents to ongoing U.S. drug control efforts.

To meet this challenge, Stares calls for a fundamental shift in the prevailing emphasis of international drug control policy from the largely ineffectual approach of the past to one that better recognizes the realities and opportunities of the contemporary world. In addition to defining the general principles and priorities that should guide future policy, he lays out a program of practical recommendations for the international community.

Due to the wide scope of this study, the author drew on the expertise and experience of many people, to whom he is profoundly grateful. In particular, he would like to thank Lieutenant Commander Stephen E. Flynn of the U.S. Coast Guard Academy, a former guest scholar at Brookings, who helped conceive the project and carry out some of the basic research while also contributing to three workshops that were convened in 1994 to discuss the nature of the problem.

The participants at the workshops, who provided many useful insights and valuable guidance to the project, were Arthur Alterman, Sergei Avdienko, Bruce Bagley, Jack Blum, Michael Brown, Ralph Bryant, Doris Buddenberg, Michael Campbell, Richard Clayton, John Coleman, William Davnie, Frank de Man, John Deal, Ernest Drucker, Jim Engleman, Georges Estievenart, Cindy Fazey, Carl Florez, George Gerbner, Arthur Gibson, Mathias Hutfless, Charles Intriago, Alison Jamieson, Klaus Jansen, Helene Kaufman, Douglas Keh, Nicholas Kozel, Alain Labrousse, Rensselaer W. Lee III, David Lodge, Alan Lopez, Wallace Mandell, Jessica Tuchman Mathews, Martin Mayer, Larry McEllynn, George Moffett, Stephen Morse, David Musto, Ethan Nadelmann, Norman Nelson, Karen Nersesyan, Nikos Passas, Greg Passic, Raphael Perl, Wolfgang Reinicke, Peter Reuter, Richard Rivers, Daniel Romer, James Rosenau, Ernesto Savona, Louise Shelley, Rainer Schmidt-Nothen, Brian Sheridan, John Steinbruner, Kalman Szendrei, Mateen Thobani, Francisco Thoumi, Francis Tims, LaMond Tullis, Hilde Van Lindt, David Westrate, and Phil Williams. The support of the Walter Annenberg School for Communication at the University of Pennsylvania, which hosted the second of the three workshops, is also gratefully acknowledged.

In addition, the author received generous assistance from the United Nations International Drug Control Program in Vienna, the Drugs Unit of the Commission of the European Communities in Brussels, the ICPO-INTERPOL in Lyons, the Pompidou Group of the Council of Europe in Strasbourg, the Customs Cooperation Council in Brussels, the Observatoire Geopolitique des Drogues in Paris, and the U.S. Drug Enforcement Adminstration and the National Institute on Drug Abuse, both in Washington. The DEA's library and its director, Mort Goren, were invaluable resources throughout the project. Furthermore, during an extensive research visit to Europe, Humphry Crum-Ewing, affiliated with the Centre for Defence and International Security Studies of Lancaster University, opened many useful doors in London.

The author would also like to thank John Coleman, Rensselaer W. Lee III, LaMond Tullis, and Phil Williams for painstakingly reviewing early drafts of the study. Valuable comments were also received from Marc Eliany, Cindy Fazey, Alison Jamieson, and Peter Reuter. Bruce Blair, Martin Binkin, Joshua M. Epstein, and Thomas L. McNaugher provided additional support, encouragement, and advice. Finally, an immense debt of gratitude is owed to Sonni Efron for her ready wisdom, unstinting support, and patient forbearance at critical junctures.

The final manuscript was edited by Nancy D. Davidson and its factual content verified by Andrew Solomon. Charlotte Hebebrand, Scott Kennedy, and Daniel Turner provided research assistance. Susan L. Woollen prepared the manuscript for publication, and Max Franke prepared the index. At different times Annette Leak, Maureen Merella, and Trisha L. Brandon also provided adminstrative assistance. To each, the author gives thanks.

Funding for the study was provided in part by the Carnegie Corporation of New York, the John D. and Catherine T. MacArthur Foundation, and the National Institute of Research Advancement in Japan, to which the Brookings Institution extends its gratitude.

The views expressed in this book are solely those of the author and should not be attributed to the persons or organizations whose assistance is acknowledged, or to the trustees, officers, or other staff members of the Brookings Institution.

Michael H. Armacost
President

January 1996
Washington, D.C.

Contents

1 | The Global Drug Challenge

W HAT WAS ONCE CALLED "the American disease" is fast becoming a global habit.[1] By all
indications, the market for illicit drugs is expanding inexorably around
the world. Simply put, more kinds of drugs are becoming more available in more places than ever before. Indeed, there are few, if any,
countries that have not registered growing concern about the expansion of the drug trade in recent years.[2] The rising apprehension felt
around the world, however, stems from the changing character of the
problem as much as from its increasing dimensions. The drug trade
has ceased to be a marginal area of criminal activity and has now
become a major global enterprise controlled by formidable interests
that threaten much more than the health of those who consume psychoactive substances. Moreover, there are good reasons to fear that
the global market for drugs will continue to expand in the foreseeable
future, with potentially serious consequences for many countries and
communities around the world.

There are few businesses—licit or illicit—that are more lucrative
than the drug trade. The Organization for Economic Cooperation and
Development calculates that as much as $122 billion is spent each year
in the United States and Europe on heroin, cocaine, and cannabis—
the most popular illicit drugs.[3] Of this, 50 to 70 percent, or as much

1

as $85 billion, is estimated to be laundered and invested in other enterprises. If this figure is true, the rewards of the drug trade are larger than the gross national product of three-fourths of the 207 economies of the world.[4] Estimates of the value of all global retail sales of illicit psychoactive substances range between $180 billion and more than $300 billion annually, making the drug trade one of the biggest commercial activities in the world.[5]

The growth of the international drug trade from what was in essence a cottage industry into the enormous business enterprise that it is today can be traced to the massive surge in the demand for mind-altering drugs that occurred in the United States and Western Europe during the 1960s and 1970s. This in turn triggered an equally dramatic expansion in the worldwide production of illicit drugs during the 1970s and especially the 1980s.[6] As output expanded, the amount seized by police and customs officials also rose steadily, although the proportion of seized drugs to the totals being produced probably stayed the same, judging by the price and purity levels in key markets.[7]

In the process, the drug trade became deeply rooted in certain regions. The cultivation of opium poppy and its subsequent processing into morphine and heroin is now heavily concentrated in the "Golden Triangle" countries of Southeast Asia (Laos, Thailand, and Myanmar—formerly Burma) and the "Golden Crescent" countries of Southwest Asia (Afghanistan, Pakistan, and Iran). Meanwhile, coca cultivation is carried out almost exclusively among the Andean countries of South America (Peru, Bolivia, and Colombia), while around 70 percent of the subsequent processing into cocaine takes place in Colombia. In contrast, cannabis cultivation and the production of its principal derivatives, marijuana and hashish, has remained more geographically dispersed, although some countries have emerged as significant source areas for the international market. Afghanistan, Pakistan, Lebanon, and Morocco, for example, are major hashish producers, while Mexico, Jamaica, Colombia, and Thailand are leading marijuana exporters. Similarly, the illicit manufacture of synthetic stimulants, depressants, and hallucinogens has also sprung up in many places around the world, with certain countries dominating the supply of particular regional markets. During the 1970s and 1980s new trafficking groups also emerged and expanded their operations internationally, notably the Colombian cocaine cartels, the Turkish heroin syndicates, and, more recently, the ethnic Nigerian organizations.

Emerging Trends

Since the late 1980s several new trends in the global drug market have become discernible.

Drug Production. The cultivation of opium poppy and coca in the main source areas has apparently leveled off and in some areas may even have decreased, although this may be the temporary result of bad weather and crop disease.[8] In addition, there are reports that processing efficiencies continue to improve in some areas and that coca farmers in Bolivia and Colombia have raised their average per hectare yield.[9] There are also numerous reports that drug cultivation has migrated to adjoining areas or sprung up in entirely new regions, such as the former Soviet republics of Central Asia. Production in these areas may or may not be included in the overall estimates. Meanwhile, worldwide cannabis production—to the extent that it can be gauged—appears to be undiminished and is probably expanding. It is also noteworthy that cannabis growers in North America and western Europe have been steadily increasing the amount of tetrahydrocannabinol (THC)—the mind-altering component—in their product. Finally, the production of illicit synthetic drugs is apparently continuing to expand, judging by their increased availability on the world market.

There are signs, furthermore, that drug production is becoming even more entrenched in key areas. Some of the established drug producers have diversified into other products. Colombia, for example, has become a source of heroin, while opium fields have been found recently in Peru.[10] Similarly, Lebanon, known more for hashish and heroin refinement, has evidently developed a capacity to process cocaine base. Meanwhile, some sectors of the drug industry are integrating forward in the supply chain to gain more of the value added. Thus the farmers of Bolivia and Peru are apparently increasingly involved in processing coca leaves into cocaine base and even fully refined cocaine.[11] Similarly, Afghani drug suppliers are developing the capacity to refine the opium they cultivate, while Turkish trafficking syndicates are evidently processing more of the heroin they subsequently distribute.

Drug Trafficking. As noted at the outset, the growing availability of an expanding array of drugs shows no sign of declining in the main markets, despite record seizures by law enforcement authorities.[12] Part of the reason is that the major trafficking organizations increasingly transport drugs in high-volume commercial conveyance systems like container ships and tractor trailers, as well as long-range jet aircraft, so that it is no longer uncommon for multi-ton deliveries to take place.[13] New trafficking groups also continue to emerge to replace or join the ranks of existing ones. Although their organizational sophistication and business acumen still vary considerably, the overall standard, by all accounts, continues to improve. This is evident in such areas as drug processing and transportation, operational security, product marketing, money laundering, and the use of technologies to evade law enforcement. Whereas high-level drug-trafficking organizations typically specialized in distributing one kind of drug, a growing number now seem to market several. Cooperative arrangements, if not formal alliances, between trafficking groups have also become more common, principally to exploit comparative advantages and opportunities in different functional and geographic areas, to share and minimize risks, and generally to expand into new markets.[14]

Drug Consumption. Although the North American and western European markets continue to be the largest in both the number of consumers and aggregate financial value, the overall number of people taking drugs has fallen since the early 1980s. This general trend masks a more complex picture, however. The number of regular "hard core" drug users in the United States has apparently not fallen and may even have grown.[15] The popularity of some drugs has also increased in some cities, judging from local epidemiological reports, while drug use among young adolescents also now appears to be rising.[16] Trends are harder to discern in Europe, given the heterogenous nature of the market. Amid reports of generally stable or declining levels of drug use are others that indicate that the problem has grown worse in certain areas, especially some inner-city neighborhoods, and that some drugs, particularly synthetic types, have become more fashionable.[17]

Elsewhere, the general trend appears to be one of growth. Almost all the formerly communist countries of central and eastern Europe, as well as the successor states of the Soviet Union undergoing the transition from communism to the free market, have reported rising levels of drug consumption following the end of the cold war. The same is apparently also true in China. Judging by press reports and some scientific surveys, drug consumption is rising in many parts of the developing world, particularly in those areas close to the main production zones and along the principal transit routes to the United States and western Europe. This has been evident in Latin America, Southeast Europe, East Asia, and Africa. Large domestic markets have also developed in some countries, such as Pakistan, Iran, and, to a lesser extent, Thailand. Although the consumption of mind-altering substances is hardly a novel phenomenon in many of these areas, the increasing use of the refined product of drug crops that were domestically cultivated and previously destined for foreign markets is a relatively new trend.[18]

Globalization and the Drug Trade

These trends can be seen as the result of the interaction of local events and much larger global processes that are progressively bringing the world closer together while simultaneously diminishing the ability and, paradoxically in some cases, the willingness of states to exercise their sovereign prerogatives to control what comes across their territorial borders and what takes place within them. Revolutionary advances in communications, transportation, and information technology have made it possible for goods, services, people, information, and ideas to travel across international boundaries with unprecedented speed and efficiency. As the natural barriers to trade and travel have fallen, economic and political ones have had to follow suit in a self-reinforcing process.[19] In order to stay competitive and sustain growth, many states have embarked on wholesale privatization and deregulation of their economies and simultaneous reduction of border controls and trade tariffs. Although these trends are most advanced in the European Union, they are also taking place in almost every region of the world. Similarly, the imperatives unleashed by these same forces undoubtedly hastened the end of the cold war and the demise of communism. The political events that prompted the fall of the Berlin Wall were the culmination of the same undercurrents that progressively made socialism and centrally planned economies untenable in the modern world. The net result, as some have observed, is a world that is becoming increasingly "borderless," in which nongovernmental or "transnational" actors play an ever-growing role in shaping the social, political, and economic life of the planet.[20]

The drug trade, as a consequence, has increasingly become a transnational phenomenon, driven and fashioned in critical ways by transnational forces and transnational actors.[21] Thus the global diffusion of technical expertise and the internationalization of manufacturing have made it possible to cultivate and refine drugs in remote places of the world and still be within reach of distant markets. And just as legitimate transnational entrepreneurs have been able to exploit the opportunities of a globalizing free market economy, so have criminal ones, particularly drug-trafficking organizations.[22] The expansion in trade, transportation networks, and tourism has not only made it easier for them to distribute drugs to the long-established markets of North America and western Europe, but it has also opened up new parts of the world to exploit. The growing integration of the global financial system, moreover, with its rapidly expanding array of services and instruments, has also provided traffickers with many more opportunities to launder money and invest in other activities—licit or illicit. This is especially true in the embryonic but still poorly regulated financial systems of postcommunist and developing nations. And finally, expanding personal mobility and, in particular, the growth of the mass media and global telecommunications have undoubtedly increased the global awareness of drugs and propagation of drug fashions around the world.

The effects of these global trends on the drug trade show no signs of abating. On the supply side, the economic incentives to cultivate and manufacture drugs—because of the livelihood they provide where few alternatives exist—will most likely continue to exert a powerful influence in the key source areas of the world. Given the desperate conditions that will almost certainly prevail as a consequence of overpopulation, environmental degradation, chronic underdevelopment, and civil strife in many parts of the developing world, similar pressures will most likely be present elsewhere. At the same time, powerful interests in the form of the drug-trafficking organizations will surely seek to sustain and extend the global habit for psychoactive drugs because of the immense profits that can be made. They have already created de facto sanctuaries in many countries where state authority is nonexistent or weak and therefore vulnerable to corruption and intimidation. The wealth amassed from selling drugs has lent them enormous power to perpetuate this process, allowing them to further orchestrate their operations with virtual impunity. Given the breakdown of law and order in many areas of the world, the opportunities to create such sanctuaries can also be expected to increase. Indeed, the overthrow or removal of central governmental authority could become an increasingly common motive for drug trafficking. Separatist groups and terrorist organizations in such diverse places as Peru, Colombia, Afghanistan, Pakistan, Lebanon, Northern Ireland, Somalia, and Turkey are now believed to purchase weaponry and supplies with money derived from the drug trade.

The ability to market drugs locally and globally is also likely to increase, given current trends in the creation of free trade zones and the general extension of cheap and efficient transportation systems worldwide. In the postcommunist world, diminished border surveillance and weakened law enforcement are providing more opportunities to smuggle drugs to the West and establish local distribution networks. As local currencies become convertible, these countries' attraction for drug traffickers will only grow. There is also no reason to expect a contraction in the supply of desperate people willing to risk legal sanctions to transport and distribute drugs, particularly within immigrant communities and in the increasingly overcrowded cities of the developing world.

Combined with the growing incentives and opportunities to supply illicit drugs, equally strong undercurrents are converging to increase the level of demand in many areas of the world. As noted earlier, there are recent indications that the downward trend of the last decade in the United States and western Europe has stalled and drug use is now moving in the opposite direction, at least among teenagers. With a new wave of teenagers expected to crest at the turn of the century as the children of the baby boom generation reach adolescence, there will be many more people in the age group generally considered to be at the greatest risk of taking drugs.[23] Given other social and economic trends as well as the likelihood that drugs will become even more available, overall consumption could increase significantly.

The rising level of drug use in the postcommunist countries of Europe and Asia also seems likely to continue, at least in the short term. For the reasons discussed above, a wider range of drugs is becoming more available to many more people. Their attraction also seems undiminished, for various reasons. Not only do Western fashions and lifestyles have a strong influence on the youth culture of the postcommunist world, but social and economic upheavals are causing many people to experience the feelings of frustration, despair, ennui, and personal loss that have frequently motivated others elsewhere to take drugs. At the same time, the same changes are undermining many of the formal and informal social controls that can help constrain drug use.

In the developing world, the prospects do not look any better, and they may turn out much worse over the long term. Several trends could precipitate a major surge in the demand for illicit drugs. The most ominous is the explosive growth in the world's population that is anticipated to occur over the next twenty-five to fifty years, mainly in the poorest countries. This has several implications. Not only will there be many more people at risk of taking drugs, but, because of the resultant social and economic pressures, many of them will live in dire conditions that could make drug use and trafficking especially appealing. At the same time, the environmental degradation, poverty, unemployment, overcrowding, and general hopelessness that could motivate people to take drugs are likely to erode protective social controls. Ethnic strife and other types of conflict, which have become more common in these parts of the world, will only exacerbate this process. Together, these factors point to the likely emergence of large regional markets supplied by local sources of production.

Judging by the experience of countries that have suffered significant levels of illicit drug use, the social and economic costs to society will be considerable. The damage to public safety, economic productivity, and citizens' personal health, educational accomplishment, professional advancement, and social relationships can be enormous. These are burdens that any country would rather not have to bear, especially those struggling to raise their general level of development while adapting to democracy and the free market.

However, it is the threat that an expanding global drug market poses to the integrity and legitimacy of governments and public institutions, as well as to the prosperity and stability of communities, that is the cause for the greatest concern. Although the illicit drug industry has provided employment and subsistence to many in the principal source countries, its overall effect on their economic development is widely considered to have been detrimental. Moreover, many countries in the developing and postcommunist world are ill prepared and institutionally too weak to resist the drug traffickers' insidious encroachment. As past experience has demonstrated, once these criminal organizations become embedded in a particular area, they are exceedingly difficult to dislodge. Not only are they able to consolidate their power through public corruption, but they often branch out into other criminal enterprises, spreading their roots and enhancing their power base in the process. In numerous cases, trafficking groups have even managed to infiltrate national political institutions and co-opt public officials at the highest levels. Recent events in Mexico and Colombia illustrate how widespread and pernicious this process can become. The presence and influence of these groups further delegitimize the state while undermining its economic and political development. As noted above, in many areas drug trafficking has also become an increasingly common way to underwrite violent challenges to state authority for political purposes.

These are serious implications, not just for the countries that appear to be most at risk from an expansion of the global drug market, but also for the United States and western Europe. In an increasingly interdependent world, the adverse effects of the drug trade in distant places could reverberate in unpredictable and unwelcome ways. The West has a great deal to lose if former communist states and developing countries come under the influence of criminal organizations or are destabilized as a result of political movements underwritten by profits from the drug trade. Neither is it in the interests of the West to see the power and influence of drug-trafficking organizations grow and extend into other types of transnational crime such as illegal immigration and arms smuggling.

Meeting the Challenge

Despite these ominous trends and implications, the potential evolution of the global drug market and the problems this may bring have received little, if any, systematic attention among drug policymakers and relevant experts. To my knowledge, no in-depth forward-looking assessment has been carried out. In fact, despite rising worldwide concern, basic appreciation of the drug problem as a *global* phenomenon remains poorly developed. Although there have been numerous studies and extensive research on the foreign or international dimensions of the drug phenomenon, their focus has by and large been narrow. Such studies have typically concentrated on one component, such as the cocaine or heroin trade or the operations of particular drug-trafficking groups.[24] To the extent that broader, more inclusive international assessments have been undertaken, they have either focused on a specific region or have been collections of individual country profiles.[25] In the process, important linkages between different components of the drug trade and between different regions of the world have either gone unrecognized or have not received the attention they deserve. Similarly, while many studies acknowledge the relationship between the drug phenomenon and its immediate social, political, or economic context—for example, underdevelopment, unemployment, urban decay, and youth culture—the extent to which it is propelled and shaped by much broader global forces of the type described above has barely been noticed, let alone understood.

Greater understanding of the problem is also not helped by the general inclination of most drug-related studies to focus on either the supply or demand aspects of the phenomenon, but rarely on both. Thus discussions of rising drug production in a particular area or of new international trafficking patterns frequently contain little or no reference to what might be influencing the demand and vice versa. Likewise, production estimates, seizure and arrest statistics, and polling data on consumption are rarely compared to test hypotheses, uncover anomalies, or detect changing patterns of behavior.[26]

These fundamental shortcomings are understandable up to a point. The subject encompasses a vast and extremely complex set of activities that cut across social, economic, ethnic, national, and regional boundaries and involve an enormous and continually expanding range of mind-altering substances. The temptation to focus on the specific rather than the general is extremely strong. The disciplinary fragmentation of most academic studies and policy analysis reinforces this inclination. Government-sponsored assessments are generally no different. The standard partition of most bureaucracies ensures that only those aspects of the problem that directly affect the sponsor's interests are studied. Since bureaucracies usually respond to existing problems rather than anticipate new ones, forward-looking assessments are rare. Even in the drug control agencies of international organizations like the European Union and the United Nations, which possess a natural constituency and an underlying imperative for broad-based assessments, the results have generally been disappointing.

The single greatest barrier to better understanding of the drug problem, however, remains the paucity of good information.[27] It is hard to think of a public policy issue of comparable significance for which the data are so bad and the methodological barriers to getting better information are so high. The illicit nature of drug production, trafficking, and consumption obviously limits what can be observed and measured. For example, it is relatively easy to identify specific countries as the main source of certain types of drugs, either because large areas have been observed under cultivation or because large quantities of drugs have been seized in or close to these areas. The precise amounts being cultivated and subsequently refined, however, remain a mystery. Sometimes the estimates differ by such wide margins that their validity becomes especially suspect. Production estimates, moreover, have been notoriously manipulated to serve policy preferences and to demonstrate programmatic success.[28] Some regions have also received closer scrutiny and assessment than others, which has produced major variations and even gaps in the level of information. For example, the principal collector of intelligence, the United States, has concentrated heavily on assessing the production of cocaine, the drug that is of most concern to Americans.

Consequently, less attention has been given to the opium-producing areas of the world.

Trafficking data are not much better. Some idea of emerging trafficking patterns can be gained from seizure reports, but no one has a firm idea of what proportion of the total amount being transported has been seized. Competing law enforcement agencies have also been known to claim credit for the same drug seizure, resulting in double accounting.[29] The final destination of the confiscated drugs is also difficult to determine, since trafficking organizations often use very circuitous routes to avoid law enforcement and a single shipment can be distributed to many different places. Informants and criminal prosecutions sometimes reveal more information, but the picture is typically incomplete and murky. The key personnel and operating practices of these organizations change frequently, making such information highly perishable.

And finally, although consumption of illicit drugs has been observed almost everywhere in the world, very little is known about how much is consumed and by whom. The United States has probably carried out the longest and most intensive monitoring of drug street prices and consumption levels anywhere in the world. Western Europe, Canada, and Australia have also initiated comprehensive data collection programs. Even so, precious little is understood about what motivates some people and not others to consume drugs. It is stunning, for example, to find how little research has been conducted on the elasticities of demand.[30] Beyond the advanced industrialized countries, in the nations now at the greatest risk, the level of knowledge drops precipitously. Many of the countries that are obliged to report annually to the United Nations on the state of drug control efforts fail to do so, while many more file incomplete information.[31]

With general understanding of the global drug phenomenon so poorly developed, it is no surprise that there has also been little or no effort to consider whether current international drug control efforts are appropriate to meet the likely challenge ahead. Judging by how poorly these efforts have succeeded to date, the signs are not encouraging, to say the least.

Since the early 1900s the international community, led most forcefully by the United States, has attempted, through the progressive extension of international conventions and domestic legislation, to prohibit and suppress the market for illicit drugs. This global prohibition regime has entailed far-reaching and costly efforts to eradicate illegal drug cultivation and destroy the drug-processing centers, to intercept smuggled drug shipments before they reach the main retail markets, and to deter drug traffickers and consumers alike with the threat of legal penalties that have varied in severity around the world. As such, the global prohibition regime has become overwhelmingly biased toward the application of sanction-based or "negative control" measures to deter or deny participation in the global drug market. In contrast, reward-based or "positive control" measures—such as those that have attempted to improve the economic alternatives for those engaged in drug production, discourage drug use through education and mass education programs that emphasize the benefits of healthy drug-free lifestyles, and treat those who have succumbed to drug addiction so that they may reestablish productive lives—have been pursued belatedly and in a generally limited manner.

The overwhelming approach to international drug control has clearly failed in its ultimate objective, as the global market has continued to expand. Many of the negative control measures have also been perversely counterproductive. Illicit drug production and trafficking, as noted above, have adapted to the forces of prohibition by gravitating to areas of the world where the ability of governments to enforce drug control policies is limited, if not hopeless. Drug smugglers have also grown more sophisticated and adept at developing new routes and methods as old ones are exposed and countered. Meanwhile, enough drug consumers have remained undeterred by law enforcement to generate the necessary demand.

Some believe that the rising level of concern around the world and the end of the cold war have opened up major opportunities to improve international cooperation and make the current global prohibition regime truly effective.[32] There is something to be said for this. During much of the 1970s and 1980s, growing friction and resentment between the net "consumer" countries of the advanced industrialized world and the net "producer" countries of the developing world did not help matters. The former felt that not enough was being done to curb supply of the drugs at the source or in transit, while the latter felt that they were powerless to do anything while the currents of demand remained so strong. No doubt some in the developing world believed that the drug trade brought welcome employment and income to many poor areas and that the repatriated profits represented a fair redistribution of wealth from the first world to the third world. In Latin America, these arguments were colored, moreover, by suspicions that the U.S.-inspired antidrug crusade was just the latest brand of "Yanqui imperialism." The politics of the cold war was also never far below the surface. On numerous occasions the United States showed little hesitation to sacrifice the goal of drug control on the altar of superpower geopolitics.[33] Meanwhile, the orthodox communist line throughout most of this period was that drug abuse was a decadent capitalist or Western vice that simply did not exist behind the iron curtain, a belief that some Islamic countries would later echo.

The convergence of concern and the end of the cold war have undoubtedly improved the climate for international drug control cooperation. Yet there is little reason to believe that more of the same will prove any more successful in the future than in the past—quite the contrary. For as long as the incentives and opportunities to participate in the drug market remain so high, the dominant emphasis on negative drug control measures is unlikely to succeed and may only make matters worse. Drugs can be produced too easily in too many places for source-country suppression efforts to have any significant or sustained effect on the worldwide supply of drugs, certainly while the demand exists. Likewise, drugs can be smuggled too easily in too many ways for interdiction efforts to have any sustained or significant effect on market availability—again, while the demand exerts such a powerful draw. And finally, the sale and consumption of drugs can take place too easily and in too many places to be effectively stopped by law enforcement or permanently deterred by the imposition of harsher penalties. Given the trends in the growth of global trade, tourism, personal mobility, and financial transactions, the task confronting police and customs officials is unlikely to get any easier.

Unfortunately, the international community seems as habituated in its response to the drug problem as many addicts are to their drug of choice. Furthermore, despite ample evidence of the transnational qualities of the drug problem and the erosion of national sovereignty by many of the global processes described above, international drug control efforts, particularly in the area of law enforcement, continue to be encumbered by the need to observe the traditional legal prerogatives and territorial precepts of the nation-state as if nothing had changed. Ironically, the transnational trafficking organizations are able in many respects to operate more extensively and freely than state actors that have more resources and legitimacy.[34]

By focusing on the drug problem as a global phenomenon and bringing much-needed attention to its likely evolution, the ultimate purpose of this book is to promote a fundamental reorientation of current international drug control policies so that they may better meet the challenge ahead. This does not entail what might be concluded from the brief appraisal above, namely, the removal of prohibitionist controls and the "legalization" of the illicit drug trade—certainly not until a great deal more study has been carried out. While offering the tantalizing prospect that some of the most pernicious features of the black market for drugs—notably its crime, corruption, and violence—would end overnight, legalization would most likely entail considerable regulation that would raise serious doubts about how it would be implemented and, moreover, whether many of its putative benefits would actually be realized. Too many critical questions still remain either unanswered or unanswerable, short of implementation, for this option to be responsibly proposed. Ultimately, it might just substitute one set of problems for another that has equal if not greater costs to society.

What is proposed here, beyond a call for monitoring and analyzing the evolution of the global drug phenomenon more rigorously and comprehensively, is placing the primary emphasis of international drug control on positive rather than negative control measures. This is not the same as substituting demand reduction for supply reduction, although minimizing the level of drug consumption to tolerable levels is the ultimate objective. It also does not mean abandoning many of the international law enforcement programs designed to combat drug trafficking. The international community should continue to target these and other forms of organized crime to prevent the accumulation of threatening levels of wealth and power. In doing so, states will have to recognize that their slavish devotion to safeguarding national sovereignty is not only increasingly meaningless in a borderless world but also a major hindrance to collective international action. This applies equally to many other transnational problems such as illegal migration, terrorism, environmental degradation, and the illicit arms trade. Although each is different in its own way, they all transcend the ability of any one state to solve them. In this respect, the general approach advocated here for responding to the illicit drug trade could have much broader application to many similar problems that also appear likely to grow more prominent in the twenty-first century.

2 | The Rise of the Global Drug Market

TODAY'S GLOBAL MARKET for illicit drugs is the product of a complex evolutionary process that began in the early years of this century. Although historians and anthropologists rightly point out that mind-altering drugs have been traded and consumed since antiquity, it was not until the twentieth century that this activity gained its distinctly illicit character. In response to growing public alarm over high levels of drug use and addiction in America, Europe, and parts of Asia, the great powers took their first steps to control what they had previously sanctioned and, in some cases, actively promoted. Through a series of international conventions buttressed by domestic laws, the production, sale, and consumption of a wide range of drugs for anything other than medical and scientific purposes were progressively prohibited around the world.

What had started out, however, as a campaign to control a legal, albeit unregulated, area of commerce became increasingly directed at suppressing the illicit trade in drugs that sprang up in the wake of prohibition. Restricting public access to drugs produced the intended result of reducing consumption, but it did not entirely eliminate the demand for drugs. Criminal enterprises, drawn by the promise of black market profits, soon filled the vacuum left by legal suppliers. It was not until a mass market for drugs in America and Western Europe arose during the 1960s and

1970s, however, that the illicit drug trade became a serious source of international concern rather than a relatively minor irritant. Largely at the urging of the United States, the global prohibition regime was subsequently strengthened and broadened to include a wider range of drugs while efforts were stepped up to disable the international trafficking networks and eradicate production at the source. The few successes proved short lived, however, as the global drug market adapted to each new assault and became larger, better organized, more efficient, and, above all else, highly profitable. This process will become clear in the following historical account of the rise of the global drug market, which is broken up arbitrarily into five phases that correspond with key stages in the evolution of the international drug trade and the creation of the global prohibition regime from 1900 to the present day.

Origins of Prohibition, 1900–45

To understand the origins of prohibition requires briefly examining the rise of the international drug trade before 1900.[1] Although opium had been traded for centuries in the Middle East and parts of Asia, it was not until the eighteenth and particularly the nineteenth century that it became in the true sense a global commodity. For most of this period, China remained the center of the trade after Portuguese and then British merchants helped create a mass market for opium cultivated in India.[2] Although Chinese authorities at first resisted the opium trade, issuing proclamations prohibiting its importation and consumption, they were too weak to enforce them. Eventually opium was legalized in 1858, following two wars in which Great Britain in effect forced China to open up its domestic market. Thereafter, China became increasingly dependent on home-grown opium supplies, forcing foreign traders to seek new markets elsewhere. They did not have to look far, as the Dutch, Spanish, and French colonies of Southeast Asia all became significant markets and later producers in their own right.

In the last decades of the nineteenth century, the demand for opium and other drugs also grew in America and Europe. Several factors contributed to this: the advent of modern medical practices, including the discovery of morphine and later heroin (both derived from opium), as well as the invention of the hypodermic needle to administer them; the massive social and economic transformation brought about by industrialization, which increased the popularity of a wide range of natural stimulants; the influx of foreign labor, notably from China; the development of long distance transportation that lowered the cost of importing goods from foreign sources; and the rise of mass consumption habits brought about by new marketing techniques and modern communications.

Although opium was by far the most important component of the international drug trade, cocaine-based tonics and medicines also became popular in Europe, America, and Japan.[3] By the turn of the century, however, opposition to the opium trade had grown increasingly vocal in the United States and Great Britain as a result of reports of widespread opiate addiction and concern that drugs in general were eroding public morals and promoting criminal behavior. Religious groups, temperance societies, and missionaries, in particular, began lobbying the governments of both countries to end the trade in opium.[4] It was not until the discovery in 1902 of a large addict population in the Philippines, which had been acquired after the war with Spain, that the United States took up the cause of prohibition. Having little at stake economically in the opium trade and seeing the opportunity to enhance its influence with China, where the problem had become particularly acute,[5] the U.S. government took the initiative in sponsoring an international conference to convince the principal producer countries to curtail their output. Convened in Shanghai in 1909, the International Opium Commission achieved very little in persuading the twelve participating countries to change their policies other than to gain their assent to a nonbinding resolution pledging each "to take measures for the gradual suppression of the practice of opium smoking in its own territories and possessions."[6]

Nevertheless, with the United States again the prime sponsor, another international conference was convened at The Hague in 1911. This time the countries in favor of greater regulation, which by now included Great Britain, succeeded in getting the conference to widen its focus beyond opium to include morphine and cocaine. The widespread use of cocaine and its perceived association with violence and deviant behavior, particularly in America, had by now also made it a target for prohibitionist groups. The majority of those present at The Hague, however, remained at best lukewarm, if not directly opposed to more stringent controls.[7] The results of the conference were, as a consequence, modest. Although the final resolutions moved beyond the recommendations of the Shanghai commission in committing each of the signatories to enact domestic legislation controlling the manufacture and distribution of medicinal opium, heroin, cocaine, and any other derivative of similar properties, implementation of the convention was made conditional on its worldwide acceptance at the insistence of Germany (by then the largest cocaine producer).[8] As one historian has commented, "In this way did narcotics control get its global approach."[9] This condition delayed the Hague convention from going into effect until after World War I, when the Versailles peace treaty incorporated the various agreements.

In the meantime, the United States went ahead and enacted the Harrison Act in 1914 to comply with its international obligations. This landmark piece of legislation required distributors and medical prescribers of specified drugs to be registered and subjected to taxation. Unregistered or unprescribed possession of narcotics was deemed unlawful. The Harrison Act would remain the basis of U.S. narcotics regulation for the next fifty years.[10] Britain and other European nations passed similar domestic legislation in the 1920s.

The involvement of the League of Nations marked the beginning of a new approach to international drug control. Instead of reliance on voluntary national laws, emphasis was now placed on the creation of mandatory international controls supervised by standing international bodies. The league established the Opium Advisory Committee, which in turn created the Opium Control Board to oversee compliance with the terms of the Hague convention. In 1925 two separate commissions met in Geneva under league auspices: one to limit the sale of opium in the Far East to government monopolies, with the goal of phasing out production over a fifteen-year period, and the other to establish an international accounting system to which states would be obliged to submit statistics on the production, refinement, and consumption of drugs.[11] To monitor compliance and enforce these new restrictions, the Opium Control Board was reconstituted as the Permanent Central Board and charged with determining the amount of drugs that each state legitimately needed for medical and scientific purposes. It also established an import certification system to manage this process, with itself as the controlling body.

Although the Geneva agreements advanced the scope of international drug control, the United States and China felt that they did not go far enough and refused to give their assent. Their objections proved well founded. The colonial administrations came to view the government monopolies more as profitable sources of revenue than as mechanisms to control production, the import restrictions were easily circumvented via nonsignatory states, and pharmaceutical companies continued to oversupply the world market for manufactured drugs.[12] Additional measures introduced by the league in 1931 to limit drug production (and also prohibit heroin use) assuaged many of the U.S. concerns, however, and the United States became a signatory.[13] By 1934 worldwide production of opium had fallen to a total of 8,000 tons—a drop of 82 percent from the 1906 level of 42,000 tons.[14]

However, as access to drugs became more restricted, illicit drug manufacturers and traffickers emerged to meet the demand of those who could no longer satisfy their needs by legal means. In the United States, the passage of the Harrison Act reduced the number of opiate addicts, reinforcing a trend that had begun earlier, but it also marked the beginning of a black market in drugs and the involvement of criminal suppliers attracted by the promise of large profits.[15] The same was true in Europe. In both cases heroin and morphine diverted from licit sources were the drugs in highest demand and circulation. But as the League of Nations began to impose tighter controls over pharmaceutical companies, making diversion more difficult, the search for alternative illicit sources of supply began.[16]

The initial tactic was to set up licensed factories working almost exclusively for the illicit trade.[17] But as the league cracked down on this activity, clandestine manufacturing laboratories began to spring up, primarily outside of Europe and North America. In the early 1930s, European criminal groups moved to Istanbul to obtain heroin and morphine and then on to China, whose weak government and proximity to the sources of supply made it an attractive base of operations. By 1934 U.S. officials in China were reporting a major influx of European drug traffickers of mainly Greek and Russian nationality.[18] From China they established supply routes back to Europe and also the United States, notably with the involvement of Jewish criminal groups in New York.

Although international and domestic efforts had drastically reduced the worldwide production and export of opium, China and Southeast Asia still remained the world's largest drug market. As Luiz Simmons and Abdul Said observe: "The Far East was riddled with opium smugglers, corrupt government and police officials, and a throbbing domestic market which would not yield to the deceptively simple logic of suppression."[19] Paradoxically, the control efforts had produced unintended consequences: the suppression of opium poppy cultivation in certain Chinese provinces stimulated its spread to others and, more ominously, a shift to foreign-produced heroin and the consumption of morphine in China.[20] As the supply of drugs diverted from European pharmaceutical companies began to dry up as a result of the league's actions, China and particularly the port of Shanghai emerged as a major center for the illicit manufacture of heroin and morphine.

The political instability of China at the time undoubtedly allowed the drug trade to flourish. The Nationalist government under Chiang Kai-shek not only used the opium trade to consolidate its hold on the portions of China it controlled, but it also allowed the activities of the most powerful trafficking group—Shanghai's Green Gang—to operate un-molested and become "Asia's first major heroin producing syndicate in the 1930s."[21] Meanwhile, in northern China, the occupying Japanese forces were actively promoting drug trafficking and consumption as part of a deliberate campaign to undermine the Chinese state.[22] To the con-sternation of U.S. officials, opium, morphine, and heroin from Japanese-controlled areas began to show up with increasing frequency on the West Coast, starting in the mid-1930s. India, Burma, and the Malay States also reported being flooded with large amounts of cocaine that were also believed to be the result of Japanese-sponsored efforts.

With the growth of the illicit drug trade, the League of Nations and its Opium Advisory Committee became increasingly intent on eliminating it. In 1936 the league sponsored a conference for "the Suppression of the Illicit Traffic in Dangerous Drugs." The resulting convention set severe penalties for participation in the illicit drug trade, established extradition procedures to bring traffickers to justice, and directed each of the signa-tories to set up a central office to supervise and coordinate enforcement of the convention.[23] Of the forty-two governments that participated in the conference, however, only twenty-six signed the convention. The U.S. government, echoing earlier sentiments, again refused on the grounds that it did not go far enough and contained too many loopholes.

This proved to be the last act of the league before World War II intervened. By interrupting and, in some areas, severely curtailing inter-national trade, the war actually did more to restrict illicit traffic than any existing statute or convention.[24] While some trafficking continued in the Persian Gulf, the eastern Mediterranean, and the Japanese-occupied areas of Asia, it declined dramatically in Europe and the United States.[25] As supplies dwindled in the United States, thefts of drugs from stores in-creased, as did falsification of medical prescriptions. Overall, however, the drop in supply "forced many users into periods of involuntary absti-nence." As an editorial in *Time* magazine remarked in 1942, "The war is probably the best thing that ever happened to U.S. drug addicts."[26]

Regeneration and Consolidation, 1946–61

With the onset of peace, the newly created United Nations assumed the functions of the League of Nations, including the various international drug control conventions. In 1946 the Commission on Narcotic Drugs was created to replace the old Opium Advisory Committee, and in 1948 a protocol was signed extending the coverage of the 1931 convention to other addiction-forming drugs.[27] Meanwhile, many of the old trafficking networks, particularly in China and Southeast Asia, began to reestablish themselves.

The civil war between Nationalist and Communist forces put an end to what little there was in the way of drug control in China.[28] The victory of Communist forces in 1949, however, had profound consequences for China's hitherto dominant position in the global drug market and for the subsequent development of illicit trafficking in the region. After taking power, Mao Zedong introduced a comprehensive anti-opium campaign linked to land reform that not only virtually eliminated poppy cultivation but also radically altered public attitudes toward opium consumption.[29] The immediate result, however, was to displace the Shanghai-based operations to Hong Kong. By the mid-1950s smaller criminal syndicates from other parts of China had pushed out the once dominant Green Gang. Using the latter's chemists, these groups began turning Hong Kong into a major heroin-processing center and one of the principal conduits of drugs to the West by virtue of its growing international transportation links.[30]

At the same time, the remnants of Chiang Kai-shek's defeated Kuomintang forces fled over the border into the Shan region of northern Burma. From here, with covert U.S. assistance, they mounted a series of abortive armed incursions into China aimed at inciting a general insurrection and ultimately regaining control. The failure of these operations caused the United States to cut back its financial support, leaving the Chinese irregulars to seek alternative sources of funding. Given their location, the opium trade was the obvious solution. The Shan region had already become a significant poppy-growing area during Thailand's brief military occupation in World War II. The end of the colonial opium monopolies that had supplied Hong Kong and the cities of Southeast Asia also meant that a ready and lucrative market beckoned. It did not take long, therefore, to establish the necessary political and logistical connections and organize production and trafficking. The U.S. Central Intelligence Agency, which was only too pleased to see its anti-Communist clients stay in business, is believed to have provided at least tacit support and perhaps more.[31]

The same kind of arrangement was apparently also taking place in Indochina between French intelligence officers and tribal groups in the highlands of what is now Laos and northern Vietnam. Again, cutbacks in funding to fight Communist forces provided the stimulus for using the drug trade to underwrite further covert operations and more generally to solicit local support against Communist forces in Southeast Asia. The end of the French opium monopoly in 1950 had also left Saigon in need of alternative sources of supply. With French intelligence agents providing the aircraft, the poppy fields of Laos became connected to the opium dens of Saigon. Following France's withdrawal from Indochina, the CIA inherited many of its covert links with the opium-growing tribesmen of Laos. Although it is unclear whether the CIA actively participated in the drug trade, it certainly took a complicit role for much the same reasons as the French had. More generally, as William O. Walker has observed, "Opium control had become something of a hostage to U.S. national security policy by 1950."[32]

It would be some time before the West would feel the consequences of U.S. and French actions in helping to lay the foundations of what later became known as the Golden Triangle. For most of the 1950s, only relatively modest amounts of Asian-produced morphine and heroin made their way overseas. The war, as discussed earlier, effectively halted the connection between the Shanghai syndicates and Jewish criminal groups in New York. As the latter were supplanted by the Italian mafia, a new set of players in the U.S. drug market emerged with a different set of international connections.

In the immediate postwar period, most of the heroin reaching the United States had been illicitly diverted from Italian pharmaceutical companies. The infamous mobster Charles "Lucky" Luciano evidently played a leading role in organizing its shipment to America via Cuba.[33] After his deportation to Italy in 1946, Luciano began establishing several heroin-processing laboratories in Sicily. Using expertise and contacts developed primarily for cigarette smuggling, the Sicilian mafia was able to import Turkish morphine by sea from Lebanon and Syria for processing into heroin. Luciano's organization simultaneously began to develop ties with Corsican criminal groups in Marseilles that had also started to refine heroin. Marseilles was in many respects an ideal center for drug production and trafficking. Besides being a major seaport with links throughout the Mediterranean and beyond, its proximity to the perfume-producing area of southern France provided ready access to acetic anhydride, a key ingredient for refining morphine into heroin.[34] So began the infamous "French connection."

After the Italian authorities cracked down on the pharmaceutical companies in 1952, the illicit processing centers expanded production and consolidated their ties with the five major mafia families in New York.[35] The evidence of the New York mafia's subsequent involvement in the drug trade is somewhat contradictory, however. Although it has been estimated that the five families controlled around 95 percent of all the heroin entering the United States at this time, the American mafia's early relationship with the drug trade has also been described as uncomfortable, to the extent that its members were explicitly prohibited by decree from becoming involved.[36] It has also been argued that this self-imposed ban allowed Cuban and other Latin American criminal groups to become more active in the drug trade.[37]

For most of the immediate postwar period, Latin America's involvement in the international drug trade was neglible by contemporary standards. With the exception of Mexican cannabis and brown heroin, which were smuggled into the southwest United States, Latin America was not yet a major source of drugs for the U.S. market.[38] The cocaine trade remained very small in this period, as indicated by the low level of seizures reported by law enforcement officials.[39] A major reason was that the technical skills necessary to convert coca leaf into cocaine hydrochloride were not generally available in the areas where it was cultivated, yet coca leaf was too bulky to smuggle to the areas where this expertise existed.

Sometime after World War II, however, an embryonic capability to produce coca sulfate, more commonly known as coca paste, developed in Peru with the use of chemicals that had become more widely available.[40] Criminal groups based in Mexico City and Havana then began obtaining supplies of coca paste for processing into cocaine at clandestine laboratories. In the 1950s, as communication and air transportation to South America improved, similar connections were made to coca paste producers in Bolivia. By the end of the decade, Bolivia had became the primary source for the coca paste illicitly refined in Havana. The fall of the Batista regime in Cuba in 1958 terminated this operation, but many of the Cubans involved in the drug trade emigrated to Miami and other locations and reestablished their connections later.

In 1961 the United Nations, after lengthy negotiations, agreed to consolidate the existing multilateral agreements into the Single Convention on Narcotic Drugs. At the same time the UN's drug control machinery was also streamlined.[41] The Single Convention, however, offered only modest advances in drug control, reflecting inevitable compromises among the various interests represented.[42] Cannabis cultivation was prohibited, but producers were given a twenty-five-year grace period to comply. Similarly, the provisions of the 1953 convention that would have limited production of virtually all organic drugs were dropped. The industrialized countries also rejected all attempts to bring the burgeoning collection of synthetic drugs into the same control regime. It would take the massive expansion of the global drug trade in the 1960s and 1970s for more stringent measures to be taken.

From the Margins to the Mainstream, 1962–73

Starting at the beginning of the 1960s, a wide range of illicit drugs became increasingly popular in the United States. What had been generally confined to the margins of society in the postwar period now became part of the mainstream.[43] The creation of a mass market for drugs in America had a profound effect on the global market and effectively transformed it into the enormous business that it is today.

No single reason accounts for the sudden upsurge of U.S. consumption in the 1960s. Rather, a confluence of forces came together in this period, most notably the passage of the baby boom generation through ages 15–24, resulting in a 50 percent increase in this cohort by the end of the decade; the widespread rejection of the values, norms, and socializing institutions of the 1950s, which came to be seen as conformist, constraining, and hypocritical; a concomitant shift toward the celebration of feelings, spontaneity, and intuitiveness that drugs were seen to promote; a surge in discretionary income (U.S. GNP doubled in the 1960s), leading to the rise of consumerism and with it rising expectations for continual stimulation and instant gratification; and widespread political alienation along generational lines, exacerbated by the Vietnam War.[44]

The collective impact of these changes produced an epidemic of drug use in America, though its precise dimensions remain unclear. A national survey in 1971 estimated that "24 million Americans over 11 years of age had smoked marijuana at least once," while the number of heroin users is believed to have grown from around 50,000 in 1960 to more than 250,000 by the end of the decade.[45] Much the same phenomenon took place in Western Europe at the same time for similar reasons, with America's growing cultural influence an added factor.

The increasing consumption of drugs, however, could not have been sustained without a commensurate increase in their supply. Mexico and to a lesser extent Jamaica became the principal suppliers of marijuana to the U.S. market.[46] More diverse sources in North Africa, the Middle East, and Southwest Asia supplied the European market. Second only to marijuana in popularity were a plethora of synthetic drugs that had been invented since 1945 and had not yet been subjected to systematic international control.[47] As one observer noted:

> Recently compounded psychotropic agents were enthusiastically introduced and effectively promoted, with the consequence of exposing the national consciousness to an impressive catalog of chemical temptations—sedatives, tranquilizers, stimulants, anti-depressants, analgesics, and hallucinogens—which could offer fresh inspiration as well as simple and immediate relief from fear, anxiety, tension, frustration, and boredom.[48]

The vast majority of these drugs were either prescribed or illegally acquired from licit sources. Some, such as LSD, began to be produced clandestinely in small laboratories in America and Europe.

As for heroin, the "French connection" became the single most important source for the U.S. market throughout the 1960s and early 1970s. It is unclear whether internecine struggles among the Sicilian mafia or the comparative economic advantages of Marseilles allowed the Corsican crime syndicates to become dominant, but by 1972 French heroin processed from Turkish morphine base was estimated to account for 80 percent of the total amount entering the United States.[49] The output of the heroin-processing laboratories in Marseilles expanded, while the main supply pipeline into New York was augmented by more circuitous routes through Canada, Mexico, the Caribbean, and even South America.[50] Whatever self-imposed restrictions the American mafia had about dealing in drugs also apparently went by the wayside, doubtless because the business had become too lucrative to ignore.

Although heroin from Southeast Asia evidently made up a tiny proportion of the U.S. market in the 1960s, two events during this period would set this area on course to later become the largest source of heroin in the world. The first was the 1962 military coup in Burma, which resulted in the nationalization of its businesses and banks. For many, particularly the numerous warring factions seeking independence from Rangoon in the remote upland areas of Burma, opium increasingly became the "only viable crop and medium of exchange."[51] To counter these rebel groups, the military government also established a paramilitary organization—the Ka Kwe Ye—and actively helped it smuggle opium to make it essentially self-financing. One of its leaders, Khun Sa, would become the largest and most notorious heroin trafficker in the Golden Triangle.

The second event was the Vietnam War, which provided a new source of demand for the opium and heroin producers of the Golden Triangle. Many American soldiers sampled and in turn developed a substantial habit for No. 4 heroin, colloquially known as "China White" for its high purity. Although details are sparse, the Hong Kong-based criminal syndicates reportedly controlled much of this trade and helped establish a cluster of heroin laboratories in the Golden Triangle area during the late 1960s to meet the rising demand. A White House–sponsored committee reported in 1973 that an estimated 34 percent of all the U.S. troops in Vietnam had "commonly used" heroin.[52] When U.S. combat forces began withdrawing from Southeast Asia in 1971, the syndicates naturally began to look elsewhere for new markets.

Beginning in the late 1960s, the popularity of cocaine also started to grow in the United States, albeit still among a relatively small portion of the population. It is unclear what initiated this upturn, although Peruvian coca cultivation started to increase steadily after 1964 despite a pledge by the Peruvian government to limit production as part of its commitment to the UN Single Convention of 1961. At the same time, new centers of cocaine production began to spring up in Chile and, to a lesser extent, Colombia, apparently the handiwork of Cuban traffickers displaced from Havana after the revolution. Using connections to the large expatriate community in Miami, the Cubans began to become more active players in the U.S. drug trade.[53] However, following the fall of the Allende government in 1973 and the subsequent imposition of martial law by the Pinochet regime, cocaine trafficking from Chile abruptly ceased. In its place Colombia would emerge as the preeminent cocaine producer in the world.

As the illicit drug trade expanded and gathered momentum throughout the 1960s, the United States began to put more emphasis on unilateral and bilateral initiatives to respond to the problem, although still concentrating overwhelmingly on suppressing supply. This reflected not only frustration with the results of multilateral diplomacy but also America's growing recognition of its global influence. Thus, starting in the early 1960s, the number of special agents assigned by the Federal Bureau of Narcotics to U.S. embassies abroad steadily increased.[54] The real watershed occurred between 1969 and 1973, when the Nixon administration declared a "total war" on drugs. Not only did the number of American law enforcement officers abroad leap dramatically, but the Nixon administration launched several high-profile initiatives to reduce the amount of illicit drugs entering the country.[55]

Chief among these were the campaigns against marijuana trafficking from Mexico and heroin smuggling from Europe. In September 1969 Operation Intercept was launched, requiring every person and vehicle crossing into the United States from Mexico to be searched at the border. Although very few drugs were discovered, cross-border traffic came to a virtual standstill, wreaking economic havoc on those dependent on traveling back and forth. After seventeen days, during which U.S.-Mexican relations seriously deteriorated, the operation was called off. Bowing to U.S. pressure, Mexico agreed to allow U.S. agents to be stationed on its territory and conduct surveillance of its poppy and marijuana fields. It also agreed to carry out an eradication program. For many, Operation Intercept exposed the folly of trying to seal the borders in a world growing more interdependent.[56]

As marijuana trafficking and consumption came to be viewed as lesser evils—and in any case practically unstoppable—attention turned to the heroin menace. In addition to providing French law enforcement with more support to dismantle the French connection, the Nixon administration put pressure on the Turkish government to end poppy cultivation. Responding to the "carrot" of financial compensation for its poppy growers and the "stick" of threatened withdrawal of U.S. foreign aid, Turkey announced that it would no longer produce opium after 1972.[57] At the same time, French police, supported by U.S. agents, broke up the Corsican drug syndicate in Marseilles.[58]

Although these actions signaled a relative shift in U.S. drug control policy, the Nixon administration did not entirely abandon multilateral diplomacy. Since the completion of the UN Single Convention, the United States had been trying to strengthen it, particularly by including synthetic drugs, which had been deliberately left out in 1961. The surge in their popularity during the 1960s had convinced many of the need to bring them under tighter international control. The result was the 1971 Convention on Psychotropic Substances.[59] The United States introduced additional domestic legislation to restrict the sale and consumption of synthetic drugs, especially amphetamines.[60]

Global Expansion, 1974–88

The breakup of the French connection and the cessation of Turkish opium production were followed by an immediate decline in the amount of heroin seized and the estimated number of addicts in the United States. The benefits of these drug control initiatives would be short lived, however. New sources of heroin emerged to fill the vacuum, while the popularity of other drugs increased. Indeed, during the period from 1974 to 1988 there was an explosive worldwide growth in the production and trafficking of virtually all types of illicit drugs.

The search for new markets for the heroin produced in the Golden Triangle after the U.S departure from Vietnam was reflected in a marked increase in the level of heroin trafficking to Australia and Europe.[61] The principal conduits of the trade were the established Chinese immigrant communities around the Pacific rim and in the major seaports of northwest Europe. Here the drug-trafficking syndicates could exploit family and regional ties while operating relatively inconspicuously. In Europe, Amsterdam and Rotterdam became major distribution centers, with U.S. servicemen stationed in Germany a prime target. Likewise, London, with its large community of Hong Kong Chinese, became another major hub for heroin distribution.[62] The end of heroin processing in Marseilles, furthermore, only temporarily disrupted the supply of Turkish-derived narcotics to Europe. Turkish drug-trafficking syndicates began to take advantage of the commercial links through the Balkans and the growing number of Turkish guest workers in Germany.[63]

Meanwhile, in the United States heroin from Mexico began to fill the void created by the severing of the French connection. From having accounted for only a modest share of the U.S. market in 1970, by 1975 Mexico had become the source of an estimated 70 to 80 percent of the heroin entering the United States.[64] Not only had Mexico failed to carry out its promise of an eradication program after the aborted Operation Intercept, but also opium poppy cultivation had spread beyond the traditional growing areas and harvesting was now being done almost continuously rather than seasonally.[65] In response to further U.S. pressure, however, the Mexican government initiated an aggressive new crop eradication program—Operation Condor—using aerial spraying in place of manual uprooting. The results were impressive: Mexican poppy cultivation fell drastically by 1977, while Mexican heroin's share of the U.S. market subsequently dropped from 75 percent in 1976 to 24 percent in 1980.[66]

Mexican marijuana production also did not escape this new eradication effort, and it too declined in this period. Mexican marijuana also fell out of favor with U.S. consumers because of fears that it had become contaminated with the herbicide paraquat.[67] At about the same time,

Jamaica took similar steps to stamp out its marijuana cultivation. Since the early 1970s, Jamaican trafficking organizations had become particularly adept at smuggling bulk shipments of homegrown marijuana into the United States through southern Florida. Using much the same tactics as the Chinese drug traffickers, they also forged links with the many Jamaican immigrant communities in Canada and Great Britain. By the mid-1970s the Jamaican government had become so alarmed about the growth of these organizations and the associated crime that it also embarked on a major eradication program.[68] The supply of marijuana from Jamaica immediately declined.

Although successful in the short term, the Mexican and Jamaican antidrug campaigns did not deliver the mortal blow to their respective trafficking organizations that many had hoped for. As one journalist later commented with respect to Mexico, "The fittest of the traffickers not only survived but prospered. . . . Operation Condor/Trizo did them a great service by winnowing out the competition."[69] In fact, by the mid-1980s Mexican heroin production and trafficking had rebounded with a vengeance and had even spread to neighboring Central American countries.[70] The twin assault on Mexican and Jamaican marijuana, moreover, had the unintended effect of opening the door for Colombia's ascendancy to the big leagues of drug trafficking.

Starting in the late 1960s, Colombians began organizing a highly sophisticated marijuana production and trafficking operation centered on the Guajira peninsula, an area in the far north of the country where the government exercised only limited control. Using DC-7 and Super-Constellation aircraft as well as large seagoing vessels known as "motherships," they began shipping multi-ton quantities of marijuana into the United States. By the late 1970s Colombian marijuana was estimated to account for three-quarters of the U.S. market.[71] This was probably the zenith of the Colombian marijuana trade, however, as U.S. marijuana consumption peaked at about this time, and more potent homegrown marijuana began to attract a growing clientele.[72] More important, the Colombians realized that bigger profits now lay in the burgeoning U.S appetite for cocaine.

Cocaine's popularity in America began to gather momentum during the first half of the 1970s. In 1973 the *New York Times* ran more stories on cocaine than on heroin, and in the following year the National Household Survey on Drug Abuse—a U.S. federally funded program that interviewed the occupants of randomly selected homes—estimated that 5.4 million Americans had tried cocaine at least once.[73] Although it is difficult to separate or assign relative weight to the numerous factors that contributed to the surge in U.S. cocaine consumption, several stand out. The drug's capacity to produce intense feelings of euphoria as well as the fact it did not have to be smoked or injected were clearly important. Earlier reports indicating it was not addictive may also have made a difference. It is also possible that domestic legislation placing strict controls on amphetamines and other synthetic drugs in the early 1970s may have deflected drug consumption toward cocaine as a substitute.[74] Finally, America's growing appetite for cocaine was undoubtedly fueled by its growing availability.

Judging by the amounts seized and the street price of cocaine, its flow to the United States expanded rapidly throughout the 1970s, primarily because of the activities of the Colombians.[75] After the Pinochet regime terminated the Chilean connection in 1973, Colombian groups forged their own ties to Peruvian and Bolivian coca growers and developed an independent cocaine-refining operation centered on the city of Medellin.[76] From the 1940s to the early 1970s, Medellin had flourished primarily as a center for textile manufacturing. But with the imposition of import tariffs by Europe in the late 1960s and increasing competition from the Far East, the Colombian textile industry went into recession and ultimately withered. This had two important consequences. The first was to send a wave of unemployed textile workers to the United States, particularly New York, where Colombian immigrants witnessed firsthand the explosion in drug use in America and, moreover, provided the nucleus of a distribution network for marijuana and later cocaine. The second consequence of the recession was to stimulate an already active black market in smuggled consumer goods that had been given an earlier boost by the Colombian government's imposition of exchange controls and import restrictions in the mid-1970s. With a long tradition of smuggling, notably of emeralds, Medellin's mafia was evidently "organized, hardworking, and highly competitive. Worldlier than most provincial crooks, they used their access to good air connections, communications, and international banks to great advantage."[77]

A more important factor in the rise of Colombia and specifically Medellin as the dominant center of the cocaine business was the delegitimation of government authority that had been taking place in the postwar period.[78] The failure of urban and rural reforms after a sustained period of civil violence from the late 1940s to the early 1950s fatally eroded the legitimacy of the state and its institutions, leaving large areas of the country under weak or limited government control. Black marketeers and smugglers exploited these conditions and in turn perpetuated them, especially after they diversified into the drug trade.

Beginning in the late 1970s, the involvement and organization of the Colombian traffickers became increasingly evident in three ways. The first, as already indicated, was in developing independent links to the primary coca-growing areas in Peru and Bolivia. By the 1970s events had conspired to make these areas especially receptive to the stimulus of external demand. In the upper Huallaga valley of Peru, the combination of rural migration, the failure of land reform, underdevelopment, and a decline in the profitability of traditional crops had turned coca into almost the only viable agricultural product.[79] There was little resistance, therefore, when Peruvian and Colombian cocaine traffickers began sponsoring a dramatic increase in coca cultivation in this valley, boosting it from an estimated 12,000 hectares in 1978 (already up from 2,400 hectares in 1964) to approximately 35,000 hectares in 1983.[80]

In Bolivia, the collapse of world cotton prices in the mid-1970s evidently prompted the cotton growers in the Santa Cruz region to diversify and plant coca bushes.[81] Farmers from the drought-stricken area around Cochabamba began to do the same in the sparsely populated Chapare region. Following a precipitous fall in world tin prices in the mid-1980s, the nascent coca industry in Chapare suddenly became a magnet for the huge number of unemployed Bolivian miners in search of a living. Coca cultivation and coca paste processing rose dramatically as a consequence, increasing 75 percent between 1977 and 1981.[82] The Bolivian government's decision in 1983 to decouple the peso from the U.S. dollar provided further incentives by stimulating hyperinflation and making the hard currency earnings potential of the coca trade even more alluring.[83]

Facilitating the transformation of Peru and Bolivia into the world's leading sources of coca was the impotence and, in some cases, direct complicity of their governments in the drug trade. As the coca-growing interests became more entrenched economically and politically in both countries, the incentives declined for the central government to confront them directly or for the growers to be attracted by alternative sources of income. The financial returns from the trade, moreover, provided ample amounts for corrupting local government officials and military officers directed to suppress it. By the mid-1980s, the Sendero Luminoso (Shining Path) and Tupac Amaru Revolutionary Movement guerrilla groups had also established themselves in the prime coca areas of Peru, further limiting the government's freedom of action. In return for protection from government forces, these groups extracted payment from the growers.[84]

In Bolivia, the situation was arguably worse. It is now generally accepted that members of the Banzer government, before its demise in 1978, and the Meza military dictatorship after 1980 were heavily involved in the drug trade.[85]

The second way the Colombian traffickers made their presence felt was in organizing the bulk transportation of cocaine. Having already demonstrated their prowess in smuggling marijuana, the Colombians perfected the use of light aircraft to ship coca paste from Peru and Bolivia to the processing labs in Colombia and the refined cocaine from there into the United States. These aircraft had become commonplace in South America, principally because of their ability to operate from small make-shift airfields in remote rural areas. Their size made them harder to detect by radar, yet was also perfectly adequate to shift large amounts of high-value coca paste and cocaine.[86] Carlos Lehder Rivas, who became one of the most successful Colombian cocaine traffickers, is widely credited with conceiving the idea of employing light aircraft to smuggle drugs into the United States, which others then emulated. Lehder eventually bought a Bahamian island with the explicit purpose of using it as a transit center for smuggling cocaine into South Florida.[87]

The third way was wholesale distribution, where the real profits of the drug trade could be realized. Beginning in 1978, the Colombians set about wresting control of cocaine distribution from the Cubans in South Florida in what become known as the "cocaine wars." At the same time, the Colombians started developing their own cocaine distribution networks in many of the major metropolitan centers of America. By 1982 their domination of the cocaine market was complete. With almost the entire business in their hands, the Colombians wielded—for a brief period at least—cartel-like influence over the availability and price of cocaine in the United States.[88]

Once in control of cocaine distribution, the Colombian trafficking groups soon realized that the U.S demand for the drug was outstripping their capacity to satisfy it. The scale of operations and the level of organization had to be expanded and even better organized if the market was to be fully exploited. As a result, a new, more enterprising, and more sophisticated group of Colombian traffickers came to the forefront. Of these, Pablo Escobar, the Ochoa brothers, and Jose Gonzalo Rodriguez-Gacha became the most powerful in orchestrating large-scale cocaine smuggling. This new generation of traffickers distinguished themselves from their predecessors in several important ways: integrating and sub-contracting various logistical functions, establishing large-scale processing laboratories, acquiring their own security forces, using advanced technologies for smuggling, and developing sophisticated money-laundering operations.[89] Moreover, they developed an increasingly strong working relationship, in part apparently as a consequence of the need to jointly resist the threat of kidnapping and extortion by Colombian guerrilla groups.[90] Although Medellin remained the center of the Colombian cocaine industry, a smaller group also began operating from Cali. Like their Medellin counterparts, the Cali traffickers had started out in the early 1970s as a gang involved in other criminal enterprises, notably counterfeiting and kidnapping, and only later diversified into the drug business.[91]

By the early 1980s, cocaine use in the United States had reached epidemic proportions. U.S. drug control policy consequently became increasingly oriented toward Latin America and more specifically toward curbing the cocaine trade. The first manifestation of the changing emphasis was the creation of the South Florida Task Force in 1982, with the goal of reducing the sudden surge in drug trafficking and related violence in that part of the country.[92] Although the task force's initiatives are credited with reducing the level of drug-related crime and smuggling in South Florida, their net effect was to shift the primary axis of cocaine trafficking to Central America and the Mexican border. At the same time, because the stepped-up border surveillance off Florida proved to be particularly effective against marijuana smuggling, it probably helped Mexican and domestic U.S. producers gain a larger market share.[93]

With the introduction of cheap, smokable, and highly addictive "crack" cocaine in 1985, public concern over the drug problem intensified. Although it is unclear to what extent the original creation of crack reflected a deliberate marketing ploy by the traffickers to expand cocaine consumption, that was its effect. In any case, its potential was quickly recognized by wholesalers and retailers alike. The cocaine phenomenon, which had largely been confined to affluent users, rapidly spread to lower-income groups, particularly in many inner-city areas of America. The crack explosion and the equally dramatic surge in violent crime that accompanied it in turn triggered a series of new antidrug laws imposing severe penalties for those caught trafficking.[94] At the same time, the United States stepped up its efforts to stem the tide of drugs at the source by involving the military for the first time in a significant way.[95]

Several operations aimed at disabling the processing centers and interdicting the supply routes in Peru and Bolivia were mounted in the 1980s with the use of U.S. military advisers and equipment. Although they disrupted the drug trade temporarily, they achieved few lasting results. The net effect in most cases was to alienate the local population and stir anti-American sentiment in the host countries. This phase in U.S. policy culminated with the U.S. invasion of Panama in December 1989 to apprehend General Manuel Noriega for complicity in cocaine trafficking. Although the invasion achieved its primary aim, drug trafficking and money laundering in Panama soon rebounded, and, by some accounts, they now exceed previous levels.[96]

Meanwhile, as the United States concentrated on its cocaine problem, the worldwide production of opium and heroin underwent a massive expansion. Although Southeast Asia—the Golden Triangle, particularly Burma—remained the largest source, in the 1980s Southwest Asia—the "Golden Crescent"—emerged as a major source of heroin. Three events in 1979 helped transform the region's role in the global drug market.[97] The first was the Iranian revolution in February 1979, after which the Khomeini regime prohibited drug production and imposed severe penalties for trafficking. Many Iranian dealers fled to Pakistan, where they set up business, providing capital to start illicit poppy cultivation and the know-how to process heroin. Iranian production did not cease, moreover, since many of the traditional opium-growing areas remained effectively beyond the government's reach.[98] If anything, the resultant black market for heroin in Iran probably stimulated production in these areas.

The second event was the decision by General Muhammad Zia ul-Haq's military regime in Pakistan to ban the licit cultivation and distribution of opium. Although this program proved successful in some regions, it left many farmers without a viable agricultural alternative and in effect "pushed the opium business underground and into the hands of the old smuggling networks in the North-West Frontier Province and Punjab."[99] Faced with a surplus of opium due to the combination of the government edict and an unusually productive harvest in 1979, the tribal groups in these remote and mountainous areas of Pakistan turned to refining heroin for the foreign market. It is believed that sometime in mid-1979 chemists from Southeast Asia were imported for this purpose.[100]

Drug production in the Golden Crescent received an additional boost from a third event: the Soviet invasion of Afghanistan in December 1979. Afghanistan had been a long-standing supplier of opium to the Iranian market (and of hashish to Western Europe) before 1979. The combined effect of Khomeini's antidrug campaign and the Soviet occupation was to deflect the opium trade into Pakistan, where the nascent processing centers turned opium into heroin. More important, the mujahedin resistance fighters, who controlled many of the traditional growing areas, increasingly began to view the opium and heroin trade as a lucrative source of income to buy arms. With the knowledge (if not direct support) of Pakistan's intelligence service and even of the U.S. CIA, the covert supply of arms to the Afghan resistance movement and the drug trade became inextricably linked. Thus, in a way reminiscent of the patterns of the early years of the Golden Triangle, drug control evidently became subordinated to larger geostrategic goals. Opium production in Afghanistan and heroin refinement and trafficking in Pakistan subsequently blossomed throughout the 1980s, leading to widespread corruption of public officials.[101]

The expansion of Southwest Asian heroin production stimulated and in turn became largely sustained by the rise of large regional drug markets. Pakistan, in particular, experienced a rapid increase in opiate addiction, which had been nearly unknown before 1979. By the end of the 1980s, Pakistan was estimated to have over a million heroin addicts.[102] Comparable levels of opiate addiction also persisted in Iran, despite the government's draconian policy.[103] India likewise became a significant drug market, although most of its opium evidently came from illicit diversions of legally produced supplies.[104]

Heroin and morphine base not destined for these regional markets began to be smuggled to Europe and the United States in increasing amounts from the early 1980s on, as indicated by seizure statistics. A severe drought that depressed opium production in the Golden Triangle between 1978 and 1980, as well as the successful disabling of several ethnic Chinese drug-trafficking networks in Europe, apparently helped heroin from Southwest Asia to gain a foothold in Europe.[105] Large immigrant communities from Turkey, Pakistan, and Iran that had grown up during the 1970s also undoubtedly provided traffickers from these countries with the necessary connections and recruits to develop extensive distribution networks. By the early 1980s almost all the West European countries had experienced steep increases in heroin use. For some—notably Spain, Portugal, and Switzerland—the increase occurred somewhat later in the decade.[106] In the United States, the decline in the availability of Mexican heroin in the early 1980s presented a similar opportunity for heroin from Southwest Asia to increase its market share. Again, resident aliens from the region acted as the principal wholesale distributors, although the Italian American mafia groups also began to play a more active role in the heroin trade.[107]

By the middle of the 1980s, however, heroin from Southeast Asia had once again become more available in the U.S. and European markets. As if to compensate for the setback caused by the 1979–80 drought, 1984 brought a bumper harvest in the Golden Triangle, and opium production soared, especially in Burma. Since the 1970s, the rebel factions in the highlands of Burma had become even more dependent on the opium trade to sustain their operations.[108] Mexican heroin also made a comeback in the mid-1980s with the advent of a crudely processed but potent version known as "Black Tar." Its popularity in the United States reportedly spurred Mexican poppy growers to double their output between 1984 and 1988. In response, the Mexican government instituted yet another eradication program, but this may have inadvertently contributed to the spread of poppy cultivation to neighboring Guatemala.[109] Lebanon also emerged as a significant heroin producer in the 1980s as a result of a now familiar set of circumstances. Although cannabis had long been a staple crop in parts of Lebanon, the civil war that racked the country in the 1980s provided fertile conditions for large-scale poppy cultivation and heroin refinement to take root and flourish. According to official U.S. estimates, opium production leapt from 3.75 metric tons in 1985 to 30 metric tons in 1988, principally in the Bekaa valley, occupied by Syrian forces. In the process, the number of heroin addicts in Lebanon grew "exponentially" in the late 1980s.[110]

As concern over the expanding drug trade grew around the world, pressure increased on the United Nations to take action and expand the existing multilateral drug control framework. In 1987 the UN sponsored an International Conference on Drug Abuse and Illicit Traffic to discuss the various options and lay out a blueprint of sorts: the "Comprehensive Multidisciplinary Outline of Future Activities in Drug Abuse Control." Although this document contained only nonbinding recommendations, it is noteworthy because for the first time drug prevention and addict treatment received equal attention with supply-sided control efforts.[111] Nevertheless, the subsequent UN Convention against Illicit Traffic in Narcotic Drugs and Psychotropic Substances, signed in 1988, focused solely on giving force to the supply-sided recommendations of the Comprehensive Multidisciplinary Outline. Among other things, it committed signatories to share law enforcement evidence and provide mutual legal assistance, seize drug-related assets, criminalize money laundering and relax bank secrecy laws, extradite individuals charged with drug law violations, control shipment of precursor and essential chemicals, and redouble crop eradication and reduction efforts.[112] The 1988 convention represented a significant extension of existing international drug controls, but the global drug trade was already expanding in new areas and new ways even before the convention formally took effect.

Emerging Markets, 1989–95

By the end of the 1980s drug use in America had fallen considerably from its peak at the start of the decade. Although marijuana remained popular among many teenagers and young adults, overall consumption had declined. The number of cocaine users had also plummeted from an estimated 12 million in 1985 to half that figure by 1990.[113] And although the population of heroin addicts remained about the same, fewer new recruits appeared to be joining their ranks. These trends can be attributed to the rise of an antidrug ethos in America that stemmed from several sources: public education programs, workplace initiatives, media campaigns, the publicity attending the death of several well-known sports and entertainment personalities from drug overdoses, the threat of disease (most notably AIDS), and, more generally, the growing emphasis on healthy lifestyles as the baby boom generation grew older.[114] The increased severity of criminal sanctions for drug trafficking and the incarceration of large numbers of people for drug-related offenses may also have affected consumption habits.[115] Drug use in western Europe, though not as well documented, had by the decade's end also stabilized and even declined in some categories, probably for similar reasons.

Both markets, nevertheless, remained a powerful attraction to drug traffickers because of the immense profits that could still be made. In the United States, for example, evidence suggests that a rise in the number of "heavy" cocaine users compensated for the decline in the number of "light" or casual users.[116] Increasing amounts of drugs entered both markets, despite record seizures by customs and police. Discounting some brief or localized interruptions, the availability of drugs continued to grow steadily, as indicated by falling prices and rising levels of purity.[117] The increasing sophistication of the principal trafficking organizations undoubtedly contributed to the growing availability of drugs. In addition, the production of the principal categories of drugs continued to rise, albeit more slowly than in the 1980s.[118]

In response, the Bush administration intensified its efforts to curb the supply of drugs entering the United States. This took two forms. One was a massive increase in the involvement of the U.S. military in border surveillance and interdiction efforts.[119] The second was the Andean initiative, unveiled in September 1989, to encourage the principal cocaine-producing nations to become more involved in controlling the supply at the source. In addition to exerting diplomatic pressure, the Bush administration authorized a package of measures to help the military and police forces of Colombia, Peru, and Bolivia take on the drug traffickers.[120]

In Colombia, the results appeared promising at first. Bowing to U.S. pressure as well as growing domestic alarm over the power wielded by the cocaine-trafficking organizations, the Colombian government launched a vigorous campaign to crack down on their operations at home. This succeeded in slashing coca leaf prices in the main producing areas and boosting retail prices on the streets of America. The effect was temporary, however, as prices rebounded to their former levels after only a few months. The temporary drop in coca leaf prices may also have encouraged the Bolivian traffickers to shift to coca base production because of its higher value added.[121] Moreover, because the Colombian government's campaign was focused primarily on the Medellin cartel and in particular one of its most notorious leaders, Pablo Escobar, the cartel's rival in Cali was able to consolidate its growing position. By 1993 the Cali cartel's domination of the cocaine market was nearly complete. The incarceration of many key figures of the Medellin cartel and the death of Rodriguez-Gacha and later Escobar in a shoot-out with government forces left the Cali cartel in control of an estimated 80 percent of the cocaine processed and distributed around the world.[122]

Since the late 1980s, the Cali cartel had been quietly building up its base of operations, keeping a much lower profile than the more violent Medellin groups and thus attracting less attention from the authorities. Demonstrating a much higher level of business acumen and organization, the Cali cartel strengthened its ties to the main supplier groups in Peru and Bolivia while contracting out various key activities such as processing, transportation, and money laundering to other Colombian groups that had developed an expertise in these areas.[123] Cooperative arrangements were also made with trafficking groups in nearby Ecuador, Venezuela, and especially Mexico to transship cocaine into the United States.[124] Increasingly, the preferred smuggling routes became commercial shipping into the main West and East Coast ports of America or light aircraft through Central America and then tractor-trailers across the long and porous southwest border.[125] To receive and distribute the drugs, the Cali cartel also built up an extremely well organized wholesale network of semiautonomous but tightly controlled "cells" in the main metropolitan areas of the United States.[126] These in turn dealt with the numerous

Jamaican, Dominican, Mexican, and African American gangs that by now controlled retail cocaine distribution in the inner cities of America.

Either in response to changing consumption trends in the United States or because of a natural desire to replicate its success elsewhere, the Cali cartel began in the late 1980s to direct more of its attention to developing a mass market for cocaine in Europe. The steadily rising level of cocaine seizures by European customs and police officials in this period reflects this new marketing strategy.[127] The general prosperity of western Europe and higher retail prices for cocaine were obvious incentives. The decision of the European Community to progressively lower internal customs controls with the aim of creating a single market must also have added to Europe's attraction as a place to do business. The traffickers could also utilize the long-established ethnic ties between Europe and Latin America as well as the presence of sizable numbers of Colombian immigrants. Not surprisingly, the Iberian peninsula became the main gateway into western Europe, with Spain accounting for 25 to 50 percent of the total amount of cocaine seized in Europe from 1988 to 1993. The diverse and burgeoning trade links between South America and Europe presented additional opportunities for the traffickers. And with the end of the cold war and the subsequent opening up of trade to the former communist bloc, central and eastern Europe became another conduit into western Europe, judging by the large amounts of cocaine seized in Poland, Russia, and the Czech and Slovak republics.[128]

As the Colombians broadened their operations, they repeated the practice of reaching cooperative partnerships with other trafficking groups that enjoyed a comparative market advantage. In southern Europe the Italian mafia groups evidently became the principal partners to distribute cocaine.[129] Similar links are believed to have also been made with organized criminal groups in Poland and the former Soviet Union. Furthermore, at around the same time the Colombians apparently agreed to ship cocaine base to Lebanon for refinement and distribution in the Middle East. Japan became another target, judging by the reports of numerous Colombian overtures to the local Yakuza criminal organizations.[130]

These efforts appear to have paid off to some extent as cocaine consumption began to rise in Spain and Italy, and the presence of crack cocaine in several inner-city areas of Great Britain also became a larger problem. By 1995, however, there were still no signs of a cocaine epidemic on the scale seen earlier in the United States.[131] The same is true for Japan, where cocaine consumption has reportedly increased, but not significantly.[132] Nevertheless, the rise of the cocaine industry in South

America has evidently had a "spillover" effect on local consumption. The smoking of coca paste (known locally as *basuco*) has increased considerably throughout the region since the early 1980s. Cocaine use is also reportedly more prevalent in many transit countries such as Argentina, Brazil, Chile, and Venezuela, as well as some Central American states such as Costa Rica and Mexico.[133]

Sometime at the end of the 1980s, the Cali cartel also made the decision to diversify into heroin production by sponsoring the local cultivation of opium and hiring foreign chemists to provide guidance and training.[134] The relative saturation of the U.S. cocaine market and the higher retail price for heroin were almost certainly the prime factor, although declining coffee prices in the late 1980s might also have contributed to the decision of many Colombian farmers to participate in poppy cultivation. Starting in 1988, Colombian heroin production and trafficking steadily increased, with the U.S. market the prime focus. Although details are scarce, the Cali cartel's Ivan Urdinola faction reportedly took charge of the cultivation and processing of opium base in Colombia, while smaller independent trafficking organizations were contracted out to transport and smuggle the processed heroin into the United States, usually by couriers traveling on commercial airlines.[135] The Cali cartel's well-established network of "cells" in the main U.S. cities then handled wholesale distribution. As with the cocaine trade, the Colombians have again demonstrated their business acumen by carefully targeting areas where their principal competitors—the ethnic Chinese trafficking groups—are weak, while offering their existing clientele free samples of much purer (80–90 percent) and therefore smokable heroin that can be purchased at a price lower than the going market rate. These tactics have evidently paid off, as demand for Colombian heroin has apparently increased in the United States.

Although Colombian heroin has become a significant and ominous addition to the U.S. market, it remains dwarfed by the output of the traditional source areas of Southeast and Southwest Asia. After the dramatic growth of the 1980s, production in the Golden Triangle region began to show signs of leveling off, although this appears to have been the result of poor weather in Burma.[136] However, a stepped-up eradication and crop substitution program in Thailand did succeed in lowering domestic opium production and heroin processing in the northern hill areas. As a result, most of the refining centers were displaced across the Burmese border into the areas controlled by the various separatist groups, thereby increasing their already heavy involvement in the heroin trade.[137]

In 1990 the military junta in Burma, which had seized power in 1988 and renamed the country Myanmar, offered two of these separatist movements—the United Wa State Army and the Kokang Chinese—some degree of political autonomy and development assistance in exchange for a commitment to end their independence campaigns. Although opium production in the areas controlled by the Kokang apparently declined, the Wa have increased their output. The Shan United Army (also known as the Mong Tai Army), led by Khun Sa, has continued to be fully active despite a new military campaign launched by the government in 1994.[138]

The displacement of heroin production evidently resulted in a sharp increase in heroin use in Myanmar during the late 1980s and early 1990s.[139] In Thailand, which remained the primary trafficking route from the Golden Triangle, heroin consumption also rose in the main urban areas and in the traditional opium-smoking upland regions. The latter is attributed, ironically, to the success of the opium eradication program in those areas.[140] Arguably, the most significant development in the region, however, has been the increase in opium smoking and heroin use in China, particularly in the southern Yunnan and Guangdong provinces. According to Chinese officials, drug use has subsequently spread from these border areas to the inner provinces and from rural to urban areas.[141] Although some of this can be attributed to an upsurge in domestic Chinese opium cultivation first reported in the late 1980s, the main reason appears to have been the opening up of a major new trafficking route from the Golden Triangle through the southern Chinese cities of Kunming and Guangzhou to Taiwan and Hong Kong as a consequence of China's economic liberalization policies and associated relaxation of border controls.[142] Since 1989, Taiwanese officials have also reported a dramatic increase in the number of morphine and heroin addicts. The same has also evidently occurred in Vietnam.[143]

The numerous ethnic Chinese organized criminal groups, known as Triads, continue to be the principal distributors of Southeast Asian heroin. From their main base of operations in Hong Kong, the Triads deal directly with the various ethnic Chinese and Thai groups connected to the principal opium producers in Myanmar while also overseeing shipment to their affiliated gangs in the United States (especially New York), western Europe, and numerous cities around the Pacific rim.[144] As a result of the surge in heroin output from Southeast Asia as well as the operations of the Triads, heroin from Southeast Asia had become the most prevalent kind sold on American streets by the 1990s.[145] By contrast, the source of most of the heroin reaching Europe continues to be Southwest

Asia, although Southeast Asian heroin is common in the cities where Chinese trafficking groups remain powerful.

After increasing throughout the 1980s, opium production in the Golden Crescent leveled off at the end of the decade, only to pick up again in the early 1990s. The withdrawal of Soviet forces from Afghanistan in 1989 and the return of refugees to areas where few other economic opportunities existed has apparently contributed to the upturn in opium cultivation.[146] Although the center of heroin processing continued to be in the North-West Frontier Province of Pakistan, Afghan groups are believed to have started developing their own processing capability sometime in the early 1990s.[147] Unlike the Southeast Asian trade, the smuggling and distribution of heroin from the Golden Crescent is controlled by a larger and more ethnically diverse collection of traffickers from Pakistan, Iran, Turkey, and Lebanon. These supply the large regional markets, particularly in Pakistan and Iran, and distribute drugs by numerous routes to the Middle East, Europe, and North America.[148]

Since the mid-1980s, trafficking groups from Nigeria have also emerged as major players in the heroin trade from both Southeast and Southwest Asia.[149] The collapse of oil prices during the 1980s hit Nigeria particularly hard, causing the World Bank to classify it as a low-income country for the first time in 1989. The combination of worsening economic conditions and inadequate government services, especially in the already overcrowded cities, spawned a crime wave during the 1980s that eventually developed a drug component. Meanwhile, many Nigerian students who had gone abroad with the help of generous educational subsidies were suddenly stranded when their financial support was terminated as a result of cutbacks in government spending. Some of these turned initially to financial fraud, and later to international drug trafficking, to support themselves. By 1990, 26 percent of the heroin intercepted coming into the United States was credited to West African traffickers. With Lagos as the principal center of their operations, the Nigerian trafficking organizations have recruited hundreds of individual couriers to smuggle drugs, using the international airline network. By 1994 INTERPOL rated Nigerians as the third largest ethnic group engaged in drug smuggling.[150]

Like their cocaine-smuggling counterparts, the heroin traffickers have also been quick to grasp the opportunities presented by the end of the cold war, particularly the expansion of trade through central and eastern Europe, to reach markets in the West. Since the beginning of the 1990s new tributaries of the main overland "Balkan route" from Pakistan, Iran, and Turkey (which is estimated to carry 80 to 90 percent of the heroin entering Europe) have sprung up through Bulgaria, Romania, Hungary, and the Czech and Slovak Republics.[151] The war in the former Yugoslavia and the ensuing disruption to transportation links in the Balkans gave further impetus to this trend. Following an old pattern, refugees displaced by the Yugoslav conflict have also become more involved in trafficking drugs in western Europe. Ethnic Albanians from the Yugoslav province of Kosovo, for example, have become the principal trafficking group supplying heroin to the large Swiss market.[152] The breakup of the Soviet Union likewise led to new trafficking routes through the newly independent states of central Asia, which had been largely off limits due to the strict border surveillance.[153]

By all accounts, drug consumption inside the former communist bloc has also risen—in some cases considerably—since the fall of the Berlin Wall.[154] In addition to the long-standing consumption of domestically produced cannabis and poppy straw extract, new patterns of drug use have emerged. Bulgaria, the former Yugoslavia, Romania, and the Czech and Slovak Republics have all reported rising heroin use, in part the result of these countries' becoming a major conduit for traffic of drugs to the West.[155] Some of the Central Asian republics have experienced rising opiate use as well, though it is unclear whether this is because of increased cross-border traffic or because of the availability of locally grown opium, which is reported to have expanded since the early 1990s, particularly in Uzbekistan, Tajikistan, and Turkmenistan.[156]

The most significant new development has been a sizable market for synthetic drugs in many of the former communist countries. The Czech and Slovak Republics, Hungary, and Poland all report the growing use of illicitly produced amphetamines and illicitly diverted pharmaceutical drugs. These are also being exported to the West by local criminal organizations. Poland, for example, has become the second largest producer of amphetamines in Europe. There has also been a spate of reports from other countries in the former communist bloc of illicit diversion from state-run pharmaceutical factories and the establishment of illicit laboratories.[157] In the former Soviet Union, ephedrine and ephedrone made from pharmaceutical preparations or extracted from wild-growing *Ephedra vulgaris* plants has also become common in some cities.[158]

The popularity of synthetic drugs in the postcommunist world appears to be part of a larger trend that has been gathering momentum since the late 1980s. As a result of the diffusion of pharmaceutical expertise, the production of illicit synthetic drugs has sprung up in many places around the world, as have sizable local markets. In western Europe, Holland has become the main source of clandestinely manufactured amphetamines, although illicit processing labs have been discovered in Germany, Britain, France, and Belgium in recent years. After declining in the 1970s, lysergic acid diethylamide (LSD) appears to have made something of a comeback in both western Europe and the United States.[159] Outgrowing LSD in popularity—certainly in Europe—is 3,4-methylenedioxymethamphetamine (MDMA), more popularly known as "ecstasy." Again, the Netherlands is a major source country (where a variant, MDEA, is also produced), along with Belgium and to a lesser extent France, Germany, and Britain. Mexico, Brazil, and Canada have also reportedly become source countries for MDMA.

Meanwhile, in East Asia the most popular synthetic drugs appear to be methamphetamine and d-methamphetamine hydrochloride ("ice"). Trafficking groups operating in Taiwan, South Korea, the Philippines, and Japan are apparently the main suppliers to the local Asian markets as well as Hawaii, where amphetamines are the drug of choice. On the West Coast of the United States, Mexican trafficking groups are also reportedly involved in producing and distributing methamphetamine.[160] In recent years, the production of methcathinone ("CAT"), judged to be one-and-one-half times as strong as methamphetamine, has also become more widespread in the United States. Easy and cheap to make, methcathinone is considered by many to have great potential to grow in general availability and popularity.[161] In the category of depressants, the production of methaqualone (Quaalude or Mandrax) for the U.S. market has apparently ceased, although counterfeit varieties continue to surface. This is not true in southern Africa, however, where there is a thriving market for illicitly produced methaqualone from the Indian subcontinent. The trade in Mandrax to southern and eastern Africa is evidently dominated by Indian criminal organizations.[162]

Since the late 1980s, several noteworthy developments have also occurred in the worldwide trade in cannabis products. Mexico has remained the single largest producer of marijuana according to U.S. estimates, but both Jamaica and particularly Colombia have increased their output in recent years.[163] Colombian traffickers, moreover, are reportedly devoting increasing attention to supplying marijuana to the European market.[164] Meanwhile, domestic U.S. marijuana growers have succeeded in developing new, more potent strains of cannabis plant, as measured by the level of tetrahydrocannabinol (THC).[165] This latter trend has also been evident among European, notably Dutch, marijuana growers.[166]

In Europe, hashish from Afghanistan, Pakistan, and Lebanon continues to arrive overland through Turkey or by sea through the Mediterranean. As with other types of drugs, however, container ships are increasingly being used to transport bulk shipments through the major European
ports, such as Antwerp, Rotterdam, and Barcelona.[167] In recent years,
the importance of Morocco as a major supplier to western Europe has
also grown, with Spain and Portugal the main points of entry.[168]

Although information is scarce, cannabis cultivation is believed to be
increasing in other parts of Africa. UN sources, for example, note this
trend in Ghana, Malawi, Nigeria, Uganda, Sudan, Swaziland, Zaire, and
Zambia. Independent observers also report cultivation in The Gambia,
Ivory Coast, Chad, and Niger.[169] Besides Africa, there is also growing
concern about production increasing in several republics of the former
Soviet Union. A UN fact-finding team reported in 1992 that 140,000
hectares of cannabis with a potential output of 5,000 metric tons was
growing wild in the Chu valley of Kazakstan, with an additional 60,000
hectares in Kyrgyzstan.[170] It remains unclear, however, to what extent
this is being harvested for sale on the international market.[171]

During the period from 1989 to 1995 some important new initiatives
were also taken to tighten the international drug control regime. Building
on the provisions of the 1988 convention, increasing emphasis has been
placed on controlling the diversion of precursor chemicals for illicit drug
production and limiting the opportunities for money laundering. In July
1989 the Group of Seven agreed at the Houston summit to establish a
Financial Action Task Force to find ways to tackle drug money laundering. This task force subsequently recommended a list of forty measures
for countries to adopt. A similar mechanism—the Chemical Action Task
Force—was also set up and called for new provisions to restrict illicit
diversion.[172]

By the mid-1990s, U.S. drug control policy had also begun to change.
In recognition of the futility of trying to seal the borders from drug
smuggling, the Clinton administration has significantly scaled back its
predecessor's efforts to interdict drugs at the border and in the transit
zone. The role of the U.S. military in this effort has consequently been
downgraded.[173] Source-country control efforts continue, however, albeit
with more emphasis on fostering economic development and democratic
institution building while also supporting the efforts of foreign law enforcement agencies against the major trafficking organizations. The latter
tactic, in particular, seemed to be paying off, as the senior leaders of the
Cali cartel were all apprehended in the summer of 1995. Although this

was hailed as a major coup in the war against organized crime, the history of almost a century of effort in trying to suppress the drug trade suggests that the effect will be short lived.

Conclusions

The preceding historical overview reveals the overwhelming emphasis that has been placed on limiting the production and trafficking of illicit drugs on the one hand and deterring their consumption by the threat of legal sanctions on the other. As one historian has remarked, "Paradoxical though it may seem, much of the history of national and international narcotics control can be written without reference to addicts or addiction."[174] Once the drug problem became defined predominantly as a challenge to law and order rather than public health, this underlying approach became largely self-sustaining. Although more resources were devoted to drug prevention education, mass media antidrug campaigns, and treatment programs in the 1970s and 1980s, this lopsided approach has remained in effect.

This overview also reveals how much the underlying approach to international drug control has been constrained by the inherent limits of state sovereignty, both externally and internally. From the inception of the global prohibition regime, states have for different reasons openly or covertly resisted, ignored, and sometimes even subverted its expanding provisions. Even when a common commitment has existed, the need to observe the legal and territorial precepts of the nation-state have inhibited cooperation. Similarly, drug producers, traffickers, and consumers alike have all been able to exploit the limited ability of states to control what happens within their borders and what passes across them.

Finally, the history also demonstrates how the global drug market has been pushed and pulled not only by the forces of prohibition but also by miscellaneous social, political, and economic forces operating at both the local and global level. Collectively, these have shaped both the incentives and opportunities to produce, traffic, and consume illicit drugs in different countries at different times. These will be discussed in greater detail in the following chapter.

3 | Market Dynamics and the Challenge of Control

T HE GLOBAL DRUG MARKET is fundamentally no
different from any other commodity trade in being
driven by the standard economic forces of supply and demand. As long
as people feel a need for psychoactive substances, drug producers and
traffickers will endeavor to satisfy that need in return for some reward.
The promise of further and potentially greater rewards will in turn encourage suppliers to seek ways to sustain the demand and even expand
it. The drug trade, however, differs from most other commodities markets in one crucial respect. The global prohibition regime has rendered
illegal all but carefully specified drug transactions. This distorts how the
market would no doubt otherwise function in several important ways.

The most important effect of prohibition is on prices. The supply is
artificially constricted by the strict rules affecting which drugs can be
legally produced, medically prescribed, and sold commercially and by
the many law enforcement barriers against illicit manufacturers and distributors. As the availability of a commodity in demand diminishes, its
price generally rises, all else being equal. The illegality of the market,
moreover, allows illicit suppliers to set prices at a level that compensates
them for the risk they take and the additional costs they incur in supplying the market. They exact what economists term a "crime tariff" or

"criminalization tax" from the buyer. Along with the supply constrictions, this largely accounts for the higher prices found in black markets.[1]

Prohibition also affects the behavior of both suppliers and consumers in other important respects. Given the threat of legal sanctions, suppliers are typically risk averse, seeking places to operate where law enforcement is less effective or nonexistent. They also adopt strategies to reduce their exposure to law enforcement, such as relying on close family, ethnic, and community ties, compartmentalizing activities, and using the cover of legitimate business enterprises.[2] In general, the illegality of the drug business causes it to have a relatively loose hierarchical structure compared with legal enterprises, which put a premium on functional integration, market responsiveness, and overall efficiency.[3] Thus, although the trafficking organizations play a vital role in stimulating production, they are typically not able to control it in the way that production managers in a licit business would. Information does not flow up and down the supply chain in a way that would allow output to be finely calibrated to meet the expected level of market demand. This probably accounts for a tendency for supply to be initially sluggish in periods of rising demand and for markets to become saturated from overproduction when demand begins to fall. Overproduction may also be encouraged by the risk of product seizure.[4]

To undermine, circumvent, and otherwise overcome the market barriers established by law enforcement, suppliers are also likely to resort to bribery and other corrupt practices. Because those in the supply chain have no legal recourse if "contracts" are broken or their inventory is stolen, prohibition encourages the use of physical intimidation to deter such activity and violent sanctions to punish it. Similarly, securing and maintaining control of distribution outlets or "turf" is more likely to involve such tactics rather than the conventional practices of an open legal market. Furthermore, although suppliers cannot openly advertise their product to boost sales, neither do they have to submit it to a regulatory body to pass basic safety standards or meet certain quality controls before it can be introduced into the marketplace. They have almost complete freedom to adulterate, dilute, and otherwise tamper with the standard of the product to their advantage.

Prohibition also affects consumer behavior in significant ways. Because of the threat of legal penalties, including imprisonment in some cases, consumers must also evade law enforcement to participate in the marketplace. In doing so they are in virtual collusion with the traffickers; hence drug dealing is sometimes referred to as a consensual crime. At the same time, however, consumers are largely at the mercy of the suppliers. Because it is an illicit market, consumers have a more limited choice and less leverage to affect the price or quality of the product to their advantage. Again, there is no legal recourse available or consumer watchdog organization to appeal to.[5] Switching to other sellers, reducing consumption, or desisting altogether are the ultimate ways to signal dissatisfaction, but these choices may not be available or appealing.

As the previous chapter described, prohibitionist policies have had a profound effect on how the global drug market has evolved over the past century. At the same time, numerous other factors have also helped to shape its form, character, and dimensions in complex and sometimes unpredictable ways. Although the incentives created by the promise of black market profits clearly motivate the vast majority of those involved in supplying the drug market, they do not provide a complete or sufficient explanation for why some and not others are drawn into this business despite the risks involved. Nor do they explain what motivates some and not others to consume drugs, thereby creating the critical demand that stimulates the supply. The first part of this chapter, therefore, examines the relevant factors that both motivate and facilitate the supply and demand for illicit drugs. Besides bringing greater clarity to what drives the contemporary global drug market, the discussion is also helpful in assessing its likely evolution.

These same factors have obvious bearing on the effectiveness of various drug control measures. The second half of the chapter discusses the basic challenges that confront standard efforts to control the production, trafficking, and consumption of illicit drugs. The conventional categorization of the various drug control measures is to define them according to whether they are intended to affect either the supply or the demand for drugs. This is a fundamentally flawed dichotomy, however, which has distorted and confused public debates about how best to respond to the drug problem. As the previous chapter also illustrated, the overwhelming emphasis of the global prohibition regime has been to suppress drug production and trafficking. As such, it is commonly criticized for being oriented too much toward reducing supply and not enough toward limiting demand. Yet, since the ultimate intent of classic supply-reduction programs is to reduce the consumption of drugs by making them more expensive and less available to the public, they can just as easily be defined as demand sided. Conversely, such classic demand-reduction programs as drug prevention education and drug treatment programs ultimately reduce the incentives to supply the market by lowering consumption.[6] At the same time, the imposition of laws and legal sanctions against the possession and consumption of certain kinds of drugs, which are not typically viewed as measures to reduce demand, do just that by deterring potential users and penalizing offenders.

An alternative and more useful dichotomy that will be explained in greater detail below is to distinguish drug control measures on the basis of whether they employ what can loosely be termed negative or positive control strategies to achieve the common goal of lowering drug consumption. Whereas negative control measures rely on coercive tactics to deter and deny participation in the drug market, positive control measures promote voluntary abstention through the promise of rewards rather than the threat of penalties.

Incentives, Opportunities, and Resources

Affecting the underlying supply and demand relationship that drives the global drug market is a mix of incentives, opportunities, and resources.[7] These influence participation in each of the three principal components of the market: drug production (cultivation and processing), drug trafficking (transportation, distribution, and money laundering), and drug consumption. These are encapsulated in figure 3-1.

Drug Production

For most people involved in cultivating drugs, the motivation derives less from the promise of economic gain and more from the pressure of economic necessity. It is not coincidental that almost all the principal drug-producing countries are among the most impoverished in the world or have suffered an economic setback of some kind. For example, during the 1980s, the decade in which coca production exploded in Peru, per capita GDP fell 28 percent (to $854). Neighboring Bolivia suffered even more, with GDP falling 30 percent between 1976 and 1990. In Burma, per capita GDP over the same period stagnated at around a paltry $170, while in Afghanistan it is not much more than $200.[8] These figures for entire nations, however, mask the more acute conditions that typically prevail in the areas where most of the drugs are grown. Here, cultivating drug crops may represent the *only* way to make a living, certainly relative to alternative licit sources of income. The reasons include poor agricultural conditions, underdeveloped infrastructure, lack of rural support

FIGURE 3-1. Dynamics of the Global Drug Market

	Production	Trafficking	Consumption
Incentives	Subsistence High, reliable economic returns	Market profits Political motives	"Remedial" motives "Symbolic" motives
Opportunities	Ease of growth, processing, and manufacture Weak or absent state controls	Ease of transportation Expansion of trade and communi- cations Privatization and deregulation of goods and services Weak or absent state controls Money laundering	Availability and accessibility Price Weak or absent formal social controls Weak or absent informal social controls
Resources	Abundant land Abundant labor Materials Chemicals	Abundant recruits Smuggling and migrant networks Transportation Capital Weaponry Technology to evade law enforcement	Disposable income Income in kind Drug paraphernalia

systems, population growth, migration, natural disasters, economic mis-management, political conflict, foreign competition, low or unstable commodities prices, and declining foreign aid.

The economic attractions of drug production in the main source areas are made all the stronger by the nature of the commodity.[9] The primary drug-bearing plants are all relatively easy to cultivate under a wide range of soil, climatic, and topographical conditions. They are generally drought- and disease-resistant. With such a long history, the cultivation of opium poppy, coca, and cannabis plants is generally familiar and the germ plasm for each is widely available. Coca and opium poppy, moreover, can be harvested several times a year after they reach maturity when growing conditions are particularly favorable, making them attractive cash crops. Large amounts of land are not required, therefore, to generate economically efficient quantities. Although harvesting can be labor intensive, this does not present a problem since cheap labor is typically abundant. Unpaid family members can also be used if necessary.

Once harvested, drug crops do not perish quickly or easily and therefore do not require speedy transportation to the market. Coca, for example, can be stored for months without losing volume or potency. Raw opium can be stored even longer with no deleterious effect. Subsequent processing—of coca leaves into coca paste and cocaine base or raw opium into morphine base—is also a straightforward procedure, requiring neither sophisticated equipment nor unobtainable chemicals. Marijuana and hashish production is even simpler. With the exception of hashish oil, no special solvents are needed. Although the refinement of the processed drug crop entails more sophisticated expertise, this has become more widely available as pharmaceutical knowledge and training has become more diffuse around the world. Chemists can be easily bought, especially in areas where other employment opportunities are poor.

The same is also true for the chemicals used in drug production, which all have legitimate end uses. Hydrochloric acid, for example, which is used in the refinement of both opium and coca, is "one the most widely traded chemicals in the world."[10] Although many of the chemicals used in illicit drug production are still imported from North America and western Europe, this is becoming less common as the world's chemical industry has become more dispersed. Nearly a quarter of all industrial chemicals and over 18 percent of other chemical products are now produced outside of North America, western Europe, and Japan. Increasingly, countries such as Brazil, Argentina, India, Malaysia, Pakistan, China, South Korea, and Taiwan, as well as those in the former communist bloc, supply the essential chemicals.[11]

Finally, the opportunity to engage in the illicit production and refinement of the main botanical-based drugs is made easier by the fact that these activities typically take place in areas where government authority is weak or absent. Most are geographically remote and often under the control of insurgent forces such as the Sendero Luminoso in the upper Huallaga valley of Peru, the Revolutionary Armed Forces of Colombia, and the National Liberation Army in the growing areas of Colombia; the warring clans in Afghanistan; and the miscellaneous groups operating in the Shan plateau in Myanmar. Also, one of the heaviest concentrations of heroin processing in the world, as described in chapter 2, is in the semiautonomous North-West Frontier Province of Pakistan.[12]

Drug Trafficking

For most drug traffickers, the promise of some portion of the enormous profits to be made clearly provides the primary incentive. The price structure of the drug industry, with large value added at successive stages in the supply chain, permits enormous profits to be made, particularly at the wholesale and retail level in the principal markets of North America and western Europe. Some examples of the markup at various stages in the supply chain, as estimated by the U.S. Drug Enforcement Administration, are worth citing to illustrate the profit-making potential of the drug trade.[13] In the mid-1990s Colombian traffickers were able to purchase a kilogram of cocaine base in Bolivia or Peru for $650 to $1,000, process it into cocaine hydrochoride for export at around $950 to $1,235 a kilogram, and then sell it (diluted to 83 percent purity) at the wholesale level in the United States for $13,000 to $40,000 a kilogram. This same kilogram, moreover, when further diluted (to 72 percent) and sold in grams at the retail street level would yield $17,000 to $173,000, depending on the location. At more or less the same time, heroin processed from raw opium, cultivated and sold for approximately $70 a kilogram in Burma, could be purchased at around $3,000 a kilogram in northern Thailand and sold for export at 70 to 90 percent purity for $6,000 to $10,000 a kilogram in Bangkok. Once in the United States, however, the same kilogram of heroin would wholesale at $90,000 to $200,000, which when further diluted and sold in grams at the street level would yield the equivalent of about $1 million. Similar markups exist for heroin produced in and exported from Southwest Asia. Although not as comprehensive, data collected at the retail level in selected western European cities indicate comparable markups, although the street cost of cocaine is considerably higher than in the United States while heroin is much cheaper.[14]

Not surprisingly, it is widely believed that the principal drug trafficking groups and their leaders have amassed immense personal riches. Whereas the coca farmers and processors of South America are estimated to earn less than $1 billion a year from their labor (which is less than 1 percent of the total retail earnings), the traffickers in South American countries reap around $10 billion a year from international cocaine trafficking. When the costs of doing illegal business are subtracted, the annual profit of an "average" core Colombian trafficking organization is currently calculated to be at least $300 million.[15] Much higher profits have been estimated for some of the Mexican cartels.[16] For the opium and heroin trade, the gross returns of growers and traffickers are calculated to be much less than those from cocaine—around $0.5 billion and $5.0 billion, respectively—and the trafficking profits are also shared among more groups.[17] The gross earnings from trafficking other drugs are more difficult to calculate, given their more diverse nature, but the potential earnings are no less impressive. The Japanese police, for example, calculate that the volume of methamphetamine sales in Japan is worth more than $3 billion a year. One organization importing hashish and marijuana from Thailand into the United States and Canada is estimated to have netted more than $400 million over a ten-year period.[18]

Not all trafficking is carried out for personal enrichment or even subsistence. For some, political motives are the prime concern. Drug proceeds have been used to support local insurgencies and separatist movements in such places as Afghanistan, Pakistan, Burma, Peru, and Colombia; and drug trafficking has been linked recently to the activities of the Kurdistan Workers Party, the Turkish "Grey Wolves" terrorist organization, the Irish Republican Army, and Algerian Islamic fundamentalist groups.[19] Similarly, drug sales are believed to have financed the purchase of arms for local conflicts in such diverse places as Somalia, the Chiapas region of Mexico, Liberia, Kashmir, Tajikistan, and the former Yugoslavia.[20]

In trafficking, as in production, the nature of the commodity facilitates participation. In general, drugs do not require special handling, such as refrigeration or elaborate packaging, nor do they perish easily. Time and distance to market are therefore not constraining factors. Moreover, the inflated wholesale price of drugs and their capacity to be adulterated at the retail level gives them a high value-to-weight ratio, so that large quantities do not have to be smuggled to achieve significant returns. The high value-to-weight properties of most drugs also means that enormously valuable quantities of drugs can travel by relatively low-capacity means of transportation, such as pack animals, sailboats, or light aircraft. Other characteristics of drugs permit them to be easily concealed within legitimate commerce. The drugs with the highest retail value (cocaine, heroin, synthetics) are virtually odorless and can be physically altered in a multitude of ways to disguise them as other products or objects.[21]

Any individual willing to risk arrest and possessing nothing more than a passport, visa, and airline ticket can become an international drug smuggler. In a technique the Nigerian trafficking organizations have perfected, the relatively small amounts carried by each courier can be offset by employing large numbers of them. In Nigeria, the most populous country in Africa, traffickers are helped by an almost limitless supply of potential recruits who are either easily tempted by the rewards offered by the traffickers or ignorant of the risk. And for many who understand the risks involved, even the prospect of jail is better than the life they would ordinarily face.[22]

Large pools of people in dire enough straits to be lured into drug trafficking are of course not confined to West Africa. Since the earliest days of the illicit drug trade, trafficking and distribution have also been facilitated by international migration and the networks of immigrant communities that have consequently developed in key markets. As the previous chapter described, this has happened with Chinese, Turkish, Iranian, Pakistani, Indian, Jamaican, Cuban, Colombian, Nigerian, and Yugoslavian minorities in North America and Europe. The presence of foreign-based communities provides obvious advantages. Since many of the immigrants are economically disadvantaged, there is usually no difficulty in finding recruits to transport and distribute drugs. Traffickers can travel back and forth relatively inconspicuously. A common ethnic identity, moreover, reinforces group cohesion, loyalty, and security. Discipline is enforced by the threat of exposure if the immigrant happens to be an illegal resident, and turncoats face reprisals against family members in the home country.

As personal mobility and commercial trade links have expanded throughout the world in recent years, so too have the opportunities to smuggle drugs. This has arisen from several intertwined trends. The first is the growth in privately owned long-range transportation systems such as light aircraft and maritime pleasure craft. These have become cheaper to buy and operate throughout the world and, therefore, more common. The second is advances in commercial transportation systems that have made it easier and cheaper to move people and goods on a global scale. This has been reflected in the expansion of international airline networks, containerized shipping and commercial airfreight services, and tourism. The third is the progressive reduction of economic and political barriers to personal travel and international trade.

The latter has been occurring on a global scale since World War II through the General Agreement on Tariffs and Trade and regionally with the creation of free trade zones and customs unions. The most advanced regional arrangement of this kind remains the European Union. Since the European common market was first established in the 1950s, trade barriers and border controls have been progressively reduced or eliminated within the boundaries of its member states. Such arrangements have also lifted constraints on European transportation systems. For example, in 1988 road haulage quotas were removed and permits for operating in another member country were no longer required. By March 1991 all restrictions had been removed for air cargo carriers based in one country to pick up freight in another country and deliver it to a third. And on January 1, 1993, cargo moving by road was given free access to any member state of the community.[23]

Although not as advanced or politically motivated, the same trends are evident in other regions. In the Western Hemisphere are the North American Free Trade Agreement (NAFTA) between Canada, the United States, and Mexico; MERCOSUR, comprising the South American states of Argentina, Brazil, Paraguay, and Uruguay; and CARICOM in the Caribbean. Some of these build on long-standing trading arrangements, such as a 1929 treaty between Chile, Bolivia, and Peru that allows sealed, uninspected containers to be moved through their ports. Similar arrangements exist between Bolivia and Argentina.[24] In Asia there is the Association of Southeast Asian Nations (ASEAN), and in Africa, the East African Preferential Trade Area (PTA), to name some of the more prominent. Beyond these regional arrangements, there are also numerous ports around the world that now enjoy the status of free trade zones, such as Colon, Panama, and Guangdong and Fujian Provinces in China.

In tandem with the general reduction of trade barriers, states have begun to remove their control over key sectors of the economy, including transportation, to cut costs and promote competitiveness. This can be seen in the current trend toward privatization and deregulation of transportation and port authorities that is taking place throughout Latin America.[25] In 1991 Mexico first allowed private companies to build and operate their own ports. Two years earlier, it had deregulated the trucking industry by not only lowering the barriers to entry but also allowing free movement in any city, port, or railroad station in the country. As a consequence, the number of licensed trucks rose by 62 percent in two years. Similar initiatives have been undertaken in Chile and Argentina. In 1991 the Colombian government also decided to privatize its state-run port authority. In place of Colombian national police port detachments will be private security firms, a shift that the DEA fears will increase the likelihood of corruption.[26] Furthermore, the increasing role of flags of convenience in the maritime shipping industry has also reduced oversight of what is transported on the high seas.

As economic barriers have fallen virtually everywhere, so too have many political ones. The demise of the iron curtain around central Europe and around the former Soviet Union has opened up vast areas that were previously off limits to the international drug trade. This has given traffickers the opportunity, as noted previously, to develop new routes to the lucrative markets in the West. Though more circuitous, they are also less closely monitored or more open to corruption. The end of communist rule has left many of the former eastern bloc countries poorly trained and equipped to monitor their borders, some of which are entirely new, with no prior customs or police infrastructure to build upon. Government spending cutbacks, moreover, have curtailed the ability of many of these countries to rectify the situation.[27]

Money Laundering

The globalization of financial services has also made it easier for traffickers to move money where it is needed to underwrite the many different component operations of the drug trade and to launder the proceeds successfully.[28] For many of the reasons outlined above, borders are just as porous to the movement of money as they are to drug shipments. Indeed, in many cases, drug money moves more easily, quickly, and sometimes even perfectly legally. The global financial system provides an enormous array of opportunities and loopholes to disguise the ownership, purpose, source, and final resting place of drug money. This typically entails three stages that may be carried out in discrete steps or simultaneously.[29] The first, generally known as "placement," entails depositing the cash proceeds from drug transactions into bank holdings, financial assets, or resalable goods. In the second step, called "layering," the placed proceeds are physically or procedurally moved to disguise their origin. Finally, through the process of "integration," a legitimate explanation is created for the source of income.

To carry out these different steps, money launderers have long relied on a standard menu of tactics. A common technique is the creation of multiple bank accounts in which numerous small deposits or payments are made by teams of launderers (known as "smurfing," after the diminutive cartoon characters) to avoid generating suspicion or triggering bank reporting requirements.[30] Money from these accounts is then simply wired to other banks almost anywhere in the world, from where it can be retransmitted just as easily to other destinations. Modern communications and the integration of the global financial system have dramatically expanded the scope for layering money in this way. For example, the New York Clearing House, which runs the Clearing House Interbank Payment System (CHIPS), handles 750,000 to 1.2 million orders each night. The sheer volume and the absence of a universal time stamp on transmissions means that "it is virtually impossible to untangle completed settlements and to roll back transactions."[31] Little is required to render the resultant electronic paper trail so complex as to be effectively beyond discovery.

The final resting places long favored by launderers are the many offshore banking jurisdictions—such as Aruba, the Cayman Islands, Liechtenstein, Cyprus, Hong Kong, or Luxembourg—where financial secrecy and client confidentiality are guaranteed.[32] Sometimes this is not always necessary. Certain banks have often been so anxious for infusions of capital that they have not particularly cared about the origins of the money.[33] Similarly, the competitiveness of the banking industry has led to lax supervision in places. As one State Department report observed: "There is constant pressure at banks large and small to conclude transactions rapidly, so as not to disrupt time sensitive deals or fall victim to changing exchange rates. When profits are otherwise slim, some banks, perhaps many, will ask fewer questions when taking greater risks but perhaps charging higher rates."[34] In Asia and among Asian immigrants, the existence of well-established informal banking systems—known as *hundi* in Pakistan, *hawala* in India, and by several Chinese names in Southeast Asia—provides another conduit for large sums of money to be deposited and transmitted internationally without any government supervision.[35] These highly efficient and extensive networks are used routinely for both legitimate as well as illicit purposes. Ultimately, money launderers can always physically smuggle cash across borders by exploiting more or less the same opportunities that exist for transporting drugs.[36]

Innumerable schemes can also be devised to provide a credible explanation for the large amounts of money that drug transactions typically generate. Some of the more common involve casinos and other gambling operations, real estate brokerages, precious metals and gem export and import businesses, antique and jewelry shops, and travel agencies; also common is the practice of false invoicing.[37] The general ease with which "front" companies or "shell" corporations can be established facilitates such activities. Once criminal enterprises diversify and invest in legitimate business, it becomes increasingly difficult to distinguish licit from illicit activities.

Several new money-laundering trends are also noteworthy.[38] One is the growing use of nonbank financial institutions (post offices, currency exchange houses, travel agents, credit unions, and checking services) and their principal instruments (postal money orders, travelers' checks, and certificates of deposit). This trend can be attributed in part to the introduction of money-laundering controls focused on the operations of banks, but more to the proliferation of these alternative financial systems, which are increasingly interconnected globally. Money orders and travelers' checks, for example, can be simply wired or mailed to designated recipients around the world. It is no accident, therefore, that nonbank financial services of this kind have flourished in many high-trafficking areas of the United States.[39]

Increasingly, the more sophisticated forms of money laundering are moving beyond the use of wire transfers to exploit an expanding array of other financial instruments, such as letters of credit, bonds and other securities, prime bank notes, and guarantees. Similarly, financial services companies, such as investment enterprises—which are springing up in many postcommunist and developing countries as a result of economic liberalization—are also being used to launder money. Although they are technically not banks, they perform many of the same functions without having to conform to banking practices.[40] Financial supervisors, like their customs and police counterparts, lack the resources to monitor and supervise this rapidly burgeoning sector of the international financial services market.

The liberalization of financial systems in many countries has also allowed many banks to be owned or controlled by criminal enterprises. The privatization of banking in Colombia, for example, has reportedly allowed the Cali cartel to purchase or develop an influential stake in several banks. This has apparently extended into neighboring Venezuela as a result of the growing integration of the two countries' financial industries.[41] The Italian mafia has also reportedly sought to obtain significant shareholdings in small or provincial banks.[42] Furthermore, the U.S. State Department believes that a significant proportion of the 2,000 banks operating in Russia today are now controlled by organized crime. Until relatively recently, "it has been cheaper to buy a bank than to buy a luxury auto" in Russia.[43] The red tape required to establish and register a bank can be easily circumvented through bribery or coercion. It reportedly costs only $1,200 to get the necessary documents, stamps, and signatures to open a bank in Russia, while to illegally register a bank as a business, thereby skirting banking regulations, costs a heftier but hardly prohibitive $300,000.[44]

Drug Consumption

The factors that motivate and facilitate the supply of illicit drugs are far easier to define than those that drive consumption. The question of what leads people to take psychoactive substances cannot be answered in simple terms; the basic reason is that drug use is not a homogenous activity and drug users are not a homogenous group.[45] Drug consumption covers multiple patterns of use, from brief experimentation and irregular "casual use" (which means different things to different people) to frequent "hard core" daily use that may or may not indicate some form of psychological or physiological dependence.[46] Each consumption pattern can in turn have different and multiple etiologies that vary between individuals and groups at different times.

At the group level, the dominant factors for a specific age cohort, socioeconomic stratum, or ethnic group in a specific community, region, or country are also not necessarily transferable to others, even to those who share broadly similar characteristics. In short, the forces that can affect types and levels of drug consumption are many and frequently intertwined. As one expert has observed:

> The contributing factors that may predispose a person to or protect them from drug use/abuse/dependence (initiation, continuation, progression within and across drug classes, regression, cessation, relapse) are a combination of genetic, biological, psychological, psychiatric, . . . familial, and social, structural, and cultural environmental factors.[47]

With due recognition of the inherent complexity of drug consumption and the very real limits of universal statements about it, it is possible, nevertheless, to make some generalizations about what can motivate drug use.

A helpful starting point is to distinguish between use that is driven by the expected pharmacological effects of drug consumption and use that is motivated by what it represents to the user and others.[48] The two types are by no means mutually exclusive, and in many cases they can be mutually reinforcing. Thus, for some, initiation into drug use may have less to do with the sensation that is expected to ensue than with the desire to conform to the behavior of a peer group, to observe the fashion of the moment, or to demonstrate one's independence from others and societal norms in general. For regular users and certainly those who become dependent in some way, the opposite is more likely to be true.[49]

The first type, which may be called "remedial" use, can spring from many different physical and psychological states, such as boredom, anxiety, fear, physical pain, grief, alienation, hunger, stress, exhaustion, or depression. The choice of drug is relevant because the user is looking for a specific remedy, whether it is mental or physical stimulation, release from personal inhibitions, or numbness to physical pain or longing.[50] Within this general category can be added "transcendental" use, in which drugs are taken to reach a different spiritual state, to heighten perception and understanding, and to enhance one's mental or physical capacity.[51] People who become habituated to illicit drug use as a consequence of legally prescribed drugs also fall into this category, as do those who have progressed from taking licit recreational drugs such as alcohol and tobacco. There are many different preconditions, or what epidemiologists call "risk factors," that make remedial drug use attractive and therefore more likely. Correlations have been observed between drug use and personal illness, injury and loss, psychic trauma, dysfunctional families and broken homes, failed relationships, scholastic and professional stress, failure, ennui, frustration, poverty and hunger, and conflict or war.[52]

The second kind of drug use, which may be called "symbolic" use, is etiologically no less complex. Drugs are taken to make an implicit or explicit statement about oneself, one's association with a particular group, or one's relationship to society as a whole. The choice of drug is less important, therefore, than what taking drugs is believed to represent. For young drug users, it can signify a rejection of an older generation's values, as was clearly the case in the United States and Western Europe during the 1960s and 1970s, or it can signal dissatisfaction with the prevailing sociopolitical order, as has occurred in many authoritarian countries. More commonly, it reflects general adolescent rebellion, when a variety of risk-taking activities are carried out to register independence from parental control and establish maturity or "adultness" to do things that are prohibited by what seem to be arbitrary societal rules. Peer pressure and the perceived need to conform with the behavior of a group to foster or maintain one's association and standing within it reinforce these tendencies. Adolescents are especially vulnerable to such pressures, as they are still developing confidence in their identities and are often acutely concerned with fashion trends.[53] Peer pressure or the desire to be fashionable clearly do not end with adolescence, however. Cocaine became attractive to an older cohort in the United States in part because of the lifestyle it was considered to project.[54]

Information about the real or expected effects of drugs, what society thinks of them, how popular they are, and who else is taking them influences both classes of potential users. This is broadcast or passed along in many different ways—through friends, family, school, the workplace, and such media as television, music, books, newspapers, and films. The accuracy or completeness of the information is less important than whether it sparks interest, curiosity, and desire, or, alternatively, fear, disapproval, and revulsion. Perversely, the fact that the drug-related information and images may be couched in negative terms apparently does not always deter use. The associations that are made between drugs and youth rebelliousness, antisocial behavior, and decadent lifestyles can reportedly have the counterproductive effect of spurring symbolic forms of drug use in imitation.

As personal mobility and communications have increased and as the reach of mass media has expanded globally, more people have inevitably become aware of drugs. In the same way that these trends have helped homogenize consumer tastes and created mass markets for such products as blue jeans, T-shirts, hamburgers, rock music, and Walkmans, they have also apparently influenced the internatic nal demand for drugs.[55] As noted previously, America's growing cultural influence after World War II clearly contributed to the rise of a mass market for drugs in Western Europe.[56] Anecdotal information also points to the more recent effect of Western influences on stimulating drug consumption in parts of the postcommunist and developing world.[57]

The incentives that motivate the consumption of illicit drugs can in turn be modified by the opportunities to acquire and use them. Certain drugs are clearly more available in certain areas than in others, either because these areas are close to sources of production or substantial markets have already developed. Availability, however, is more commonly defined by the price of drugs and the purchasing power of the would-be consumer.[58] For some the price may fall within the margins of their disposable income, while for others it may simply be too high. The price barrier, however, can be overcome by either acquiring more money—legally or illegally—or by using income in kind, including sexual favors. The sensitivity, or in economic terms "elasticity," of consumer demand to subsequent changes in the price of drugs is difficult to assess precisely. It is believed that occasional consumers are likely to be more sensitive than heavy ones, and the elasticity of demand is likely to be lower for drugs that can cause physical or psychological dependence, such as heroin or cocaine, than it is for others, such as marijuana. The effect of price changes on consumer demand is likely to be greater over time.[59] In addition to price, availability has another element: the time, inconvenience, and personal risk involved in obtaining drugs.[60] Some argue that this is often more critical than price in affecting the level of consumer use.[61]

Beyond these factors, the opportunities to consume drugs are nearly limitless, including that offered by the sanctuary of private property, where individuals enjoy their greatest protection from the intrusions of the state. The relative ease with which drugs can be self-administered no doubt also facilitates consumption. Although initiation usually entails the advice or example of experienced users, the act of taking most drugs is not difficult to master. In the majority of cases it is only a question of chewing, swallowing, inhaling, or snorting the drug. Special paraphernalia, while sometimes desirable to heighten the effect, are not essential for most drugs. The important exception, of course, is intravenous drug use. Hypodermic syringes are generally not difficult to acquire, however, at least in most advanced industrialized countries, and although this is a more difficult form of administration, it too can be easily learned. In some cases the ease of use is bolstered by the immediacy of effect, as with heroin or crack cocaine. That the use of some drugs is not incapacitating to some people or outwardly detectable by others may also reduce personal inhibitions about consumption.

Negative and Positive Controls

For the reasons discussed at the outset, I will not use the standard dichotomy between supply-reduction and demand-reduction measures to assess the principal control options and the challenges that each faces. Instead, I will analyze them according to whether they employ either negative or positive control strategies against each of the three principal components of the drug market. It is important to note, again for the reasons discussed earlier, that control efforts in one area of the drug market can affect others. The different measures organized in this manner are shown in figure 3-2 and will be described in turn below.

FIGURE 3-2. Negative and Positive Drug Control Measures

	Production	Trafficking	Consumption
Negative control measures	Forcible eradication Chemical controls Destruction of processing centers	Interdiction Disabling trafficking networks	Laws and legal sanctions Policing Mandatory drug testing
Positive control measures	Crop substitution Alternative development	Legal amnesty and clemency Alternative employment Trade and industry cooperation	Drug prevention education Mass media campaigns Drug treatment programs Drug-free zones Harm-reduction techniques

Controlling Production

The principal negative control method to limit the production of botanical-based drugs is forcible eradication programs. Such programs face formidable challenges. Many areas are simply off limits, at least to nonaerial forms of eradication. Even when it has been possible to gain access to the growing areas, the process of physically uprooting plants and preventing them from being recovered and grown again is time consuming and labor intensive.[62] More often than not, it is also dangerous. Since forcible eradication represents a direct threat to the livelihood of the local farmers and in some cases well-armed insurgent organizations reliant on the drug trade, it has often met with violent resistance.[63] It can also prompt costly countermeasures against the state. For example, when the Colombian government began spraying drug crops with herbicides in 1994, angry farmers occupied state-owned oil-pumping stations, significantly reducing output as well as blocking the flow of Ecuadorian oil to the Pacific coast.[64] Growers can also use other tactics, such as concealing their crops among other vegetation or legitimate crops. Aerial spraying can overcome some of these tactics and is more cost effective, but it remains unpopular because of potential environmental hazards.[65]

Eradication programs have also proven to be perversely counterproductive in many cases.[66] The threat of eradication, for example, has often caused farmers to compensate by planting more crops. Even when farmers have been offered financial inducements not to grow drug crops, they have been known to use the money to underwrite new cultivation. The biggest challenge, however, remains preventing cultivation from migrating to nearby areas or entirely different regions. The inherent mobility of most drug crops means that successful eradication in one area is merely compensated by growth in another. In the case of coca cultivation, which is geographically concentrated, a comprehensive eradication program, systematically implemented in a sustained manner by all the Andean countries, might reduce production enough to significantly raise wholesale and retail prices. However, unless such a program were carried out in conjunction with massive financial offsets as well as credible assurances about the ecological impact, the predictable backlash would soon undermine such a campaign. Given the more dispersed nature of the other principal botanical drugs, such eradication campaigns seem even less feasible.

Efforts to reduce production downstream by making it difficult for traffickers to gain access to the chemicals needed for processing also face significant challenges. As noted earlier, the increasing dispersion of the international chemical industry is hindering the task of controlling the export and end use of its products. Although the use of North American– and European-produced chemicals in illicit drug refinement has been reduced considerably through the application of tighter export restrictions, many countries in Asia, Africa, and the former communist bloc have yet to implement the international chemical control agreements or establish the necessary monitoring and enforcement structures because they lack trained personnel and funding. Many chemical suppliers take little interest in how their product is to be used, while import and export licensing authorities in many countries frequently fail to investigate end use in great depth. This fosters the practice of numerous illegal diversion tactics, such as "inaccurately reporting amounts of manufactured and stored chemicals and their intended destinations or customers; making illicit multiple sales or shipping transactions; falsely documenting or labeling chemicals; substituting shipments; establishing illegitimate, or 'front' companies; and extracting controlled substances from non-controlled mixtures."[67]

Where diversion is not possible, the trafficking organizations have been adept at substituting uncontrolled or commonly available chemicals. Gasoline and cement, for example, are now reportedly being used for cocaine refinement.[68] In 1993 Colombian police discovered a cocaine-processing device that requires only hydrochloric acid and water to operate. Traffickers are also using chemicals more efficiently through repeated recycling. Certain traffickers, for example, are reportedly able to use some chemicals up to seven times.[69]

Past campaigns to destroy the cocaine base and cocaine hydrochloride production centers illustrate the difficulty in targeting this phase of the supply chain. What success has been achieved in seeking out and disabling laboratories has proven difficult to sustain, not only because of the level of effort required and the political turbulence that such campaigns typically generate, but also because traffickers adapt by dispersing production and making laboratories more mobile and better camouflaged.[70] If necessary, they can shift to entirely new areas. Much the same is true for heroin refinement and the production of synthetic drugs.

Crop substitution programs, in which farmers growing drug crops are encouraged to switch to licit agricultural products, represent the principal positive control method for limiting the production of botanical drugs. Although there have been some successes, the overall record has also been poor. This is not always because licit alternatives cannot match or even better the economic rewards of drug crops. Some crop substitution programs have reported higher overall returns from certain licit crops. Studies have also identified other agricultural products that have the promise to be just as profitable, if not more so. The basic problem, however, is that these more lucrative crops are typically consumed locally, and local markets are not large enough to sustain a large-scale shift in production. The isolated nature of the main source areas and their poor transportation infrastructure make it difficult and costly to generate new markets beyond the immediate vicinity. Efforts to redress this problem by building roads and bridges to make distant markets more accessible have also perversely backfired in some instances by making it easier to export drug crops.[71]

Most of the nontraditional alternative crops also typically require lengthy gestation periods before the first harvest can be reaped; by this time, it is not clear whether they would still be so economically attractive. For poor, risk-averse farmers with limited resources to fall back on, drug cultivation promises a quicker, more predictable return on their investment. As a result, farmers often continue to grow their drug crops alongside the putative substitutes as an insurance policy. Their calculations are also likely to be reinforced by the traffickers who sponsor and buy their produce. Aside from offering protection or using coercion, the traffickers can easily outbid the economic inducements to grow alternative crops.[72] In the cocaine trade, the growing trend for coca leaf growers to "integrate forward" and exploit the higher value added that they can obtain by producing cocaine base can also undermine the competitiveness of alternative crops.

The relative success of some crop substitution projects has nevertheless taught some valuable lessons. The experience of Thailand in significantly reducing drug cultivation stands out in this respect.[73] The Thai government has a long-standing program (aided by considerable international donor support) to develop the opium-producing northern highland region and integrate its marginalized inhabitants, both politically and geographically, with the rest of the country through extensive road construction. The program appears to have made a significant difference in addition to demonstrating the importance of macroeconomic factors, notably the value of a rapidly expanding economy in providing alternative employment and market opportunities for those engaged in drug crop cultivation. Although the jury is still out, the more recent experience of crop substitution programs in the Chapare region of Bolivia shows some encouraging signs of confirming the Thai example. As a result of investment in the transportation infrastructure, marketing assistance, and other alternative development programs, more farmers are reportedly turning to growing licit agricultural crops than ever before.[74] Overall, however, the successes recorded in Thailand and possibly Bolivia have to be kept in proportion to the situation in these two countries' respective neighbors, Myanmar and Peru.

Controlling Trafficking

Given the expanding range of opportunities to traffic drugs internationally and launder the proceeds, the ability of states to interdict shipments before they reach their intended destination has quite clearly diminished. The probability of interception and arrest in certain areas of the world was hardly very high in the first place. The international borders of almost all the major drug-producing states in Latin America, Southeast Asia, and Southwest Asia are long and pass through physically remote and difficult terrain with few natural barriers. They are consequently very difficult, if not impossible, to monitor effectively. The advent of radar and other electronic monitoring devices has improved matters somewhat; however, judging by the ease with which light aircraft, small ships, or vehicles can evade these devices or exploit the poor response times of law enforcement, the border regions of most of the main source areas remain effectively porous to the drug trade. In Peru, for example, of the 356 registered and 40 unregistered airports, only 58 are controlled by the civilian aeronautics agency and 9 by the military.[75] In southern China, police and customs authorities face the nearly impossible task of controlling a 2,100-mile border with Burma, Vietnam, and Laos that millions of people now cross annually because travel restrictions have been eased.[76] In regions where borders cut through areas of ethnically homogenous peoples, controlling cross-border movements is doubly difficult. The Iranians have discovered this after constructing a vast system of fortifications and barriers along 840 kilometers of Iran's 2,000-kilometer border with Afghanistan and Pakistan for the purpose of sealing it from drug trafficking. Despite this expensive effort, which is estimated to have cost nearly $1 billion, the Baluchi tribesmen and Afghan refugees who straddle the border still manage to routinely pass back and forth, some ferrying drugs.[77]

Beyond the drug-producing regions and closer to the main consumer markets, border controls have traditionally presented more meaningful barriers for traffickers to overcome. The sheer volume of international transactions now taking place, however, has significantly lowered the probability of being caught. The numbers are staggering and, for law enforcement, quite sobering. Some examples help convey the magnitude of the challenge.

—In fiscal year 1994, 451 million people entered the United States by land, sea, or air. Nearly 15.6 million traveled through New York airports alone in 1993.[78]

—In 1992 Miami International Airport had a total of 132 airlines making 1,200 landings daily. In 1993 it handled 12.4 million passengers and 1.1 million tons of air cargo. Two million tropical plants from South America arrived at Houston International Airport each month during 1992.[79]

—In 1993 there were 30.7 million air travelers in Europe, 10.8 million in the Caribbean region, and 16 million in the Far East. Between 1988 and 1992, fifty new airlines were added to the Asian market, not including China, where forty airlines were operating by 1993.[80]

—In 1991 the world's top ten seaports handled 33.6 million containers, up from 11.4 million just over a decade earlier. The two largest—Singapore and Hong Kong—each handled more than 6 million containers, and the largest European and U.S. seaports—Rotterdam and Los

Angeles—handled more than 3 million and 2 million, respectively. In August 1993 Hong Kong alone handled 865,000 containers.[81]

—In 1993, 1,000 Trans International Routiers–registered trucks passed through the Kapitan Andreevo border checkpoint on the Bulgarian-Turkish border each day. In the same year 50,000 trucks passed through the border post of Gyula on the Hungarian-Romanian border. Each day, 5,000 trucks enter the United States from Mexico.[82]

With such extraordinary levels of international passenger and container traffic, the vast majority of border and customs inspections can be no more than cursory at best. Intrusive inspections must inevitably be highly selective, given the resources that are typically available and the time and effort required to carry them out. This is particularly true for container inspections, which are extremely labor intensive. As an illustration, it takes five U.S. customs officers three hours to thoroughly examine a single container.[83] Suspicious containers have to be sent to a special inspection point and "may require that the container be completely emptied, holes drilled in the container walls and floors, or interior dimensions measured."[84] Moreover, as a result of manpower reductions, the U.S. Customs Service has streamlined many of its traditional inspection controls and replaced them with automated systems and postaudits. Although this has speeded the flow of traffic at ports of entry, it has almost certainly provided more opportunities for circumvention and abuse.[85] In fact, U.S. Customs now estimates that only 3 percent of the nearly 9 million containers that enter the United States every year are checked by customs inspectors. For example, of the 5,000 trucks entering daily from Mexico, only about 200 are inspected.[86]

The difficulty of intercepting drugs in transit has led to a relative shift in the focus of law enforcement efforts toward disabling the trafficking organizations and their networks. The challenges facing this strategy are no less formidable, however. In most of the key producer and transit countries, bribery and corruption provide the first line of defense for the traffickers.[87] The relatively poor salaries of government officials, police officers, customs and tax inspectors, judges, and members of the armed services in these countries make them especially vulnerable to traffickers offering relatively large sums of money for their cooperation.[88] If bribery does not work, there is always intimidation and physical coercion. Again, in the many areas of the world where the rule of law has never been fully established or has broken down irretrievably, there is little or no deterrent to such tactics. Compounding this problem is the relative ease with which trafficking groups can acquire explosives and modern weaponry often more powerful than that available to law enforcement. Many trafficking groups have developed their own private armies to protect their property and operations from law enforcement as well as other trafficking groups.[89] Once established, such sanctuaries are extremely costly to attack, as Colombia discovered in the late 1980s.

Targeting the distribution networks also has its challenges. The standard police techniques of surveillance and undercover infiltration are more difficult to carry out within closely knit immigrant communities. Given the closed nature of these communities, where emphasis is often placed on personal connections, gaining the confidence of the traffickers is no easy task. Informants are also hard to come by for the reasons noted earlier, and some countries do not offer immunity and witness protection programs to those who do cooperate with the police. Although law enforcement bodies can exploit an impressive array of intelligence-gathering devices to eavesdrop on and monitor drug-trafficking operations, this advantage has been eroded by the increasing sophistication and commercial availability of such technical countermeasures as encrypted communications systems and antibugging devices, as well as cheap cellular phones that can be disposed of before court orders can be gained to tap them legally.[90] Attempts to collect intelligence by technical means have also been hampered, at least initially, by inadequate knowledge of the language and dialects used by the immigrant communities.[91]

Other police strategies also have their limitations. These include "controlled delivery" operations, in which drugs are allowed to transit countries so information can be collected for the entire distribution network to be later "rolled up," or "buy and bust" operations, in which undercover law enforcement officers posing as distributors purchase drugs from dealers who are then arrested for trafficking. Some countries, such as Turkey and Poland, have until recently prohibited such operations on their soil because they are seen as either entrapment or aiding and abetting a crime. Police and customs authorities have also been known to reject or ignore the larger objective of disabling a network in favor of gaining domestic credit for making a large seizure. More broadly, the need to adhere to sovereign prerogatives continues to hinder international law enforcement cooperation in such areas as intelligence dissemination, joint surveillance, "hot pursuit" across borders, evidence sharing, and extradition.[92]

In general, control strategies that focus on intercepting shipments and disabling trafficking organizations face the general substitution and adaptation problem. Drugs, for the most part, can be easily and cheaply replaced, while the trafficking organizations can reconstitute themselves or be replaced by entirely new ones. Given the price structure and profit potential of the drug trade, trafficking control efforts have to be extremely effective to overcome the powerful economic incentives to supply the market, and especially so to raise retail prices high enough to make drugs unaffordable to all but the very rich.[93] Moreover, as others have argued and the historical overview attests, trafficking organizations adapt and survive in Darwinian fashion, making subsequent control efforts ever more challenging.

In contrast, targeting the financial resources and profits of the trafficking organizations has more potential to do harm to their operations and deprive them of what ultimately motivates their activities. The basic problem, however, is the growing number of opportunities, discussed above, to launder dirty money in the global financial system. Moreover, many countries have either not adopted measures against money laundering or have failed to implement the ones they have formally agreed to observe.[94] Money laundering is still not a criminal offense in many jurisdictions. Where it is, effective monitoring mechanisms have not been put into place. Sometimes the reporting regulations are voluntary, rather than mandatory. These are not just shortcomings of countries in the developing or postcommunist world. Canada, for example, still does not require cash movements across its borders to be declared or reported.[95] As in other areas of law enforcement, cooperation continues to be hampered by inadequate sharing of information. And ultimately, as long as there are internationally sanctioned methods for legally moving and hiding clean money to evade taxation (particularly in offshore banking havens), it will be very difficult to make real inroads against money laundering.

Given the incentive structure of the illicit drug industry, positive inducements to forgo trafficking and money laundering face even greater problems than those targeted at production. Several options exist. One is to offer legal amnesty or clemency to drug traffickers in return for their cooperation with law enforcement authorities and, ultimately, the termination of further operations. Deals along these lines have been negotiated by drug traffickers and government authorities in Colombia and Myanmar with decidedly mixed results.[96] Besides attracting the ire of those who feel that such strategies essentially reward criminal acts and undermine the deterrent effect of the law, these deals have had a minimal or short-lived effect on the level of trafficking. Furthermore, such approaches have to be comprehensive in scope, or new traffickers will merely fill the vacuum left by those who have reached an accommodation with the state.

A similar but less formal strategy is the reputed tacit agreement reached in Japan between organized crime groups—the Yakuza—and police, which permits certain kinds of illicit businesses to operate according to informal rules, but forbids extensive drug trafficking.[97] This arrangement may no longer exist, given the reported increase in the albeit still relatively low levels of drug trafficking in Japan. In any case, the unique qualities of Japanese society raise doubts about the applicability of such tactics elsewhere.

In addition to these direct positive control tactics, there are indirect ones that can help curb trafficking and money laundering. Targeted investment and employment programs designed to expand the range of legal economic alternatives in high trafficking areas can reduce the potential pool of recruits. But again, the economic opportunities have to be sufficiently attractive and open to large numbers of people to make a significant dent in the problem.[98] However, to the extent that such programs may lower crime and improve the quality of life in certain neighborhoods, they can be considered more generally worthwhile.

Another indirect approach to limit drug trafficking and money laundering is to engage the active cooperation of trade and industry in identifying and reporting suspicious activities in a timely fashion to law enforcement authorities according to prescribed arrangements laid out in formal memorandums of understanding (MoU). This practice has become increasingly common not only among the banking community, as discussed above, but also among airlines and commercial conveyancy operators as a result of a British initiative at the July 1991 G-7 summit in London. The Customs Cooperation Council, representing national customs authorities around the world, has since drawn up guidelines for such MoUs, while this practice has received further impetus in the form of a UN resolution.[99] Although this kind of self-regulation can be considered another negative control measure, inasmuch as its primary purpose is to aid law enforcement, such cooperation can also have positive rewards for trade and industry. It can enhance their business reputation as "clean" operations that are less likely to be targeted and disrupted by law enforcement bodies.[100]

Controlling Consumption

Underlying all current efforts to reduce drug consumption—whether they employ negative or positive control strategies—are the laws that prohibit in varying ways the freedom to sell, acquire, possess, and take certain psychoactive substances for reasons other than medical or scientific purposes. As such, they represent society's collective disapproval, typically on the grounds of public health, of all but carefully limited types of drug use.[101] As Mark H. Moore has argued:

> The law is seen as a collective understanding about the dangers of drug use, and the establishment of individual responsibility to avoid drug use. Its promulgation seeks to remind individuals about the reasons for the law, and to increase the law's moral force and legitimacy. It produces its practical results by promoting voluntary compliance among those who are persuaded, and by authorizing others in the community to comment informally on behavior that lies well outside the law. In effect, the law and its promulgation are seen as a way of establishing, or sustaining, or giving force to a community norm.[102]

Moreover, in setting penalties for noncompliance—typically fines and imprisonment—the laws are designed to deter would-be drug users. These penalties can be buttressed and even replaced by the perceived informal social costs of legal infractions, such as the public humiliation, damage to personal relationships, and loss of employment that might follow arrest and prosecution.

As others have argued, the effectiveness of legal controls as instruments of moral suasion and deterrence is affected by numerous factors.[103] The public not only has to be aware of the laws and their sanctions, but also respect them as moral, legitimate, and fair. For some, drug use is a private matter in which the state simply has no right to intervene and set standards. Paradoxically, for others the very illegality of drugs may heighten their attraction by making them "forbidden fruit." As noted earlier, the very act of taking drugs can become a way of registering one's dissent from society. Perversely, imposition of sanctions and the stigmatization that may follow can also increase the likelihood of further infractions.

More important, it is generally accepted that informal social norms and controls play a vital—and perhaps the primary—role in promoting or discouraging drug use. Through family and kinship networks, friends, peer groups, coworkers, teachers, and community leaders, perceptions of how one should behave and how others do behave are formed and become important influences on individual attitudes toward drug use.[104] The messages—both verbal (mores, beliefs) and behavioral (customs, traditions, practices)—that are generated and transmitted through these social agents can reinforce, modify, or undermine society's formal drug use regulations and sanctions. Though constantly evolving, these norms and controls can exert a steady and important influence in shaping a person's predisposition to drugs. Thus it is generally believed that the rise in U.S. drug consumption during the 1960s, 1970s, and early 1980s was largely facilitated by more permissive social attitudes that passively or actively tolerated some types of drug use while minimizing their risks to health. Conversely, the subsequent decline has been linked to an observed increase in the perceived harmfulness and risks associated with drug use as well as the growing disapproval of peers and parents.[105]

When a society is in a state of flux or riven by conflict, the traditional informal controls on behavior can also be disrupted, weakened, and even eroded. Such upheavals may make it much more difficult for that society to acculturate to new drugs that suddenly become available. This phenomenon has been observed in countries undergoing rapid modernization that results in urbanization, population growth, and increased geographic and social mobility.[106] It may also have been a factor in rising consumption in some postcommunist countries struggling to adapt to democracy and the stress of the free market as well as in certain areas of the "postindustrial" world, particularly inner cities, that have experienced acute unemployment, capital flight, depopulation, and cutbacks in social services.[107]

Besides setting disincentives, prohibitionist laws are also intended to reduce the opportunities for drug consumption by making it difficult for buyers to find suppliers and by keeping prices as high as possible to limit the number of customers. Authoritarian regimes have generally fared better than open democratic countries in suppressing drug market activity because the state plays a more intrusive and repressive role in almost all aspects of daily life. By contrast, the capacity of liberal democratic states to reduce the availability of drugs is clearly limited by their commitment to the very principles and values upon which they are based. Even the most repressive states, however, cannot be omniscient and omnipresent, especially when the consumer is in collusion with the supplier. The Soviet

Union and the communist states of Eastern and Central Europe thus were never able to completely suppress consumption.

Increasing the penalties for illicit drug trafficking and consumption in order to deter such behavior by others also has questionable long-term value. Research in different contexts has shown that it is difficult to sustain the deterrent effect of harsher sanctions for lawbreaking.[108] As countries such as Malaysia, Iran, and Saudi Arabia have discovered, even the severest penalties for drug trafficking have failed to completely deter such activities. This also appears to have been the case in the United States following the imposition of significantly harsher penalties for trafficking and possession at the end of the 1980s. These measures not only imposed an additional financial burden but also were viewed as discriminatory by many.[109]

Law enforcement and efforts to control supply have managed to keep the cost of illicit drugs high relative to their licit counterparts, which probably has influenced some not to start consuming drugs and others to reduce their use or desist completely. Nonetheless, drug traffickers have found ways to lower the economic barriers of prohibition. The U.S. crack cocaine phenomenon is a prime example. Packaged in small but highly potent doses at a fraction of the cost of powdered cocaine, crack can be purchased by many more people. Its use brings instant and intense gratification and, for retailers, a double benefit. Not only can they expand their clientele and generate an even greater return on their investment by cheaply converting cocaine hydrochloride into crack, but the highly addictive qualities of the drug make consumers keep coming back for more—at least until it incapacitates them.

Both the incentives and opportunities for drug consumption can be targeted in ways other than through the negative sanction of the law. Public education and mass media programs, which can be considered positive control measures, are designed to persuade or help people to avoid drug use. Such programs usually fall into one of the following categories: information-only programs that emphasize the harmful psychological and physiological effects of drug use; alternative activity programs that engage adolescents in other pursuits; and social competency programs that teach problem solving and communication skills as well as techniques for rejecting drug use.[110] To the extent that these programs can be evaluated by isolating other factors, the results have in general been mixed and in some cases even counterproductive.

Information-only programs have been found to increase the level of knowledge but to have little effect on shaping attitudes and behavior. Sometimes they have actually sparked curiosity and heightened the desire to experience the reported effect of drugs.[111] Much depends on how the message is conveyed and the perceived legitimacy of the sender. Exaggerated negative claims have tended to be disbelieved, undermining the credibility of other information. As for alternative activity programs, there is little evidence that they deter or in some way displace drug use by adolescents. In some cases, when they have involved entertainment and sports activities, drug use has been known to actually increase. Social competency programs have apparently fared better, although the effect in decreasing drug use has often been short lived.[112]

More substantial and sustainable results have reportedly occurred, however, in programs that engage schools, families, and local communities in an integrated program that teaches resistance skills, reinforces nonuse norms, and informs individuals of the personal risks involved in drug use. Although these results are encouraging, it should be emphasized that they require more validation because they may simply reflect broader societal trends. It also seems reasonable that such programs are more likely to be effective with regular school attendees and with families and communities that are relatively functional, stable, and cohesive. Mass media campaigns are also difficult to assess and thus have received competing judgments about their effectiveness. Some believe that at best they have been only marginally influential in changing behavior.[113] Others dispute this, however, citing Nancy Reagan's "Just Say No" campaign and the "This Is Your Brain on Drugs" advertisement program organized by the private Partnership for a Drug-Free America in the 1980s. Although hard to prove, there are claims that these messages did resonate widely in America and that they helped rally parents and communities to take a more active antidrug stance, which in turn contributed to the general change in attitudes.[114] On balance, however, the consensus appears to be that mass media campaigns are likely to be effective only if they are used in conjunction with other prevention initiatives.

Drug treatment programs constitute the other main approach to tackling the incentives for drug use. In contrast to education and mass media programs, the emphasis is clearly more remedial than preventive. (To the extent that some education and treatment programs are designed to intervene and avert further drug use or abuse, they can obviously be considered preventive.) There is also considerable variety in the range of drug treatment programs; they differ by approach (detoxification, pharmacotherapy, counseling and psychotherapy), treatment medium (residential or outpatient), duration (short- versus long-term), and objective (drug use cessation, reduction in harm, rehabilitation).[115] Some programs, therefore, are clearly more suited for some people than others and for different types of drug use. For this basic reason, matching the appropriate treatment modality to the individual is considered to be a crucial factor in determining outcome.

Overall, however, there appears to be a general consensus that drug treatment is a cost-effective approach to reducing consumption. As one Canadian study reports after examining numerous domestic and foreign treatment programs:

> Comprehensive reviews of the literature conclude that 50–60% of individuals receiving treatment show improvement at follow-up. The data suggest further that about one-half of those who are improved will have ceased all drug or alcohol use or will have substantially reduced their consumption; the other half will have made reductions in their level of consumption and significant improvement in other life areas. From an economic point of view, the data indicate that drug and alcohol treatment is a sound investment of the health care dollar.[116]

Treatment reduces not just consumption but also rates of crime and infection. This conclusion is supported by evaluations of U.S. and foreign programs. Beyond the advanced industrialized and former communist world, however, the training and resources for drug treatment are minimal or nonexistent. India, for example, has only 250 drug treatment centers.[117]

Additional positive control methods can be employed to reduce the opportunities for drug consumption. One is to designate areas where drug use is actively discouraged to buttress the moral force and practical effect of the law. "Drug-free zones" can be established in schools, workplaces, and areas of the community to broadcast the desire and commitment of its members to keep the designated areas from being used to buy and take drugs. These declarations can be bolstered by drug-testing programs, which, depending on whether they are compulsory or voluntary, can be classified as either positive or negative control measures. Local communities—with or without police assistance—can also take action to discourage or close down known drug markets and places where drugs are being used.[118] Although such efforts are considered useful by many, the net effect may be only to displace drug use to other locales.

A completely different set of positive control tactics is what are generally known as "harm-reduction" or "harm-minimization" measures. Proponents of these measures proceed from the view that drug control should aim to be as pragmatic as possible in minimizing the adverse consequences or "harms" to society that derive from the illegal nature of drug use.[119] Again, many different initiatives fall under this general rubric. In brief, they include needle exchange programs that make hypodermic syringes legally or more readily available to reduce the risk of HIV infection and the transmission of other diseases; maintenance and prescription programs that make certain drugs—principally but not exclusively methadone—available to addicts to reduce their dependence on illicit and potentially dangerous sources of supply; informal zoning schemes that designate certain areas and facilities as places where people can purchase and consume drugs under safer conditions and seek medical and social help if desired; and changes in the law that permit the commercial sale of "soft drugs," principally cannabis products, and the removal of punitive sanctions (decriminalization) for possession and use.[120]

Harm-reduction measures of one kind or another have been implemented in many areas around the world with varying degrees of support from central governments. Some initiatives have proven more successful than others. There is now substantial evidence, for example, that needle exchange programs reduce the likelihood of HIV infection from contaminated syringes, although it is difficult to prove clearly that they have curbed transmission of the virus.[121] Methadone maintenance is also generally accepted to be beneficial in stabilizing the condition of heroin addicts, increasing their willingness to accept and stay in treatment, and reducing their illicit drug use and, to a lesser extent, criminal activity.[122] Some local jurisdictions, such as Merseyside in Britain, which have gone beyond methadone maintenance to allow medical prescription of heroin and other drugs, have also reported a lessening of related criminal activity.[123] The informal zoning schemes that could also be called "prohibition-free zones" have proved more controversial, however. The most famous was Zurich's Platzspitz, which became widely known as "Needle Park." Intended to contain Zurich's rising number of intravenous drug users in the late 1980s by allowing them to buy and consume drugs openly in one central location, the park eventually became a magnet for drug users from the rest of Switzerland, which caused the problem to grow worse and local sentiment to sour. After being shifted initially to a nearby location, the experiment was shut down altogether in 1994.[124] Similar initiatives in Berlin and Basel produced much the same outcome, although Frankfurt and Rotterdam have reported more encouraging results.[125]

Finally, some national and local jurisdictions have adopted more lenient laws affecting the sale, possession, and use of cannabis products out of a belief that cannabis is less harmful than the so-called hard drugs, such as heroin and cocaine. The most permissive examples can be found in the Netherlands, where the sale of cannabis products in "coffee shops" is permitted, providing it conforms to strict rules prohibiting advertising and sale to minors. According to official sources, this policy has not resulted in higher consumption among the indigenous Dutch population. It has, however, caused a substantial inflow of "drug tourists" from neighboring countries in similar fashion to Zurich's experience.[126] In nearby Germany, the Federal Constitutional Court has recently removed criminal penalties for the possession of small (though still to be defined) amounts of marijuana and hashish, while some states have extended this principle to other drugs.[127] During the 1970s eleven U.S. states decriminalized the possession of small amounts of marijuana, with neglible effects on the general level of consumption. One study did indicate, however, that there was an increase in the number of marijuana mentions in emergency room records but an overall decrease in the number of mentions involving other drugs, suggesting a substitution effect as users shifted from harder drugs to marijuana once the legal sanctions were removed.[128]

In conclusion, it is clear that there is no simple or universal solution to controlling the global drug market. It is too complex a phenomenon. On balance, however, while the incentives and opportunities to participate in the drug market remain high, negative control measures offer the least prospect of achieving their desired effect. As will become apparent in the next chapter, these incentives and opportunities are unlikely to diminish in the coming years, bringing into question still further the utility of negative control measures.

4 | The Future of the Global Drug Market

T HE PROGNOSIS for the future is not a promising one. On the basis of what is understood about current trends and the broad social, political, and economic factors that appear likely to affect the incentives and opportunities to produce, traffic, and consume psychoactive substances around the world, the global drug market looks poised to expand. In some countries the growth could be considerable. This assessment is discussed in greater detail below according to two time frames: the short term (to around the year 2005) and the longer term (approximately 2005–2020). Given the limited amount of hard information and the complexity of the global drug phenomenon, I will make only very general predictions. No attempt will be made to forecast specific levels of production or consumption. These projections in turn provide the context for a discussion of the potential implications of an expanding global drug market.

The Short Term

Over the next five to ten years, North America and western Europe will probably remain the largest and most lucrative markets served by the international drug trade. It is conceivable, moreover, that the size of these markets may actually increase during this period, reversing the trend of the last ten years. The primary reason is that the age cohort typically considered most at risk for taking drugs is expected to increase over the next ten years as the baby boomers' children become teenagers. The United Nations predicts that there will be about 41 million people aged 15 to 25 in North America in the year 2000 and more than 45 million by 2010.[1] To put this into some perspective for the United States, it has been calculated that in 2006 there will be 30.8 million teenagers— 900,000 more than the high-water mark of the baby boom generation in 1976 and 4.1 million more than were alive in 1969, the year of Woodstock.[2] Only after 2015 does the total for North America begin to decline. In Europe, the number of 15- to 20-year-olds is expected to peak somewhat earlier, around the turn of the century, and to decline considerably after 2005.[3]

The presence of many more people in higher-risk age groups does not, of course, automatically predispose them to take drugs. Much will clearly depend on the effect of other factors that are inherently difficult to predict. On the basis of the factors motivating symbolic and remedial forms of drug use, discussed in chapter 3, one can foresee several mutually reinforcing trends that could spur increased drug consumption.[4]

First, the antidrug norms and values developed since the early 1980s could erode in significant ways as drug taking for recreational purposes once again becomes perceived as fashionable and less risky. This phenomenon, which some have labeled "generational forgetting," has been observed with prior resurgences of drug use in American history. In essence, past lessons about the harmful consequences of heightened drug use either fade with time or fail to be transmitted across generations.[5] Some fear that this is already taking place in the United States, as suggested by recent trends in the data collected by both the National Household Survey on Drug Abuse and the University of Michigan High School Survey, which indicate rising drug use and declining perceptions of its harmfulness among youth.[6] This seems particularly true for cannabis products, which have traditionally been perceived as the least harmful illicit drugs, and for several synthetic varieties, notably LSD and ecstasy (MDMA).

Second, it is conceivable that drug taking could become more popular because of its associations with a larger generational consciousness, as it did for the baby boom generation in the 1960s and 1970s. Should members of the emerging youth generation begin to feel that their economic opportunities and quality-of-life expectations are considerably less than those of prior generations, the resultant sense of frustration, hopelessness, and even anger could promote both symbolic and remedial forms of drug use. Indeed, it is already becoming depressingly obvious to many that the quality of their life is unlikely to match, let alone exceed, that of their parents. Moreover, should the predicament of the younger generation come to be seen as the direct consequence of previous generations' selfish excesses or mismanagement, then the sense of grievance and potential for intergenerational conflict will be higher. Again, this might manifest itself in heightened drug use.

Current trends in mass media and communications technology will probably heighten the emerging youth generation's collective awareness of its attitudes, behaviors, and fashions—including those of drug use. Moreover, the speed with which this knowledge is propagated and behavior is imitated is likely to be rapid. For example, one of the fastest-growing communications mediums, the Internet, is already being used to transmit recipes for making LSD and to share advice on how to smoke heroin.

Third, current trends toward a more stratified society in North America and western Europe could also promote remedial forms of drug use. In the United States, where the process is most accentuated, some see society as being increasingly made up of three groups.[7] The first is a relatively small "overclass" living in elite suburbs or, in some cases, their own gated communities or residential compounds guarded by private security forces. Having enriched themselves during the 1980s, they now have access to good health care and education and are therefore "profitably positioned to ride the waves of change."[8] The second group is a growing underclass that is largely trapped in inner cities where high unemployment and urban flight have fueled a self-perpetuating dynamic of low investment, declining tax bases, deteriorating social services, and rising crime. In some cases, this process has been exacerbated by racial tensions, often involving immigrant groups in search of a better life. With the welfare state in retreat nearly everywhere, the prospects of those who fall into this category look particularly hopeless. The third and largest group is what has been termed the "anxious class." Although most hold jobs, global economic competition and technological advances have undermined confidence in the security of employment. Many young people entering the work force find themselves ill prepared for the modern marketplace, where specialized skills are increasingly valued. To the extent that economic opportunities exist at all for these people, they are often in low-paying, temporary jobs.[9] At the same time, increasing divorce rates are leading to more broken homes and single-parent families, while greater mobility and the vicissitudes of employment are making communities in general less stable.

Whether new or existing drugs will become more popular in the context of these trends is impossible to say. One possibility, for example, is that illicit drug producers will design a new class of nonaddictive recreational drugs or that a black market in mind-altering prescription drugs like Prozac might develop. Also possible is the emergence of what has been termed the "sober-up pill," to be taken after drug use.[10] The habits of hard-core drug users could also change. For example, heroin smoking could become more prevalent, not just because of the greater availability of purer supplies, but also because it would avoid the risk of infection from intravenous use.

In many parts of the postcommunist world, the factors that have apparently led to increased drug consumption in recent years are likely to persist, at least in the short to medium term. Western youth culture and fashions continue to exert a powerful effect on shaping adolescent behavior in former communist countries. To the extent that drug use is an element of this, imitative behavior can be expected. The availability of drugs is also likely to increase not only as traffickers use many of these areas as transit routes to the West, but also as they target them as markets in their own right. As these societies continue to adjust to the painful realities of the free market, drugs may also become appealing to many who find it difficult to cope or whose prospects look bleak. The economic transition to the free market in central and eastern Europe and the former Soviet Union has undoubtedly created new opportunities for many, but it has also caused a great deal of pain and suffering for others. Unemployment and underemployment have soared and will in all probability remain high for the foreseeable future.[11] Although some will doubtless prosper from both licit and illicit business activities, the standard of living of many others will fall and remain low. It is very difficult to predict whether drug consumption levels will eventually match those found in western Europe or North America, however.

In the developing world, the emergence of sizable regional markets seems set to continue. The impact of Western fashions, which the expansion in global communications will disseminate, as well as proximity to the principal centers of production and trafficking, can be expected to lead to increased drug consumption in the newly industrialized and developing world. As will be discussed below, this could rise dramatically after the turn of the century.

In general, there appears to be no obvious reason why the availability of.illicit drugs to meet and further stimulate demand around the world should be limited in any way. A brief overview of the incentives and opportunities to supply drugs to the major markets will confirm this.

The coca and cocaine industry remains deeply entrenched in Peru, Bolivia, and Colombia because it provides a major source of employment and subsistence in those countries. In Peru, between 150,000 and 250,000 farmers are estimated to be engaged in illegal coca cultivation; in Bolivia, around 100,000 (with perhaps another 20,000 involved in processing); and in Colombia, around 61,000. In 1991–92, this represented approximately 9 percent of the agricultural work force in Peru and Bolivia and about 1 percent in Colombia.[12] In the primary growing areas, the dependency is obviously much more pronounced. As a proportion of GDP, the coca and cocaine sector has been declining in recent years but still remains significant. In 1991 Bolivian officials estimated that the coca and cocaine economy amounted to 13 to 15 percent of GDP, or $850 million, although others considered it less. In the same year, 4.2 percent of Peru's GDP was estimated to come from the coca sector.[13]

As for foreign currency earnings, the coca and cocaine trade remains a lucrative source. In Bolivia, it is reportedly the primary source of foreign exchange, accounting for 23 to 43 percent of the country's total exports (legal and illegal) in 1990.[14] About a third of the proceeds are retained by factors of production, with the farmers benefiting the least. In contrast, the foreign exchange earnings have been much higher in Colombia because of the value added at later stages of production, though they represent a smaller proportion of total exports. Of the approximately $4 billion that the Colombian traffickers are believed to earn each year, about $1 billion is repatriated. Some believe these amounts to be conservative.[15]

The present structure of the coca and cocaine business appears to be undergoing significant change, however. In Peru, the combined effect of soil erosion, crop disease and aging, and pollution in the primary coca-growing areas of the upper Huallaga valley is apparently taking its toll on productivity. The declining power of the Sendero Luminoso following the capture of its leader, Abimael Guzman, in 1993 has also increased the Peruvian government's freedom of movement in the upper Huallaga valley. As a result, coca cultivation is reportedly migrating to neighboring areas. An estimated 2 million hectares of land are considered suitable for coca cultivation in Peru, and current output derives from around 100,000 hectares; thus the country's potential capacity is enormous.[16] The trend toward upstream processing of coca paste into cocaine base in Bolivia and Peru also promises to reinforce the economic motives for the primary producer countries to stay in business.[17] Although this development is apparently still sponsored largely by Colombian trafficking organizations, there are reports that "independent" trafficking groups in Bolivia and Peru have begun to refine cocaine and bypass the Colombians to deal directly with retail distributors in other countries. This trend could conceivably be accelerated following the arrest of the key leaders of the Cali cartel in 1995.[18] It is unlikely, however, that Colombia's role as a major center for cocaine refinement and distribution will end any time soon. The rewards of the cocaine trade will almost certainly spur the emergence of new leaders and groups to replace the old. Indeed, there were indications before the arrests of its senior leaders that generational changes and internal differences within the Cali organization were leading in this direction. Several semiautonomous groups operating with or under the control of the Cali cartel are poised to fill the vacuum.[19] Cocaine processing could also develop in Argentina and particularly Brazil because of those countries' access to indigenously produced precursor chemicals.[20]

The primary opium and heroin suppliers look equally entrenched. The likelihood that opium cultivation and heroin production will be physically dislodged from the main source areas looks remote in the short term because of the limited government influence where most of the opium cultivation and heroin refinement takes place. Afghanistan's position in the heroin trade could expand as the ongoing civil war continues to provide strong political and economic incentives. Indeed, it may already have surpassed Myanmar as the largest producer of opium in the world.[21] The reported development of an indigenous heroin-refining capability, noted earlier, will also heighten Afghanistan's importance as a major source country. Pakistan will also continue to play an important role in the heroin trade. It has been estimated that the turnover of Pakistan's heroin industry in 1992–93 is equivalent to about 5 percent of its gross domestic product. Foreign currency earnings are also calculated to amount to as much as $1.5 billion. This represents over 20 percent of Pakistan's legitimate commodity exports and more than 50 percent of its official current account deficit in recent years.[22]

Meanwhile, the supply of heroin from the Golden Triangle will probably not change dramatically anytime soon. Myanmar's current campaign against the miscellaneous insurgent groups in the Shan state may put some out of business and disrupt trafficking for a while, but the heroin trade's long history of adaptation to suppressive efforts in this region makes any long-term effect unlikely. The opportunities for cultivation and refinement to migrate elsewhere are too great. The development of a new center of refinement emerging closer to the Indian border is one possibility.[23] Beyond Myanmar, the reported increase in poppy cultivation in Vietnam and Cambodia as well as in parts of China points to a larger potential.[24] Some are also concerned that Hong Kong's reincorporation into the People's Republic of China after 1997 could give a major boost to mainland drug producers by providing greater access to international markets.[25]

Finally, it is even less likely that the availability of cannabis products will be limited in some way. Although harder to smuggle internationally than heroin, cannabis can be cultivated in many more places. The same applies even more to the manufacture of synthetic drugs.

With the barriers to entry so low and success sure to breed imitation, there would appear to be no major obstacle to the emergence of new sources of supply and new international trafficking groups. A shortage of land is unlikely to be a factor, especially since many drug crops can be grown in poor soil. Neither is there likely to be a dearth of labor or of sufficient numbers of desperate people seeking subsistence and a better life. And the materials needed to process and refine drugs are likely to be available as a result of the dispersion of chemical and pharmaceutical production capabilities to the developing world. Although government authority may be strengthened in some areas, the opposite is also likely to be true in others as a result of civil war and domestic unrest, which provide ample opportunities to produce illicit drugs. Such conditions may also be the prime motivator. The drug trade, as described earlier, has provided a major source of income for many separatist organizations and insurgent groups. Drug trafficking to support political causes could increase in the future. Since the end of the cold war, there has been an upsurge of separatist and ethnically motivated conflict for a variety of reasons. Organizations seeking to change the status quo used to be able to appeal for support from a superpower donor, but this source has effectively dried up. Drug trafficking is an obvious alternative.

The opportunities to transport and distribute illicit drugs internationally are also unlikely to diminish. Given the growing volume of international passenger travel for business and tourism as well as the continued expansion of global commercial links through free trade agreements, the capacity of trafficking groups to supply drugs to whatever market they choose does not appear to be in serious doubt.

In addition to the efforts of the World Trade Organization to promote free and expanded trade, regional organizations also appear likely to grow in the coming years. In the Western Hemisphere, NAFTA is currently enlarging its membership to include Chile, while the MERCOSUR common market arrangement is fueling rapid growth in cross-border trade and investment. Discussions to consolidate the various trading agreements to create a free trade area of the Americas by 2005 have already begun.[26] A comparable process, though not as advanced, is also under way with the Asia-Pacific Economic Cooperation (APEC) forum, made up of Australia, Brunei, Canada, Chile, China, Hong Kong, Indonesia, Japan, South Korea, Malaysia, Mexico, New Zealand, Papua New Guinea, the Philippines, Singapore, Taiwan, Thailand, and the United States. Plans are being drawn up to achieve free and open trade and investment in the region by 2020 and for the more developed economies by 2010.[27] In western Europe, the most integrated trading bloc in the world, the European Union is also expected to expand membership to include central European countries by the beginning of the next century.

The European Union is also leading the way in reducing personal passport controls within its outer boundaries as a result of the so-called Schengen agreement, named after the small town in Luxembourg where it was signed in 1992. As of March 26, 1995, the Schengen group within the EU—France, Belgium, the Netherlands, Luxembourg, Germany, Spain, and Portugal—formally abolished checks on visas and identity cards for travelers moving between them, although this decision has yet to be fully implemented. The way has also been cleared for a merger of the Schengen group and the countries of the Nordic Union—Denmark, Finland, and Sweden, as well as its non-EU members, Norway and Iceland—to abolish passport controls in an area that will effectively span from the Mediterranean to the Arctic.[28] Although the EU is bolstering its external frontiers to compensate for the progressive elimination of internal controls, they are likely to remain permeable to the determined trafficker. Given the sheer volume of commercial and personal traffic into Europe, customs and police authorities face a daunting challenge. Overall, it is hard not to agree with the assessment of one observer that "in practice, external border controls will inevitably vary in their severity and traffickers will quickly learn which entry points to use and which to avoid."[29]

The Longer Term

Over the long term, it appears reasonable to expect that the size and importance of the North American and western European drug markets will decline relative to those of the developing world. The populations of the high-income, advanced industrialized countries are progressively aging. In place of the classic pyramidal structure, the distribution by cohort is slowly becoming more evenly divided as the baby boom generation reaches retirement age.[30] In the United States the median age is already close to 35, and by the end of the first decade of the next century it will be close to 40.[31] By 2025 the largest cohort by far will be above the age of 75. Over the long term, therefore, there will be fewer people in the age group typically associated with illicit drug use.

Meanwhile, a massive surge in the population of the developing world is anticipated over the next thirty years. Despite generally falling fertility rates, almost all (95 percent) of the world's projected population growth—approximately 85 million people a year, or around 1 billion a decade—will take place in the poorest countries of the world. By the turn of the century, the total population of the world is expected to have reached the 6 billion mark, and by 2025, about 8 billion.[32]

A large proportion of the developing world's population will also be living in huge urban conurbations. Projections show that 40 percent of the population of the developing world will live in cities by 2000 and 57 percent by 2025. This translates into 4 billion city dwellers, close to three times the number in 1990.[33] Enormous megacities or "shanty cities," as some have called them, are already beginning to take shape.[34] It is estimated that by 2010 there will be fifty-nine cities with over 5 million residents, forty-seven of which will be in developing countries.[35]

These demographic trends have an inescapable relevance to the social and economic prospects of the developing world, which in turn will affect both the incentives and opportunities to consume drugs as well as to produce and traffic them. As will become clear below, there is considerable risk of large-scale drug markets' emerging in the developing world.

The World Bank's latest assessment of the global economic prospects contains probably the brightest outlook for developing countries since the 1960s because of the opportunities presented by increasing trade, capital market liberalization, and the internationalization of corporate production and distribution. However, the Bank readily admits that its general prognosis of worldwide growth masks significant differences among regions. In particular, East and South Asia are projected to do a lot better than the Middle East, Africa, and Latin America. The forecast for some countries is clearly also more promising than for others. The Bank warns, moreover, that growing economic integration has a down as well as an up side: "Greater integration into the world economy raises the payoffs to increased competitiveness but also compounds the losses from failure to act. Increasingly, it is the more efficient policy regimes that will win out."[36]

Even with overall positive growth rates, the likelihood that new jobs will be created at a rate that keeps pace with the enormous wave of new entrants to the work force does not look promising for many developing countries, and for some the prospects look exceedingly grim. The International Labor Organization (ILO) has estimated that 30 percent of the world's labor force is currently not productively employed; more than 120 million are registered as unemployed and some 700 million are believed to be underemployed.[37] The situation is likely only to grow worse for many developing countries, where the biggest surge has yet to take place. The ILO calculates that some 350 million jobs will have to be created in these countries during the 1990s alone. By 2025 the labor force in the developing countries is expected to expand to an estimated 3.1 billion people from its present level of 1.76 billion, which implies a need for some 38 million to 40 million new jobs each year.[38] Sub-Saharan Africa looks as if it will suffer the greatest disparity between the size of the work force and the number employed. The World Bank projects that annual average GDP growth rates for Africa will stay at 3.7 percent until 2002, with overall per capita income remaining below the level reached in the early 1970s.[39] Even assuming that average GDP rates in sub-Saharan Africa accelerate from 3.7 percent to about 5 percent, the ILO estimates that productive employment would still grow at only 2.4 percent a year in the 1990s while the labor force expands at an annual rate of 3.3 percent. The situation, it argues, is unlikely to be any better for parts of Latin America and South Asia.[40]

It is not obvious what job-multiplying industries will be created in the future to soak up the masses of people looking for employment. Technological advances have traditionally worked in the opposite direction to reduce labor costs in the advanced industrialized world. As Paul Kennedy asks: "If we cannot produce decent employment for millions of young people in America, Europe, Russia, perhaps even Japan now, what prospects do we offer to the emerging hundreds of millions of men and women in the developing world?"[41]

Other factors and trends make the economic prospects for many developing countries look especially bleak. For some, the burden of foreign debt cannot help but affect their overall performance and consequent pace of development. As an illustration, in 1992 the value of foreign debt as a proportion of GNP was 84 percent for Bolivia, 48 percent for Pakistan, 95 percent for Peru, and 386 percent for Zambia.[42] Although poor planning and misguided management have contributed to the dismal economic record of many developing countries, their situation has undoubtedly been made worse by the depression in commodity prices and thus export earnings during the 1980s. Again, Africa and particularly sub-Saharan Africa have been among the hardest hit.[43] Although the recent rise in nonoil commodity prices has undoubtedly given a boost to many economies of the developing countries, the World Bank predicts that for several reasons this trend is unlikely to be sustained over the long term.[44]

Not only does this trend reflect temporary market shortages that are likely to be corrected, but structural economic changes taking place in the industrialized world—the primary market for nonoil commodities—are anticipated to affect long-term demand. These include a continuing shift to service-based economies, the operation of more efficient and less commodity-intensive manufacturing industries, and the increasing substitution of synthetics and composites for traditional materials.[45] At the same time, the per capita consumption of many foodstuffs in the advanced industrialized countries has apparently reached a saturation point.[46] Over the long term, their need to import agricultural commodities may also decline as a consequence of advances in biotechnology that not only improve production efficiencies but allow the cultivation of previously imported goods. This in turn could worsen employment in the agricultural sector of many developing countries, compounding the problem discussed above. Other technological advances, notably in robotics, may also reduce the developing world's comparative advantage in labor costs.[47]

The likelihood that economic aid and foreign investment will alleviate the plight of many developing countries does not look promising, either. There is a growing climate of skepticism surrounding the value of economic aid to the developing world—a sentiment increasingly voiced in the United States and western Europe.[48] In addition, the general shortage of capital caused by declining savings rates, national deficits, and competing demands in many key donor countries promises to reduce the amount of aid to the third world just when the needs of many recipient countries will become particularly acute.[49]

The demands are extraordinarily high. For example, the World Bank calculates that about 9 percent of the GDP of sub-Saharan Africa would have to be added from external sources during the 1990s in order to attain per capita growth rates of 1 to 2 percent.[50] However, many developing countries are comparatively disadvantaged in their ability to attract foreign capital. In particular, those that are not well endowed with exploitable natural resources and have a poorly developed social and economic infrastructure will suffer the most. Even the former communist bloc has not fared well, despite expectations that investment would boom. In 1994 the total foreign direct investment in the twenty-five countries that make up the postcommunist world was roughly equal to the amount received by Mexico.[51]

Political instability and ethnic conflict will also drive capital away from many areas and deter further aid and investment. As the Mexican crisis of 1995 has revealed, the fortunes of favored countries can also change quickly. The ability of relatively localized events to resonate rapidly and unpredictably is undoubtedly another negative aspect of greater economic interconnectedness. As the World Bank has observed, "When a crisis of confidence develops, its impact can be sudden and damaging and with some spillover to other countries that market participants perceive as being in a similar situation."[52]

For these reasons, it seems probable that foreign direct investment will be increasingly concentrated—certainly in the short to medium term—on a relatively small group of politically stable countries where the economic returns look more certain. This will doubtless produce some "success stories," as has already been the case around the Pacific rim and in parts of Latin America. For many other states in the developing world, however, these trends will only exacerbate their relative backwardness and be more likely to consign them to a state of perpetual underdevelopment. Worse still, some could simply fail as functioning civil societies, sliding into general anarchy, as has occurred in Somalia and Rwanda.

Not surprisingly, many envisage a world increasingly divided between the "haves" of North America, Europe, the emerging Pacific rim, and a few other places and the "have-nots" of everywhere else, with the gap growing ever wider. The richest 20 percent of the world's population already receive 83 percent of global income, while the poorest 20 percent receive 1.4 percent. During the mid-1960s the former group, mostly living in OECD countries, was thirty times as rich as the latter, while today it is sixty times as rich. Other indicators show similar disparities in the quality of life.[53] To use Robert D. Kaplan's phrase, we are living in an increasingly "bifurcated world."[54]

Whether the demand for drugs increases in the developing world will depend, as noted earlier, on their perceived symbolic value as well as their attractiveness as remedies. It seems fair to conclude, given the trends described above, that the conditions of many living in the developing world, especially those in the cities, are going to be appalling, with little prospect of improvement. The pressure on individuals and families will be intense. Although the effect on drug consumption cannot be predicted with precision, more people will have even greater motivation to take drugs to increase productivity, dull hunger, relieve stress, or simply escape the harsh reality of the world they inhabit. At the same time, many of the formal and informal social controls—family, tribe, community organization, or workplace—that ordinarily might be expected to provide psychological, social, and economic support and moderate the level of drug use will be weakened or destroyed completely by the same forces. (In some countries, however, it is possible that Islamic fundamentalism might exert a counterinfluence.) Ethnic strife and other forms of conflict will only accelerate this process.

Whether the inhabitants of these cities will be able to afford drugs is obviously an important consideration. On the face of it, large-scale impoverishment would appear to be a major constraining factor. Yet this has not prevented drug epidemics in poverty-stricken areas of the world in the past. Production costs are low, and in many areas transportation and distribution do not add a great deal to the final price. In short, trafficking groups can be expected to recognize the large potential of the emerging markets of the developing world and price their products to put them in reach of many more people even if the profit margins on individual sales may not be very great. Something akin to this process is already unfolding in the proliferation of street children around the world. As a UN report observed, "Cities of the developing world are fast becoming warrens of destitute children trapped in a circle of poverty and drug addiction."[55] Not only are many engaged in petty crime to support themselves, but the inhalation of solvents and various commercial aerosols has become popular among street children in many large cities.

Although the growth of emerging markets would not necessarily require new sources of supply—because the world's existing productive capacity is already enormous and could probably expand—the emergence of new areas of production cannot be discounted. Since the drug trade apparently does not function as a truly efficient market, where the greater competitiveness of one supplier undermines the existence of another, there is considerable latitude for new suppliers to emerge in new locales where the conditions are ripe. And because the drug trade also does not operate according to free trade principles of equal access to global markets, local suppliers could in effect erect their own kind of trade barrier to protect their turf—violently, if necessary—while exploiting other comparative advantages.

As in the past, supplying regional and local markets is unlikely to present a major challenge, given their proximity, the poor state of border controls in many parts of the developing and postcommunist world, the strong connections that have developed from the flow of migration from rural to urban areas, and the ever-present opportunities for corruption. Neither would development of the necessary retail distribution networks. The pool of potential recruits who are likely to be economically motivated and also undeterred by the threat of legal sanctions will be almost limitless. In any case, the ability of the state to wield power and stamp out drug trafficking in the enormous shanty cities that are expected to emerge is highly doubtful.

It is conceivable that the global trend toward free trade and greater integration might stall and even be reversed under the pressure of economic nationalism and political friction. Such an outcome is unlikely to seriously affect the drug trade, however, for two reasons. First, the formation of competitive trading blocs would not affect intraregional trade and might actually boost it. Thus the capacity to grow and manufacture drugs throughout the world and distribute them to regional markets is not likely to be impeded significantly. Second, it is doubtful that interregional trade and travel would cease. Given the relatively small amounts of drugs needed to supply sizable numbers of consumers, transportation opportunities would presumably still exist. The global tourist business would also continue to expand, opening up potential new routes and markets in the process.

As a result, it is possible to envisage the emergence of two distinct tiers of trafficking groups. The first is those with global reach by virtue of their superior organizational skills, dispersed ethnic connections, and capacity to reach alliances with other trafficking groups. The primary but not exclusive focus of these trafficking organizations will continue to be the lucrative markets of North America, western Europe, and the countries along the Pacific rim where they already have well-established networks. By contrast, the second tier of trafficking organizations will be principally regional in orientation. These will nurture their own independent sources of supply and develop distribution networks centered on the rapidly expanding urban conglomerations of the developing world. A similar process has already occurred in Pakistan. As noted above, the emergence of independent cocaine trafficking groups in Latin America with ties to emerging markets in Brazil, Venezuela, and Argentina may presage the same. The vast and largely untapped regions of Amazonia could also become significant source areas. In Africa, conditions appear to be especially ripe for the already powerful Nigerian and other West African trafficking organizations to develop their own production base on the continent.[56] Similarly, Russian and other organized criminal syndicates inside the former Soviet Union with links to emerging Central Asian sources of supply could come to dominate the postcommunist bloc of countries. Some of these second-tier groups might be able to operate more widely, but their real power will derive from the control they wield over regional markets.

Implications

In assessing the likely implications of an expanding global drug market, it is important to distinguish between the consequences of the growth of illicit production and trafficking and those of the increased consumption of illicit drugs. For reasons that will be explained, the two types are not totally separable, but the general distinction serves as a useful organizing device. Both can be further divided in terms of economic, political, and social effects, but here the boundaries become more blurred because of interrelationships among these effects. Although not discussed in detail here, the drug trade has also caused significant ecological harm.[57]

Effects of the Drug Trade

The financial rewards of the drug trade will clearly continue to provide income and employment to many people in places where licit alternatives are limited. Through these people's interaction with others in the economy, these rewards will also be indirectly shared and multiplied. In the past, the opportunities provided by the drug business have helped absorb unemployed labor and ameliorate the social and economic impact of temporary or long-term declines in other industries. This was clearly the case with the mining sectors of Peru and Bolivia as well as the manufacturing industry in Medellin.[58] Similarly, at the other end of the supply chain the drug business provides income to traffickers at the retail level, where few opportunities exist. Money gained from the drug business also makes its way into the local economy with the purchase of goods and services, the capitalization of banks, and investment in real estate and legitimate businesses. Many of the settlements in the upper Huallaga valley and the Chapare, for example, became boom towns overnight as a result of the multiplier effect on the local economy. The cities of Medellin and Cali in Colombia experienced a major construction boom that is generally believed to have been financed by drug money. Several well-known drug traffickers have also been known for their local largesse and public works projects.[59] At the macro level, some have maintained that the emergence of the coca industry in Bolivia probably staved off widespread social unrest when the economy was undergoing a severe adjustment process after 1986.[60] It has even been argued that the repatriated monies gained from the drug trade are now indirectly helping the principal drug-producing countries to pay off some of their accumulated international debt and in the process are keeping many Western banks solvent.[61]

Although the drug trade will doubtless bring benefits to some, these are more than likely to be outweighed by the larger costs. If previous experience is any guide, the drug industry can impose significant indirect costs on the economies of the host nations. In Colombia and, to a lesser extent, Bolivia, the influx of foreign exchange is believed to have distorted the economy by artificially raising the value of the local currency, which in turn undermined the competitiveness of other export sectors.[62] The recent influx of U.S. currency into Colombia, much of which is believed to be drug related, has caused inflation to rise and rendered subsequent efforts to control it more difficult. With the Colombian peso continuing to appreciate in value relative to the dollar, the demand for imports has also increased, which again has affected domestic producers.[63] Although the flood of dollars has provided Colombia with more capital to repay debts and invest in national infrastructure projects through government-issued securities, much of the local investment of repatriated drug money has apparently not been carried out in a productive fashion. Economists argue that local investments have typically been in short-term speculative ventures designed more to launder money than to promote sustained economic growth.[64] The same point has also been made in relation to Chinese and Pakistani drug proceeds.[65] Moreover, the businesses and services controlled by drug interests can undercut the competitiveness of legitimate businesses.[66]

Arguably the most pernicious effect of the drug trade, however, has been in undermining the economic integrity and political legitimacy of the states where it has taken root. Successful drug traffickers not only encourage others to imitate them, but they also contribute to the growth of an underground economy by visibly demonstrating the impotence of government authorities.[67] Their ability to operate with impunity and avoid taxation infects other business practices, further corroding public confidence in the ability of state authorities to regulate economic activity equitably for the common good. They deprive the government of revenues from untaxed business activity and make its management of the economy more difficult. Moreover, the traffickers erode the state's traditional functions in providing for public safety and the security of property. This in turn stimulates the growth in private protection services, which add to the expense of doing business and further undermine public trust in the effectiveness of law enforcement agencies and the justice system in general. It also promotes the private resolution of disputes, usually by intimidation and armed force. As law and order begin to fray, local capital takes flight and potential new investment goes elsewhere.

Once set in motion, this sequence of events is difficult to stop, let alone reverse. What is happening to Rio de Janeiro is illustrative. Twenty years ago, Rio had 101 of Brazil's largest private businesses. Now it has only 65. Ten years ago, Rio's stock exchange accounted for half of the nation's total activity. Now it is only 12 percent. And, of Brazil's thirty-five largest banks, only one remains in Rio. In addition, over the last five years international tourism has been cut in half. Although a mix of factors has contributed to this outcome, high crime and violence, much related to drug trafficking by rival gangs in the burgeoning shantytowns of the city, are important ones.[68] The apparently unsuccessful campaign by the army to "cleanse" the poorer sections of Rio de Janeiro of drug-trafficking gangs illustrates the challenge that states already face and that may become an increasingly common problem in many parts of the developing world.[69] The deteriorating situation in Caracas, Lagos, and Karachi provides further examples.[70] When added to the direct costs incurred from additional law enforcement expenses, the economic impact can be substantial. The former president of Colombia, Cesar Gaviria, estimated that the country spent $1 billion annually fighting the drug trade and lost the same in foreign investment, foreign exchange, and taxes.[71]

The economic costs of the drug trade are not confined to the developing world, of course. Although some of the capital accumulated at the wholesale level by drug traffickers is invested locally or spent purchasing domestic products, some portion is transferred overseas and therefore represents a net loss to the economy. Drug trafficking and the associated crime and violence have clearly contributed to the economic decline of many inner-city areas of America and, to a lesser extent, Europe. The billions spent on drug-related policing and law enforcement, including the expenses of imprisoning offenders, must also be seen as a major opportunity cost.

Beyond these economic implications, broader social and political costs derive from the corrupting and intimidating influence of drug trafficking in many areas of the world. Not only does drug traffickers' presence and behavior undermine the authority of government institutions, but in some cases they prevent it from being properly established. The vital process of nation building becomes stalled, if not derailed, in the process.

Much of the corruption that takes place, as discussed earlier, is directed at facilitating the immediate operational goals of drug trafficking. It is typically sporadic and localized.[72] As the power of trafficking groups has grown, however, the level of corruption has often grown into more far-reaching forms that are systemic in character. Through bribery or intimidation, whole areas or institutions of the state have been made subordinate to or compliant with the wishes of the traffickers. This was evident in the case of the Peruvian military after it was directed to combat drug trafficking in the upper Huallaga valley. At the end of 1994 more than one hundred soldiers—most of them officers, including two former regional commanders for the upper Huallaga valley region—had been indicted or convicted for complicity in the drug trade.[73] The problem has been even more pervasive in Colombia, where more than 14,000 national police officers have been dismissed over the last four years for corruption.[74] Since at least the early 1980s, Haiti's military is believed to have been directly complicit in the trafficking of cocaine.[75] Nigeria's National Drug Law Enforcement Agency provides another example of this kind of pernicious corruption. Between 1989 and 1993, eighty-four agents, including one of its directors, were dismissed for corruption.[76] Similarly, it was estimated that 10 percent of metropolitan Manila's police force in 1994 were either protectors or members of Philippine drug syndicates.[77]

Numerous cases also illustrate the power of drug traffickers to infiltrate the legislative and executive arms of government through bribery or the direct funding of candidates for public office. This form of systemic corruption has the more sophisticated goal of collecting intelligence on government activities and economic policies as well as more generally ensuring that the state does not adopt programs "inimical to the interests of the drug trafficking organization."[78] This has been known to entail electing the drug traffickers to public office—most notably Pablo Escobar, who was elected to the Colombian legislature—but it is typically more subtle and indirect in nature. This pervasive phenomenon has been seen in Thailand, Turkey, the Philippines, Taiwan, Morocco, and Pakistan, to cite some recent cases from other regions of the world.[79]

Far more troubling, however, is when drug-related corruption becomes so pervasive and insidious that it reaches the highest levels of government and controls significant portions of the economy. The interests of the state and those of the trafficking organizations become entwined and mutually serving. As noted earlier, this evidently happened in Bolivia, the Bahamas, and Panama. Some fear that it has occurred or is about to occur in Colombia and Mexico. Both have already been branded "narco-democracies."[80]

In Colombia, it has been calculated that drug money accounts for 30 percent of the construction industry, while traffickers are believed to now own 3 million hectares of the best agricultural land, or about 8 to 9 percent of the total.[81] The recent privatization of banks in Colombia has reportedly provided drug-trafficking organizations with "the ability to influence covertly the policies and operations of certain banks." At least one bank has been directly linked to the Cali cartel.[82] Some calculate that as much as 10 percent of the national wealth is controlled by drug-trafficking interests.[83] The greatest concern, however, is that the Cali cartel may have funded the successful electoral campaign of President Ernesto Samper in 1994 and in the process gained undue influence at the center of power in Colombia.[84] Although many of the cartel's leaders, as noted above, have since been arrested, it remains to be seen how much the power of the Colombian trafficking organizations in general is actually curtailed.[85]

In Mexico, investigations surrounding the arrest of former deputy attorney general Mario Ruiz Massieu in 1995 have revealed how powerful Mexican drug traffickers have become. Not only were many officers within Mexico's federal judicial police and its National Institute for Combating Drugs co-opted to assist trafficking operations, but, according to one observer, the attorney general's office became "in reality an arm of drug trafficking, and organized crime's government intermediary."[86] More alarming, the assassinations of former presidential candidate Luis Donaldo Colosio, the head of the ruling Institutional Revolutionary Party, Jose Francisco Ruiz Massieu, and Cardinal Juan Jesus Posadas

Ocampo are now all considered to be drug related. Since the brother of former president Carlos Salinas de Gortari has been indicted in connection with the murder of Ruiz Massieu, the reach of the Mexican drug-trafficking organizations is believed to have extended to the highest levels of government.[87] Although President Salinas's successor, Ernesto Zedillo, has instituted a major crackdown against drug trafficking, questions have also been raised about the source of his campaign financing.[88]

The growing power and influence of drug-trafficking organizations in the economic and political life of Colombia, Mexico, and other countries has been likened to a three-stage process that is applicable to all forms of organized crime. In brief, trafficking groups evolve from an initial predatory stage, in which small-scale gangs seize control of particular businesses or turf, to the parasitical stage, whereby the state's institutions, public officials, and infrastructure become routinely corrupted and exploited for their ends, to the final symbiotic stage, in which the interests of organized crime and the state essentially coalesce to the extent that the line between licit and illicit activities becomes so blurred as to be meaningless.[89] A different metaphor is to view trafficking groups as viruses that progressively weaken the immune system of the state until they are in virtual control. With government authority weak in so many parts of the developing world and under increasing strain in many other places, the threat posed by drug traffickers and organized crime in general is readily apparent.

Given its increasingly transnational nature, this threat also transcends state borders. The regional consequences of Mexico's severe financial crisis in 1995 are a prime example. Although other factors contributed to the crisis, the large-scale flight of capital, much of which is believed to have been acquired from the drug trade, also played a significant role, as did the political instability generated by the assassinations and abuses of power discussed above.[90] The actions of drug traffickers can also introduce forms of friction into the relations between states. Colombian-Venezuelan relations, for example, became severely strained in 1995 as a result of cross-border drug trafficking.[91]

More directly, to the extent that the drug trade is used to bankroll other forms of organized crime and the networks of connections and conduits developed for drug trafficking are used to transport other types of illegal commerce, then even larger international threats will exist. This is reputedly already gaining in relation to illegal immigration and arms smuggling.[92] The most obvious other candidates include counterfeited documents and currency, pirated copyrighted material, prostitution and auto theft rings, and, most ominously, the theft and delivery of nuclear materials.

The symbiotic relationship between the different manifestations of organized crime is already becoming a serious problem in eastern and central Europe as well as the former Soviet Union. Although there has been some misunderstanding, if not exaggeration, of the impact of organized crime on the new market economies, there are nevertheless legitimate fears.[93] At the present, the amount of money generated from drugs is probably small relative to that resulting from the panoply of other criminal enterprises. This could quickly change should drug consumption increase markedly in the former Soviet bloc. If it does, criminal groups could grow rich enough to consolidate their position through corruption and extend their operations and investment to other enterprises—licit and illicit. To the extent that this stifles the operation of the free market, deters foreign investment, undermines the stability of financial institutions that have been penetrated by criminal groups, and contributes to civil disorder and ultimately the delegitimation of the state, it represents a real threat.

If extensive drug cultivation gathers momentum in some former communist states, most notably within the Central Asian republics of the former Soviet Union, a Colombia-style process could unfold.[94] Through corruption and the acquisition of weaponry, the relevant trafficking organizations may ultimately become virtual states within states. The use of drug money to underwrite political movements in this volatile part of the world is reportedly already a reality. The activities of Chechen criminal groups, who are prominent in the Russian drug trade, was also one of the declared reasons for Russia's armed intervention in the breakaway republic of Chechnya in the winter of 1994–95. Some have speculated that this rationale may be increasingly used to justify interventions by Russia in other former republics of the Soviet Union.[95] The growth of organized crime and a concomitant decline in civil order have also become potent rallying points for reactionary political forces in some former communist states.

Costs Related to Consumption

Rising consumption of prohibited psychoactive substances can also impose significant costs on society, although it is important to acknowledge that some of the harm caused by illicit drugs derives from their illicit nature, principally the lack of properly regulated quality control standards. In general, consumption-related costs can be grouped into the following categories.[96]

—Public health: Increased incidence of death from drug overdoses, physical and mental impairment from drug abuse and adulterants, including fetal deformities, more drug-related accidents, and, where intravenous drug use rises, higher prevalence of HIV infection and AIDS as well as other infectious diseases.[97]

—Employment: Greater incidence of absenteeism, lower worker productivity (at least over the long term), and more drug-related accidents and damage.

—Crime: Rise in crime, including prostitution, to pay for consumption or compensate for a failure to attain employment or substitute for its loss due to drug-related problems. The pharmacological effects of drugs may also lead to violence, child abuse, and other criminal acts.

—Education: Impairment in learning as well as a higher incidence of disciplinary problems and truancy in schools.

—Social relationships: Negative effect on family and dependents through opportunity costs of drug expenditures, loss of employment, theft and intimidation, and higher propensity of some substance abusers to threaten and inflict harm on others.

For many developing countries, such concerns may pale beside some of their other problems. Most, nevertheless, would rather avoid them. To the extent that rising consumption forces governments to divert resources into drug education, prevention, and treatment (including emergency hospitalization) and rehabilitation programs, while also increasing law enforcement and criminal justice expenditures, it costs society dearly. The same is obviously also true for many former communist countries. At a time when many are slashing public health services to the point that some are already in crisis, the burdens associated with rising drug consumption represent an additional problem that they can ill afford.

These costs should not be overshadowed by those that are incurred from the consumption of licit drugs, notably alcohol and tobacco. In the United States alone, alcohol-related costs to society—including medical spending, lost wages, and lost hours of work—have been estimated to total $128 billion a year. Automobile accidents attributed in some way to alcohol consumption are believed to incur $44 billion each year alone.[98] Similarly, annual tobacco-related health costs for the United States are estimated to be close to $100 billion.[99]

Although tobacco consumption in the United States and western Europe has reportedly declined in recent years, the same is not true for the rest of the world. Interestingly, the very countries that appear most at risk of experiencing higher illicit drug consumption are also the ones that are apparently being targeted by Western tobacco companies.[100] The inevitable costs to health and productivity will clearly be enormous. As one World Bank report states: "Recent estimates suggest a current worldwide annual toll of three million tobacco-related deaths—a quarter of which will occur in India alone—rising to more than ten million by the 2020s. Most of this increase will occur in developing countries. Fifty million Chinese alive today will die as a result of tobacco use."[101] The number of deaths worldwide from alcohol-related causes was calculated to be around 2 million in 1989, a figure that will presumably also grow.[102]

Conclusions

In conclusion, the continued expansion of the global drug market is likely to have a negative effect on each of the three broad societal transformations that are taking place in the world today.

The first is the long-standing transition in the developing world from feudalism and postcolonialism to different forms of democratic capitalism. As occurred in the advanced industrialized countries before them, this process has caused and is continuing to cause considerable societal stress and turbulence as new patterns of social, political, and economic behavior challenge and ultimately replace the old ones. For some countries and regions, the modernization process has been especially slow and painful, with little accrued benefit. Indeed, some have evidently regressed, burdened by accumulated debt, political corruption, unresolved ethnic and religious conflicts, growing demographic pressures, deteriorating levels of public health and education, and depleted natural resources.

The presence of the drug trade is likely only to complicate the transition and, in extreme cases, set it back. Besides inhibiting the development of legitimate political institutions and more generally the establishment of civil societies, the corruption and violence typically associated with the drug trade will have serious economic repercussions. The very real threat of a major expansion of drug consumption in the developing world provides additional sources of concern. The attendant social, economic, and health consequences of growing drug consumption, including the heightened incidence of HIV infection, place further burdens on these countries that most are ill prepared or able to bear. Not only do these problems pose opportunity costs that detract from other societal needs, but the inability of state authorities to respond effectively can further erode their political legitimacy. The total social, economic, and political costs could be immense.

The second is the transition under way in the postcommunist world from socialism and central economic planning to democracy and the free market. While the transition has brought political emancipation and economic opportunity to many, it has also been a profoundly disorienting and disruptive experience for others. Unemployment and underemployment, as noted above, have soared, while basic social services have declined in many areas. Although illicit drug production is still at a relatively low level, the potential for considerable growth in certain former communist states undoubtedly exists. Organized criminal groups are also becoming increasingly involved in drug trafficking, seizing the opportunities presented by the collapse of the former authoritarian regimes and the relative weakness of the state structures that have replaced them to supply drugs to the West while simultaneously promoting a burgeoning domestic market. The crime and corruption associated with the drug trade and the explosive growth of the black economy in general are threatening the vitality of the legitimate economy and represent a serious challenge to law and order. As in the developing countries, these countries also would rather not bear the added cost to law enforcement and public health services posed by the growing drug problem. Although drug consumption in the former communist states may never reach the level of the advanced industrialized states, the net costs may still be considerable.

The third is the less defined transition toward a postindustrial society in western Europe and North America. Structural changes in these countries' economies and their populations as a whole are now translating into long-term effects on society at large. Illicit drug use will continue to impose major social and economic costs in the form of higher crime, violence, special health care services, and a precipitous deterioration in the quality of life in certain neighborhoods. The drug problem will doubtless continue to strain many inner-city areas that are typically already struggling to stay solvent and viable. The tendency to identify drug trafficking with new immigrant communities and minority groups is also likely to exacerbate racial tensions and even xenophobic sentiments, as it already has in parts of the United States, Germany, France, and the United Kingdom. Moreover, if past U.S. relations with many Latin American countries are any indication, the drug problem—should it worsen and be perceived as being predominantly foreign in origin—has the potential of becoming a serious international irritant.

5 | Responding to the Challenge

THIS BOOK has endeavored to show that there is ample cause for concern about the evolution of the global market for illicit drugs. For some countries, the situation could deteriorate significantly, unleashing a range of extremely unwelcome side effects that could reverberate beyond their borders.

For the reasons elaborated earlier, the incentives and opportunities to cultivate and manufacture drugs, transport them to the main centers of demand, and distribute them locally are already great and are only likely to grow in many areas of the world. In the primary source areas for botanically derived drugs, producing drugs remains far more economically attractive than alternative legitimate sources of income and employment. This attraction is unlikely to diminish in the forseeable future. The emergence of new suppliers is likely for similar reasons. Similarly, the main trafficking organizations, as rational actors, will continue to seek new ways to extend and exploit this extraordinary source of wealth. The opportunities opened up by the end of the cold war and an expanding global economy are facilitating their activities and motivating new trafficking groups to emerge where the local conditions are propitious.

At the same time, broad social, political, economic, and demographic trends in many parts of the world appear likely to make many more people receptive to the symbolic and remedial attractions of illicit drugs.

Moreover, this temptation will be increased by the growing availability of drugs. Although consumption of most categories of drugs in North America and western Europe either fell or leveled off from the mid-1980s to the early 1990s, this trend appears to be reversing itself—certainly in the United States—if current indicators are correct. Although consumption may never return to earlier levels, it is sure to continue to pose a serious social problem for many communities. Meanwhile, new drug markets are emerging in areas of the postcommunist and developing world that have the potential for rapid growth after the turn of the century.

The central question that this prognosis prompts is, what can be done to minimize the growth of the global drug market and lessen its negative effects? Continuing on the present course certainly does not look promising. There is little reason to believe that the primary policy emphasis on negative controls to deter and deny the production, trafficking, and consumption of illicit drugs will be any more sucessful in the future than it has been in the past. The standard supply-reduction tactics—eradication and interdiction—will surely achieve periodic successes in which production or trafficking is suppressed in a specific area, but given the incentive structure of the illicit drug business, the overall effect is likely to be marginal or short lived at best. The historical record provides overwhelming evidence of this.[1] Increasing the penalties for illicit drug trafficking and consumption in order to deter others is also of dubious long-term value. Besides the costs that this imposes on society in terms of law enforcement and civil liberties, it is difficult to sustain the deterrent effect.

Because the market incentives derive essentially from the underlying policy of prohibition, many have come to view the resulting edifice of associated domestic laws and international conventions as harmful and ultimately self-defeating. This has consequently prompted periodic calls for the repeal of prohibition and the "legalization" of those drugs now considered illicit. At first blush, the arguments for doing so are attractive, which doubtless explains the support that legalization has received from prominent people in public life. A closer look, however, reveals not only the practical difficulties of repealing prohibition but, more important, its uncertain promise.

The Uncertain Promise of Legalization

There are many arguments that appear to make legalization a compelling alternative to current policies. In addition to undermining the black-market incentives to produce and sell drugs, legalization would potentially remove or significantly reduce the very problems that cause the greatest public concern: the crime, corruption, and violence that attend the operation of illicit drug markets. It would also presumably diminish the damage caused by the absence of quality controls on the drugs sold and would lower the danger of infection from needle sharing and other unhygienic practices. Furthermore, the costly and largely futile effort of suppressing the supply of illicit drugs and incarcerating drug offenders could be abandoned, and the money saved could be spent on educating people not to take drugs and treating those who have become addicted.

Beyond these generalities, however, there has been little discussion of the operational meaning of *legalization*.[2] What debate there has been on the subject has been suffused with terminological confusion, analytical imprecision, and not a little intellectual dishonesty. As a result, *legalization* has come to mean different things to different people and has often been used interchangeably with the term *decriminalization*.[3] It is also often equated—implicitly at least—with complete deregulation, which not only fails to acknowledge the extent to which the market for most licit drugs (such as alcohol and tobacco) is subject to legal controls, but also ignores the fact that some illicit drugs, including heroin and cocaine, can be acquired and used legally in some instances. The debate about prohibition versus legalization is essentially a false and meaningless one.[4] The real issue is what degree of regulation is appropriate for the common good. Regulation can take many forms and be applied to different areas of the marketplace. In the case of psychoactive substances, the more pertinent questions that define the regulatory regime can be grouped into three generic categories.

The first concerns the nature of the product: which substances could be legally acquired and consumed? All of them, including heroin and cocaine, or just some, such as cannabis? In what form would the permitted substances be made publicly available? Would the purity or potency of the permitted substances be controlled? Who would decide such regulations, and how would they be reviewed and revised if necessary?

The second concerns the terms of supply: who would produce the permitted substances? Would this be under government or private control? If the latter, what kind of certification, licensing, product reliability, safety, and security arrangements would take effect? Would restrictions be applied to the packaging of the product, as well as any self-administration devices? How would consumers gain access to the permitted substances—through privately owned businesses, government-controlled shops, or mail order services? What regulations would affect the location and operating hours of these outlets? How would they be monitored? What regulations would apply to the personnel selling, dispensing, and safeguarding the permitted substances? Would public advertising of the distribution outlets and the different products be permitted? If not, would this contravene constitutional free speech provisions? If advertising were allowed, what regulations would apply? Could every media outlet be utilized or only some? Where permitted, would the advertising have to conform to certain informational standards? Likewise, at the places selling or otherwise dispensing the drugs, would restrictions be placed on the location and display of the substances? Would product liability and safety information also be made available, and, if so, to whom, how, when, and where? How would the transactions take place: using money, special credits, ration cards, medical prescriptions, or some other means? Would transactions be taxed, registered, and otherwise reported in some way? What would happen to the tax revenues as well as the reported information? What penalties would be set for violating restrictions on the supply of permitted and unpermitted substances?

The third category concerns the terms of consumption: would restrictions be placed on *who* would have access to the permitted drugs, or on *where* they could be consumed (in special facilities or private property) as well as where they could not (schools, parks, or public transportation)? Would pregnant women be given access, and, if not, how would this be regulated? Would special identification procedures have to be followed to gain access? Would consent from a parent, guardian, or health professional be required? Would limits be set on the age and occupation of those acquiring the permitted drugs? Would restrictions apply to *when* certain drugs could be consumed? Would restrictions be placed on *how* the permitted drugs could be consumed? Would information be supplied to help consumers use the permitted drugs safely and tell them what to do in the event of accident or adverse reactions? Would limits apply to the amount of permitted drugs that could be consumed at any one time and during a specified period? Would restrictions apply to the amount that could be carried or in one's possession at any time? Would specific restrictions apply to certain activities—occupational and recreational— that could not be carried out while under the influence of the permitted drugs? Would consumers who suffer adverse physical or psychological reactions have legal recourse? What about people injured and otherwise harmed by others under the influence? In general, what would be the penalties for violating any of the consumer restrictions? Would they be harsher or less severe than existing sanctions?

It is not difficult to see that there are an enormous number of regulatory permutations for each drug. Until the principal alternatives are clearly laid out in reasonable detail, however, their potential costs and benefits cannot be responsibly assessed and compared with the present arrangements. Unfortunately, the debate over alternative legal regimes has yet to reach this stage, and until it does it will remain essentially unproductive. This basic point can be illustrated with respect to the two central questions that would probably sway public opinion: how would more permissive regulatory regimes affect the level and type of drug consumption, and how would they affect the level and type of crime?

Those who argue against relaxing restrictions on the availability of psychoactive substances typically argue that it would lead to an immediate and substantial rise in the level of their consumption. To support this claim, they point to the prevalence of opium, heroin, and cocaine addiction in various countries before international controls took effect, the rise in alcohol consumption after the Volstead Act was repealed in the United States, and some studies showing higher rates of abuse among medical professionals with greater access to prescription drugs.[5] Without explaining the basis of their calculations, some have predicted dramatic increases in the number of new addicts.[6]

In response, proponents of more permissive legal regimes concede that consumption would most probably rise but argue that it would not necessarily increase by very much or for very long.[7] They also point to the fact that consumption of opium, heroin, and cocaine had already begun to decline before international controls took effect, that alcohol consumption did not rise suddenly after Prohibition was lifted, that decriminalization of cannabis use in eleven U.S. states in the 1970s did not lead to increased use, and that public opinion polls in America indicate that most people would not rush off to experiment or binge on hitherto forbidden drugs if they suddenly became more available.[8]

Besides illustrating how the historical record can be interpreted in different ways, such exchanges generally demonstrate the futility of arguing without a fixed point of reference.[9] It is difficult to imagine that consumption of the relevant drugs would not increase if they were to become commercially available in the way that cigarettes and tobacco products are today and if the same kinds of sophisticated product packaging, marketing, and advertising campaigns were also permitted. How much consumption would increase is difficult if not impossible to predict.

In any case, the costs of increased consumption would have to be compared with the gains achieved from making some forms of drug use safer and from reducing much of the crime associated with the black market for illicit drugs.

Here again, those who argue against more permissive regulatory regimes doubt that black-market activity and its associated problems would disappear or be significantly reduced.[10] Again, this question can be addressed only in relation to the terms of supply. Under schemes where drugs would be sold openly on a commercial basis and prices would remain close to production and distribution costs, the opportunities for illicit undercutting would appear to be relatively small. Under more restrictive conditions, such as those involving government-controlled outlets or medical prescription schemes, there would be a greater likelihood that illicit sources of supply would remain or evolve to satisfy the legally unfulfilled demand. The most obvious case concerns the degree of regulation affecting access to drugs by the largest group considered to be at risk, adolescents and young adults.[11] The desire to control access in the interest of stemming consumption has to be balanced against the black-market opportunities that would arise. To the extent that illicit markets would remain, additional questions would need to be asked about their operation over time, whether they were more "benign" and therefore easier to deal with than previous ones, and more broadly, whether the trade-off with other benefits still made the effort worthwhile.[12]

A whole set of additional questions surrounds the international repercussions of different regulatory regimes. How would the current international conventions be affected? Would every nation have to conform to a new set of general rules, or could major variations exist? If the latter, what would be the impact? For example, would more permissive countries be suddenly swamped by drugs and drug consumers, or would traffickers focus on the countries where the profits were higher as a result of tighter restrictions? This is not an abstract question, as demonstrated by the problems caused by "drug tourists" in the Netherlands or in Zurich. What would happen to the principal suppliers of illicit drugs if restrictions on the commercial sale of the same drugs were lifted in some or all the main markets? Would the trafficking organizations adapt and become legal businesses, or would they turn to other illicit enterprises? What would be the effect on the source countries? These questions have not even been posed in a systematic way, let alone seriously studied.

Although greater precision in defining terms and alternative regulatory regimes is critical to evaluating their costs and benefits, considerable uncertainty is still likely to remain without experimentation and implementation.[13] This is particularly true for those regulatory alternatives that would amount to the greatest departure from current policies. These are also the ones that would represent the biggest legislative and regulatory challenge for most countries to enact. Reducing the uncertainty, however, is still a worthwhile pursuit even though it cannot be entirely eliminated. It would be helpful, for example, if a range of hypothetical regulatory regimes could be assessed according to a common set of variables to bring greater clarity to their potential costs, benefits, and trade-offs. In addition to instilling some much-needed rigor into the debate over regulatory alternatives, such an exercise would also bring the limits and contradictions of current policy choices into sharper focus.

Unfortunately, governments have been reluctant to support such research, apparently because it might suggest that their commitment to prohibition is wavering. This seems particularly true in the United States, where opposition remains high.[14] This position is usually justified on the grounds that such studies are unnecessary because it is self-evidently true that legalization would promote higher drug consumption. Public opinion surveys indicating opposition to legalization for apparently the same reason bolster this position.[15] Yet, for the reasons outlined above, this is not a public policy issue that lends itself to such simplistic discussion. Perhaps with more information about the alternatives and what they may have to offer, public opinion might be quite different. At the very least, such information might stimulate an honest discussion about the role of drugs—both licit and illicit—in society.

Ultimately, however, the prospects for a radical departure from the prevailing prohibitionist stance look remote. Reversing or jettisoning nearly a century of effort when the putative benefits are so uncertain and the potential costs are so high would represent a herculean leap of faith. Only an extremely severe and widespread deterioration of the situation globally is likely to produce the level of consensus that would have to be attained—domestically and internationally—to bring about such an attitudinal shift and generate the necessary political impetus. Acknowledging realities, however, does not mean accepting the status quo. International drug control policy can be made more effective and less counterproductive within the existing legal framework.

A Global Prescription: Priorities, Principles, and Programs

Making international drug control policy more effective must begin with a restatement of its principal goals and priorities. The primary objective should be to minimize the consumption of psychoactive substances that are deemed harmful to one's health and to the safety of others. This goal accepts that drug consumption can never be eliminated entirely, but that it is possible to keep it to tolerable levels in a way that minimizes its costs to society. Acknowledging that a drug-free society is impractical, however, should not be confused with condoning drug use. This objective also accepts that identifying the drugs that society deems harmful and dangerous will continue to rest on arbitrary legal distinctions. The inherent contradictions of this position can be minimized, however, by more actively discouraging and constraining the consumption of *legal* psychoactive substances that pose equal if not greater risks to health and safety. Finally, acknowledging the likelihood of persistent illicit drug use means accepting the continued existence of illicit drug suppliers. The goal should be to prevent trafficking groups and other forms of organized crime from acquiring sufficient concentrations of wealth from the sale of drugs and other illicit activities to corrupt, threaten, and otherwise wield undue influence on the legitimate political and economic processes of governments at the local, regional, and national levels.

Attaining these more pragmatic goals requires both a major shift in policy emphasis and a more discriminating use of resources. Although the primacy of negative control sanctions should be maintained and where possible made more effective to combat high-level drug trafficking organizations, positive control measures should now become the dominant means of reducing the production and consumption of illicit drugs. This formula is different from what is often proposed within the general framework of prohibition. It is not, for example, the same as advocating the abandonment of supply reduction in favor of demand reduction. For the reasons discussed previously, these terms are misleading and not helpful for policy prescription. Neither is it the same as advocating a more balanced multipronged drug control policy. Although many pay lip service to this general approach, it is more likely to lead to the augmentation of existing programs with others such as drug education and treatment rather than to any real reordering of priorities and allocation of resources. Before describing what the proposed course of action means in practical programmatic terms, it is important to lay out the three basic operating principles that should guide future policy.

First, international drug control should be explicitly integrated into or "embedded" in larger policy initiatives that enjoy general support and indirectly serve the same objectives.[16] These include fostering global economic development, free trade, stable democracies, safe and lawful communities, and healthy and productive citizens. Too often in the past, drug control policies have been carried out as stand-alone initiatives, which by definition marginalizes them organizationally and reduces the political investment in their success. Harnessing drug control to complementary policy initiatives not only increases the possibility of synergistic benefits, but it also promotes organizational control and efficiency while reducing duplication, poor coordination, and bureaucratic rivalry.

Second, international drug control policies must not do more harm than the problems they are designed to alleviate. This basic philosophy underlies the "harm-reduction" or "harm-minimalization" movement but is more generally applicable. Although associated more with alleviating the adverse effects of prohibition on public health, this basic principle can also be applied to law enforcement efforts.[17] As the historical account revealed, the net effect of many such programs in the past has been to displace rather than resolve the problem, sometimes making it worse in the process.

Third, international drug control policies must recognize the value of policy differentiation and problem discrimination. It is not appropriate to design a global blueprint applicable to all. The specific social, political, economic, and cultural characteristics of individual countries should clearly guide what is appropriate and feasible. Similarly, programs should be better focused on problem groups and areas, as well as on the drugs that constitute the greatest threat to public health and welfare.

In addition to observing these basic principles, it cannot be stressed enough that international drug control policy formulation and evaluation must be based on more reliable data and better analysis of market trends and forecasts. This is particularly true for the countries that are now at greatest risk. At present, policy is largely pursued in a vacuum, devoid of detailed, accurate information on everything from drug production to consumption patterns. It is extraordinary if not reprehensible that so little is known about a problem that has been a major source of international concern for so long and that routinely absorbs enormous societal resources. The small pockets of knowledge that do exist, moreover, are rarely joined to create a larger picture. The frequency with which well-intentioned policies cause unintended and often counterproductive results is just one indication of this shortcoming. The general state of ignorance has also allowed fear and dogma to prevail in too many cases.

A Global Monitoring and Evaluation Network. A primary program initiative, therefore, should be the creation of a global drug-monitoring and evaluation network to measure more accurately the nature of the problem. This would comprise a system of interlinked regional centers in North America, Latin America, Europe, Africa, Southwest Asia (including the Middle East), and Southeast Asia and the Pacific that would be funded and established under the auspices of the principal regional organizations and coordinated by the United Nations International Drug Control Program (UNDCP). Each of the centers would compose a core group of staff recruited from existing national agencies, as well as some on temporary loan, who would sponsor and coordinate the collection of drug-related production, trafficking, and consumption data for their area. Common data collection, registration, classification, and analysis standards would be employed to allow cross-national and cross-regional comparisons. These centers should also endeavor to anticipate future developments rather than just assess current ones. In this respect, it might even be possible to develop a set of early warning indicators to draw attention to emerging trends and problems so that timely interventions can be made. Information collected at each regional center would in turn provide the basis for an annual global drug net assessment to be carried out by the UNDCP. This would replace the existing annual review by the International Narcotics Control Board.

Although the primary goal of the network would be to collect, collate, and assess data on the global drug market, it might also develop a policy evaluation function. In the short term, the centers could act as clearinghouses for sharing information on the effectiveness of specific drug control programs and initiatives. This should be focused more on collecting information on drug prevention efforts, particularly where the knowledge base is skimpy. Eventually, the centers could develop their own sections for monitoring and evaluating implementation.

Elements of such a network are already in existence or planned. For example, the European Monitoring Centre for Drugs and Drug Addiction, which is now being established in Lisbon, together with an associated network of national systems (the European Information Network on Drugs and Drug Addiction, or REITOX), provides a model for how a regional system might operate.[18] In the United States, the National Institute on Drug Abuse has for over a decade run a Community Epidemiology Work Group, which monitors drug-related trends in selected North American cities. It has also been instrumental in promoting the establishment of similar networks in other regions of the world.[19]

A Global Drug Use Prevention Program. Given the difficulty of reducing the supply of drugs while the incentives and opportunities remain high, positive control programs should focus primarily on discouraging the use of drugs in the context of their general and, in some cases, growing availability. The goal should be to promote a general antidrug ethos through integrated education, workplace, community, and mass media programs that stress how drugs can do harm to one's health, personal relationships, educational progress, and professional prospects. Although this effort would be designed to appeal in dispassionate ways to the self-interest of potential users, the ultimate effect can be likened to strengthening society's immunological defenses against the widespread presence of drugs. It does not help, however, if the messages that society endeavors to transmit about the health and safety consequences of illicit drugs are contradicted by open or tacit approval of licit ones like alcohol and tobacco, which are now acknowledged to cause more social harm in terms of personal impairment, injury to others, loss of productivity, and, in some countries, crime.[20]

Many countries in the advanced industrialized world already operate a variety of drug prevention programs with varying degrees of success. It is fair to state, however, that the resources devoted to such programs have been considerably less than those given to drug-related law enforcement, and in many cases they appear to have been implemented in a largely haphazard and unintegrated fashion. Beyond North America and western Europe, such programs receive even less emphasis, if they exist at all. With these shortcomings in mind, the UNDCP and the World Health Organization (WHO) should establish a global drug use prevention program with the goal of actively promoting and aiding countries to devote more resources to preventing drug consumption.

As an urgent priority, the first task of this program should be to conduct or sponsor a comprehensive evaluation of existing national drug use prevention programs that have been carried out in schools, colleges, local communities, and workplaces as well as those using the mass media. The basic aim of the study would be to determine more precisely which programs have proven to be more successful than others so as to develop a general inventory of useful methodologies.[21] The results of this study could then be used to advise governments on how to design and implement their own drug use prevention programs. In practice, this would probably entail mixing and matching specific approaches to countries that share similar characteristics. "Program packages" would be tailored to the specific needs and conditions of individual countries. In some, for example, more emphasis may have to be placed on mass media programs to compensate for low levels of enrollment in public education.[22] Although the intent is to encourage countries to make such programs the main priority of their antidrug efforts, some outside financial and technical assistance will probably be needed. Given the magnitude of the task and the shortage of resources, a prioritizing scheme would be desirable that identified countries according to levels of risk.

A Global Drug Treatment Training Program. In parallel with their drug prevention efforts, the UNDCP and WHO should also establish a global drug treatment training program. Again, the first task would be to carry out a comprehensive evaluation of existing drug treatment and rehabilitation programs to determine which have achieved more success than others. On the basis of its findings, an international training program should be created focused primarily on raising the level of expertise among health professionals in many postcommunist and developing countries, where the current resources are minimal or nonexistent. In practice, this might include running instructional courses on the latest methods as well as educational exchange programs for public health professionals. The long-term goal would be to create a cadre of trained individuals who can in turn instruct others. Something akin to this, but on a terribly small scale, is already operational with the Hubert H. Humphrey Fellowship Program run by the Johns Hopkins University School of Hygiene and Public Health in Baltimore. The success of this program is suggestive of a larger potential.

A Global Drug Crisis Response Program. It is not unreasonable to expect that prevention efforts and treatment resources will be insufficient to curb a rapid increase in drug use and abuse in some areas of the world. Under such circumstances, the best that may be achieved is to contain the epidemic and reduce its most harmful consequences. For such contingencies, an international drug crisis response program could be established to provide rapid assistance for badly affected areas. Depending on the nature of the problem, this might include the offer of medical advice on drug-related emergency cases and assistance in implementing some of the harm-reduction programs mentioned earlier to minimize the spread of HIV infection. Although such assistance would necessarily be short term, it could provide critical momentum for a sustained effort by local authorities.

Efforts to Reduce Production. Given the many challenges that exist, expectations should not be high about significantly reducing the world-wide production of illicit drugs. In the case of botanical-based drugs, there seems little reason to believe that forced eradication methods will yield any better results in the future. The success of some crop substitution programs carried out in conjunction with other forms of development assistance does offer some hope, however, of improving conditions in some areas. The critical factors that appear to have made the difference now seem to be well known. At the local level, they include infrastructure improvements to permit the transportation of alternative crops, farming and marketing advice, credit schemes, and direct engagement of local groups and community leaders in the process. At the national level, macroeconomic adjustments to create market and employment opportunities are important, as are efforts to integrate remote growing areas into the political life of the country and strengthen the presence of government authority. Since much broader nation-building goals are being served, assistance should be given to countries willing to carry out such programs in a carefully planned manner. Because resources are limited, debt relief and debt swap programs could be utilized to help finance such initiatives.[23]

Efforts to Combat Organized Crime. For similar reasons, combating international drug trafficking will remain an uphill battle. Once trafficking groups establish a relatively safe base of operations, they are very difficult to dislodge. From there they can exploit the numerous and growing opportunities to distribute drugs, launder money, and diversify into other activities—licit as well as illicit—increasing their wealth and power in the process. Clearly some countries are more vulnerable than others to such developments. Some also have more resources available to take on criminal groups once they become entrenched. Since the threat from such groups transcends national borders, the international community has a direct interest in helping others to both prevent the growth of large trafficking groups and transnational criminal organizations and disable them before they become too powerful. Although the conditions that promote the rise of organized criminal groups in certain areas can be addressed only through much larger initiatives, states can nevertheless provide assistance to bolster the criminal justice and law enforcement systems of countries at risk.

There are several obstacles to providing assistance of this kind, whether it be financial aid, equipment, or technical advice. For donor countries, the principal concern is that it is not squandered or applied in ways that contravene basic human rights. However, recipient countries typically resist oversight of how the assistance is implemented or application of specific conditionalities to its use, because these implicitly challenge their national sovereignty. Such sensitivities can be alleviated somewhat through the use of multilateral institutions that enjoy general legitimacy. The use of the UNDCP to coordinate and channel law enforcement assistance to the countries of the former Soviet Union is an example of this approach.

On a more fundamental level, when it comes to combating criminal organizations that routinely flout traditional notions of national sovereignty, states will have to accept that to regain some de facto control over what comes across their territorial borders and takes place within them they will have to reconsider their staunch defense of de jure principles that are becoming increasingly meaningless. These sovereign prerogatives are clearly not going to vanish overnight, but there are ways to work around them and reduce their effect on operational performance. Just as many military forces have accepted the value if not the necessity of confronting common security threats through collective action— which has in turn required the capability to function in multinational formations with interoperable equipment and common procedures that are at times placed under the direction of officers from a foreign but allied country—so police forces and criminal justice systems will have to see that similar practices can have benefits in their own field of work.[24]

The same logic can also be applied to the organization of national antidrug-trafficking efforts. It makes no sense to have many different agencies dedicated to the same task, as is presently the case in the United States, where the panoply of agencies dealing with drug trafficking includes the Drug Enforcement Adminstration, the Central Intelligence Agency, the Federal Bureau of Investigation, the National Drug Intelligence Center, and the Department of the Treasury. Neither does it make sense to have many more agencies separately tackling other connected forms of organized crime such as money laundering, illegal immigration, terrorism, and counterfeiting. For this reason, many European countries have consolidated the work of previously disaggregated departments, as in the cases of Germany's Federal Criminal Agency, Holland's National Criminal Intelligence Service, and Britain's National Criminal Intelligence Service. Although there are legitimate concerns about concentrating too much power in one organization, these can be alleviated with the appropriate constitutional checks and oversight mechanisms.

The Europeans have also probably done more to foster joint action at the international level. The Trevi Group, made up of representatives from the Justice and Home Affairs Ministries of member states of the European Union, has been meeting regularly since the mid-1980s to coordinate responses to the threat of drug trafficking, illegal immigration, terrorism, and other forms of international crime. With the treaty on European Union that came into force on October 29, 1993, these activities have been subsumed under the auspices of the K.4 Coordinating Committee.[25] In 1991 the EU's European Council approved the establishment of the European Police Office (Europol) to exchange intelligence and coordinate common action. Some members, notably Germany, have envisaged the eventual evolution of Europol into an organization with real operational, even supranational, law enforcement authority. Others, notably France and Great Britain, have stiffly resisted this vision out of concern that it would represent an unacceptable erosion of their sovereignty. Some countries, such as Holland, have also been apprehensive about whether personal data and the privacy of individuals can be properly safeguarded. These concerns have delayed agreement on a convention governing the operation of Europol, but the European Union nevertheless proceeded by establishing in June 1993 a Europol Drugs Unit to collect and exchange relevant intelligence, headquartered in The Hague.[26]

Recognizing the almost limitless opportunities to smuggle drugs does not mean forgoing all forms of control. It is still desirable to reduce the ease with which traffickers can conduct routine large-scale deliveries that significantly increase the availability of drugs in a particular market. The vast worldwide commercial conveyancy network, as discussed previously, is becoming the most efficient way of delivering drugs internationally. Since these networks are also exploited for other illicit purposes, such as the illegal movement of people, arms, chemicals, or radioactive materials, drug interdiction efforts should be made part of a broader international effort to bring greater transparency and regulation to the movement of global trade.

Again, this calls for much closer international cooperation between national customs and immigration services along the lines laid out above for combating organized crime. The Europeans are pointing the way here too in the development of common procedures and standards as well as information-sharing systems.[27] Several other initiatives also bear investigating, including tighter disclosure rules, electronic tagging devices, antitampering mechanisms, and nonintrusive rapid inspection systems. These could significantly narrow the latitude for abuse without impeding the free movement of goods.[28] I would also encourage the growing practice of engaging the active cooperation of trade and industry in identifying suspicious activities and reporting them in a timely fashion to law enforcement agencies according to prescribed arrangements laid out in formal memoranda of understanding.

In a similar fashion, the existence of a multitude of ways to launder drug money should not deter efforts to reduce the opportunities or raise the costs of doing so. These efforts should be institutionally consolidated and made part of a broader campaign to bring greater transparency and accountability to the international financial system. To a great extent, this is already being pursued under such initiatives as the Basel Committee's Minimum Standards Report and the Financial Action Task Force's forty recommendations, which set down basic norms and standards for international banking with the aim of having them universally accepted.[29] A parallel process is also under way to convince the offshore banking community that it is in their interest to be seen as a "clean place to do business." Otherwise, legitimate clients will go elsewhere. With competition for capital so intense, the fear of becoming stigmatized can be a powerful inducement for banks to clean up their act. The carrots, however, will have to be backed up with some formidable sticks, such as making managers personally accountable for criminal transgressions and denying access to the international financial system for banks known to be used by criminal enterprises.[30]

In conclusion, the effectiveness of reorienting drug control policy to curb the global habit will ultimately rest on the international community's willingness to address much larger concerns to which the drug problem is inextricably linked. These include the looming and interrelated problems of population growth, environmental degradation, underdevelopment, poverty, illiteracy, mass unemployment, ethnic strife, and disease. Thus drug prevention based on the message that drugs do not promote a healthy and successful life is likely to be rendered meaningless if people have little reason to expect such a life. Similarly, the attraction of trafficking drugs is not going to diminish while the economic prospects of so many people look so bleak. The fight against organized crime will continue to be a constant struggle for as long as there are places where the rule of law has broken down or has never been properly established. The same is true also for initiatives against money laundering while the international community continues to sanction the existence of offshore tax havens. Drug control, therefore, can be seen not only as a necessary component of the efforts to address these larger issues but also as a direct beneficiary. Only by recognizing this fundamental relationship and the realistic expectations that it implies can meaningful progress be made.

Notes

Chapter One

1. The term comes from David Musto, *The American Disease: Origins of Narcotic Control,* expanded ed. (Oxford University Press, 1987).

2. One has only to casually peruse either the U.S. State Department's annual *International Narcotics Control Strategy Report* or the United Nations' *Report of the International Narcotics Control Board* to get a sense of how pervasive the drug trade has become. Further confirmation is provided by the large number of countries represented at the UN Special Session on Drugs held in New York in October 1993.

3. Organization for Economic Cooperation and Development, Financial Action Task Force on Money Laundering, *Report* (Paris, February 7, 1990). Another estimate calculates that approximately $50 billion is spent annually on drugs in the United States. See William Rhodes and others, "What America's Users Spend on Illegal Drugs, 1988–1993," prepared for the Office of National Drug Control Policy, Abt Associates, Cambridge, Mass., 1995, p. 3. By contrast, the worldwide licit market for controlled drugs used principally for pharmaceutical purposes has been estimated at $150 million. See "Opium Firm Plans to Go Public," *International Herald Tribune,* June 19, 1995.

4. United Nations International Drug Control Program, "The Social and Economic Impact of Drug Abuse and Control," position paper, United Nations System, June 19, 1994, p. 29.

5. See Sid Zabludoff, "Economics and Narcotics: A Perspective," in *Economics of the Narcotics Industry,* report of conference sponsored by U.S. Department of State, Bureau of Intelligence and Research, and Central Intelligence Agency,

November 21–22, 1994; and United Nations Economic and Social Council, Commission on Narcotic Drugs, "Illicit Drug Traffic and Supply, Including Reports from Subsidiary Bodies and Evaluation of Their Activities," E/CN.7/1995/ 7, February 10, 1995, p. 23. Other estimates put the total at around $500 billion. See LaMond Tullis, *Handbook of Research on the Illicit Drug Traffic: Socioeconomic and Political Consequences* (Westport, Conn.: Greenwood Press, 1991), p. xvii; and Stephen Fidler, "U.S. Tries to Break the Vicious Circle," *Financial Times*, November 5, 1993, p. 5.

6. Paul B. Stares, "The Global Drug Phenomenon: Implications for Policy," in Georges Estievenart, ed., *Policies and Strategies to Combat Drugs in Europe: The Treaty on European Union: Framework for a New European Strategy to Combat Drugs?* (Netherlands: Martinus Nijhoff, 1995), pp. 7–14.

7. Ibid., pp. 16–19.

8. Bureau of International Narcotics Matters, *International Narcotics Control Strategy Report*, Publication 10246 (U.S. Department of State, March 1995), p. 27. (Hereafter *1995 INCSR*.)

9. Patrick Clawson, "How Profitable for Farmers Is Cultivation of Coca Leaves?" and Rensselaer W. Lee, "The Global Narcotics Trade: Economic Patterns and Implications," in *Economics of the Narcotics Industry*.

10. *1995 INCSR*, p. 100; and "Experts Discuss Threat of Poppy Replacing Coca," *El Peruano*, January 25, 1994, pp. A6–7, in Joint Publications Research Service, *Narcotics*, February 7, 1994, pp. 12–13. (Hereafter JPRS, *Narcotics*.)

11. Peter A. Lupsha, "From Leaf to Nose: An Analysis of Trends and Directions in the Cocaine Industry," in *Strategic Organizational Drug Intelligence Symposium Compendium* (National Drug Intelligence Center and Ridgeway Center for International Security Studies, March 16, 1995), pp. 11–18.

12. UNESCO, "Illicit Drug Traffic and Supply," p. 8.

13. Tim Golden, "Agents of Graft—A Special Report," *New York Times*, April 19, 1995, p. A1.

14. See the excellent discussion on strategic alliances among criminal organizations in Phil Williams, "Drug Trafficking, Risk Management and Strategic Alliances," in *Economics of the Narcotics Industry*; and Williams, "Transnational Criminal Organizations: Strategic Alliances," *Washington Quarterly*, vol. 18 (Winter 1995), pp. 57–72.

15. C. Peter Rydell and Susan S. Everingham, *Controlling Cocaine: Supply versus Demand Programs*, RAND/MR-331-ONDCP/A/DPRC (Santa Monica, Calif.: RAND Corp., 1994); Office of National Drug Control Policy, *National Drug Control Strategy: Reclaiming Our Communities from Drugs and Violence* (The White House, February 1994), pp. 12–14; and Rhodes and others, "What America's Users Spend on Illegal Drugs," pp. 3–24.

16. National Institute on Drug Abuse, *Epidemiologic Trends in Drug Abuse*, vol. 1: *Highlights and Executive Summary* (U.S. Department of Health and Human Services, June 1994); Abigail Trafford, "The Snare of Illegal Drugs," *Washington Post Health*, December 12, 1995, p. 6; Substance Abuse and Mental Health Services Administration, Office of Applied Studies, *National Household Survey on Drug Abuse: Population Estimates, 1993* (U.S. Department of Health and

Human Services, October 1994); and Lloyd D. Johnston, Patrick O'Malley, and Jerald Bachman, "National Survey Results on Drug Use," in *The Monitoring the Future Study, 1975–1995*, vol. 1: *Secondary School Students* (National Institute on Drug Abuse, forthcoming).

17. See H. Klingemann and others, "European Summary on Drug Abuse, First Report (1985–1990)," EUR/ICP/ADA 527/A, World Health Organization, Regional Office for Europe, Copenhagen, 1992; and Richard Hartnoll, "Drug Misuse Trends in Thirteen European Cities: Synthesis of Individual City Reports," Pompidou Group, Strasbourg, France, 1993.

18. United Nations International Drug Control Program, "Drugs and Development," discussion paper prepared for the World Summit on Social Development, June 1994, p. 3.

19. See Ralph C. Bryant, "Global Change: Increasing Economic Integration and Eroding Political Sovereignty," *Brookings Review*, vol. 12 (Fall 1994), pp. 42–45.

20. The term *borderless world* is taken from Ken'ichi Omae, *The Borderless World: Power and Strategy in the Interlinked Economy* (Harper Business, 1990). The term *transnational* is used here in reference to the myriad interactions of people, goods, services, and ideas across state boundaries that are not exclusively, if at all, state sponsored or controlled. Some emphasize the private and nongovernmental nature of transnational relations. See Joseph S. Nye Jr. and Robert O. Keohane, eds., *Transnational Relations and World Politics* (Harvard University Press, 1970), pp. ix–xxii. Others, however, adopt a more inclusive definition. See Samuel P. Huntington, "Transnational Organizations in World Politics," *World Politics*, vol. 25 (April 1973), pp. 334–35.

21. The drug trade has been characterized as a transnational phenomenon before, although not always very explicitly or in great detail. See, for example, Luiz R. S. Simmons and Abdul A. Said, "The Politics of Addiction," in Luiz R. S. Simmons and Abdul A. Said, eds., *Drugs, Politics, and Diplomacy: The International Connection* (Beverly Hills and London: Sage, 1975), p. 3; Michael J. Dziedzic, "The Transnational Drug Trade and Regional Security," *Survival*, vol. 31 (November–December 1989), p. 533; and Ethan A. Nadelmann, "Global Prohibition Regimes: The Evolution of Norms in International Society," *International Organization*, vol. 44 (Autumn 1990), p. 512. The connection between transnationalism and the drug trade was also made by Stephen E. Flynn, *The Transnational Drug Challenge and the New World Order*, a report of the Center for Strategic and International Studies Project on the Global Drug Trade in the Post–Cold War Era (Washington: CSIS, 1993); and Flynn, "Worldwide Drug Scourge: The Expanding Trade in Illicit Drugs," *Brookings Review*, vol. 11 (Winter 1993), pp. 6–11.

22. See Phil Williams, "Transnational Criminal Organisations and International Security," *Survival*, vol. 36 (Spring 1994), pp. 96–113.

23. I am grateful to Richard R. Clayton for bringing this possibility to my attention in his presentation, "Drugs vs. Public Health: Assessing the Risk of a Global Drug Epidemic," prepared for the Brookings Institution Workshop on "The International Implications of the Transnational Drug Phenomenon," Uni-

versity of Pennsylvania, April 18–19, 1994. See also UNDCP, "Drugs and Development," p. 3.

24. For an extremely comprehensive and useful review of the literature on the international drug trade, see Tullis, *Handbook of Research on the Illicit Drug Traffic*, pp. 254–610.

25. This is not to impugn the quality of all of the research that has been carried out. Examples of excellent studies include Mary H. Cooper, *The Business of Drugs* (Washington: Congressional Quarterly Press, 1990); Peter H. Smith, ed., *Drug Policy in the Americas* (Boulder, Colo.: Westview Press, 1992); Alfred W. McCoy and Alan A. Block, eds., *War on Drugs: Studies in the Failure of U.S. Narcotics Policy* (Boulder, Colo.: Westview Press, 1992); and Scott B. MacDonald and Bruce Zagaris, eds., *International Handbook on Drug Control* (Westport, Conn.: Greenwood Press, 1992). The best nongovernmental update on the global drug trade is the monthly *Geopolitical Drug Dispatch* (Paris: Observatoire Geopolitique des Drouges).

26. To its credit, the RAND Corporation has endeavored to carry out such "systemic" analyses of the trade in different categories of drugs. See Bonnie Dombey-Moore, Susan Resetar, and Michael Childress, "A Systems Description of the Cocaine Trade," WD-6043-A/AF (July 1992); Childress, "A Systems Description of the Heroin Trade," WD-6194-A/DPRC (October 1992); and Childress, "A Systems Description of the Marijuana Trade," WD-6195-A/DPRC (March 1993). See also Rhodes and others, "What America's Users Spend on Illegal Drugs."

27. This is a long-standing lament of almost everyone who ventures into this field of study. See, for example, Peter Reuter, "The (Continued) Vitality of Mythical Numbers," *Public Interest*, no. 75 (Spring 1984), pp. 135–47; and Reuter, "Prevalence Estimation and Policy Formulation," *Journal of Drug Issues*, vol. 23 (Spring 1993), pp. 167–84.

28. LaMond Tullis, "Illicit Drugs: Production, Consumption, Traffic and Control," report prepared for the United Nations Development Program, November 1993, p. 2.

29. Interview at Customs Cooperation Council, Brussels, June 1993.

30. This point is made by Jonathan P. Caulkins, "Evaluating the Effectiveness of Interdiction and Source Country Control," in *Economics of the Narcotics Industry*.

31. See UNDCP, "Social and Economic Impact of Drug Abuse and Control," pp. 6–7.

32. See Office of National Drug Control Policy, *National Drug Control Strategy*, p. 49; and Raphael F. Perl, ed., *Drugs and Foreign Policy: A Critical Review* (Boulder, Colo.: Westview Press, 1994).

33. Richard B. Craig, "Review Essay: Everybody Talks about the War on Drugs . . .," *Orbis*, vol. 37 (Winter 1993), pp. 135–47; and William O. Walker III, "U.S. Narcotics Foreign Policy in the Twentieth Century: An Analytical Overview," in Perl, ed., *Drugs and Foreign Policy*, pp. 7–35.

34. Williams, "Transnational Criminal Organisations and International Security."

Chapter Two

1. Unless indicated otherwise, the following discussion draws heavily on Alfred W. McCoy, "Heroin as a Global Commodity: A History of Southeast Asia's Opium Trade," in Alfred W. McCoy and Alan A. Block, eds., *War on Drugs: Studies in the Failure of U.S. Narcotics Policy* (Boulder, Colo.: Westview Press, 1992), pp. 237–55; Peter D. Lowes, *The Genesis of International Narcotics Control* (New York: Arno Press, 1981); Arnold H. Taylor, *American Diplomacy and the Narcotics Traffic, 1900–1939: A Study in International Humanitarian Reform* (Duke University Press, 1969); Ethan A. Nadelmann, "Global Prohibition Regimes: The Evolution of Norms in International Society," *International Organization*, vol. 44 (Autumn 1990), pp. 408–513; and Luiz R. S. Simmons and Abdul A. Said, "The Politics of Addiction," in Luiz R. S. Simmons and Abdul A. Said, eds., *Drugs, Politics, and Diplomacy: The International Connection* (Beverly Hills and London: Sage Publications, 1974), pp. 3–48.

2. American merchantmen also transported Turkish opium and later Indian opium to the Chinese market.

3. The alkaloid cocaine had first been isolated from coca leaf in 1859. While coca cultivation has long been associated with South America and particularly the Andes region, a major source at this time was Java, now modern-day Indonesia. See James A. Inciardi, *The War on Drugs II: The Continuing Epic of Heroin, Cocaine, Crack, Crime, AIDS, and Public Policy* (Mountain View, Calif.: Mayfield Publishing, 1992), pp. 6–8.

4. Some estimates put the number of opiate addicts in the United States during this period as high as 3 million. See Inciardi, *War on Drugs II*, p. 6. Other indicators suggest the number to be lower but still high. Apparently the number of addicts peaked in the 1890s and thereafter declined, primarily as a result of more stringent medical practices. See David T. Courtwright, *Dark Paradise: Opiate Addiction in America before 1940* (Harvard University Press, 1982), p. 2; and David F. Musto, "Patterns in U.S. Drug Abuse and Response," in Peter H. Smith, ed., *Drug Policy in the Americas* (Boulder, Colo.: Westview Press, 1992), p. 31.

5. By 1906 over a quarter of all adult Chinese males were estimated to be regular opium smokers. See Taylor, *American Diplomacy and the Narcotics Traffic*, p. 6.

6. Lowes, *Genesis of International Narcotics Control*, p. 199. See also David F. Musto, *The American Disease: Origins of Narcotic Control*, expanded ed. (Oxford University Press, 1987), pp. 35–37.

7. See Musto, "Patterns in U.S. Drug Abuse and Response," p. 37; and Musto, *American Disease*, pp. 50–51.

8. For a full account of the conference, see Taylor, *American Diplomacy and the Narcotics Traffic*, pp. 82–122.

9. Lowes, *Genesis of International Narcotics Control*, p. 178.

10. Bureau of Justice Statistics, *Drugs, Crime, and the Justice System*, N/CJ-133652 (U.S. Department of Justice, 1992), p. 77. A brief but useful overview of subsequent domestic legislation is provided on pp. 78–81.

11. See William B. McAllister, "Conflicts of Interest in the International Drug Control System," *Journal of Policy History*, vol. 3, no. 4 (1991), p. 497.

12. Simmons and Said, "Politics of Addiction," p. 5. For a more detailed discussion of U.S. objections, see Taylor, *American Diplomacy and the Narcotics Traffic*, p. 200.

13. Taylor, *American Diplomacy and the Narcotics Traffic*, pp. 252–53; and Musto, *American Disease*, pp. 214–15. Even so, since the 1931 agreement exempted colonial possessions, it achieved less than the advocates of drug control hoped. See McAllister, "Conflicts of Interest in the International Drug Control System," pp. 497–98.

14. McCoy, "Heroin as a Global Commodity," p. 251.

15. Courtwright, *Dark Paradise*, pp. 2–3; and Simmons and Said, "Politics of Addiction," pp. 27–28.

16. See Bertil A. Renborg, *International Drug Control: A Study of International Administration by and through the League of Nations* (Washington: Carnegie Endowment for International Peace, 1947), p. 145.

17. Ibid., p. 146.

18. McCoy, "Heroin as a Global Commodity," p. 253.

19. Simmons and Said, "Politics of Addiction," p. 28.

20. McCoy, "Heroin as a Global Commodity," p. 252.

21. Ibid., p. 255. See also William O. Walker, *Opium and Foreign Policy: The Anglo-American Search for Order in Asia, 1912–1954* (University of North Carolina Press, 1991), chaps. 3, 4.

22. McCoy, "Heroin as a Global Commodity," p. 254; Taylor, *American Diplomacy and the Narcotics Traffic*, pp. 281–83; and Renborg, *International Drug Control*, p. 147.

23. Taylor, *American Diplomacy and the Narcotics Traffic*, pp. 294–95; and Renborg, *International Drug Control*, pp. 148–53.

24. Simmons and Said, "Politics of Addiction," pp. 7–8.

25. Renborg, *International Drug Control*, p. 235.

26. Courtwright, *Dark Paradise*, p. 6; and Inciardi, *War on Drugs II*, p. 24.

27. Taylor, *American Diplomacy and the Narcotics Traffic*, pp. 334–35.

28. At the same time, the commitment by the European powers to phase out their opium monopolies as a result of pressure from the United States and its general anticolonial campaign was also diluted and in some cases ignored by the local colonial administrations. See Walker, *Opium and Foreign Policy*, chap. 8.

29. See Paul Lowinger, "How the People's Republic of China Solved the Drug Abuse Problem," *American Journal of Chinese Medicine*, vol. 1, no. 2 (1973), pp. 275–82. I am grateful to Jasper Woodcock of the Institute for the Study of Drug Dependence, London, for bringing this article to my attention.

30. McCoy, "Heroin as a Global Commodity," p. 255.

31. See Bertil Lintner, "Heroin and Highland Insurgency in the Golden Triangle," in McCoy and Block, eds., *War on Drugs*, p. 288.

32. Walker, *Opium and Foreign Policy*, p. xiii.

33. See August Bequai, *Organized Crime: The Fifth Estate* (Lexington, Mass.: Lexington Books, 1979), p. 137; and Peter A. Lupsha, "La Cosa Nostra in Drug

Trafficking," in Timothy S. Bynum, ed., *Organized Crime in America: Concepts and Controversies* (Monsey, N.Y.: Criminal Justice Press, 1982), p. 32.

34. See Frank Robertson, *Triangle of Death: The Inside Story of the Triads—the Chinese Mafia* (London: Routledge and Kegan Paul, 1977), pp. 83–87. Although the bulk of the heroin produced in Marseilles was also from Turkish morphine, it is likely that the Corsican groups also imported some from French-controlled Indochina.

35. Although details are sparse and somewhat contradictory, various intermediaries were used and a series of summit meetings was convened to smooth the logistical arrangements. See Bequai, *Organized Crime*, pp. 138–41; Raimondo Catanzaro, *Men of Respect: A Social History of the Sicilian Mafia* (Free Press, 1988), pp. 192–95; and Lupsha, "La Cosa Nostra in Drug Trafficking," pp. 33–35.

36. Catanzaro, *Men of Respect*, p. 192; and Lupsha, "La Cosa Nostra in Drug Trafficking," p. 35. The timing of this alleged decree, however, varies in the public sources; some say it was as early as 1948, while others peg it much later, in the 1950s.

37. Robert J. Kelly, ed., *Organized Crime: A Global Perspective* (Totowa, N.J.: Rowman and Littlefield, 1986), p. 6; and Catherine Lamour and Michel R. Lamberti, *The International Connection: Opium from Growers to Pushers*, trans. Peter and Betty Ross (New York: Pantheon Books, 1974), p. 22. A possible alternative explanation is that the Cuban trafficking groups became more active in the drug trade after the New York families began to disengage from Cuba in the late 1950s as a result of increasing domestic turmoil. See Catanzaro, *Men of Respect*, pp. 192–93.

38. Ironically, Mexico had been encouraged to grow opium poppies during World War II as an alternative source of morphine for the U.S. pharmaceutical industry. Immediately after the war, the amount of illicit heroin reaching the United States from Mexico was larger than that from Turkey, Iran, and India combined. See William O. Walker, *Drug Control in the Americas*, rev. ed. (University of New Mexico Press, 1989), p. 178.

39. See Kettil Bruun, Lynn Pan, and Ingemar Rexed, *The Gentlemen's Club: International Control of Drugs and Alcohol* (University of Chicago Press, 1975), pp. 228, 233; and Walker, *Drug Control in the Americas*, p. 189.

40. The following discussion draws heavily on *International Narcotics Control Study Missions to Latin America and Jamaica, Hawaii, Hong Kong, Thailand, Burma, Pakistan, Turkey, and Italy*, H. Rept. 98-951, 98 Cong. 2 sess. (Government Printing Office, 1984), pp. 17–18, 47–48. (Hereafter *International Narcotics Control Study Mission Report*.)

41. Robin Rolley, "United Nations Activities in International Drug Control," in Scott B. MacDonald and Bruce Zagaris, eds., *International Handbook on Drug Control* (Westport, Conn.: Greenwood Press, 1992), p. 417. The only previous convention that was not incorporated into the Single Convention was that relating to the suppression of illicit traffic.

42. McAllister, "Conflicts of Interest in the International Drug Control System," p. 503.

43. Inciardi, *War on Drugs II*, p. 33.

44. Ibid., pp. 33–34; Musto, *American Disease*, pp. 253–54; Lloyd D. Johnston, "Toward a Theory of Drug Epidemics," in Lewis Donohew, Howard E. Sypher, and William J. Bukoski, eds., *Persuasive Communication and Drug Abuse Prevention* (Hillsdale, N.J.: Erlbaum Associates, 1991), pp. 93–132; and Todd Gitlin, "On Drugs and Mass Media in America's Consumer Society," in Hank Resnick, ed., *Youth and Drugs: Society's Mixed Messages*, OSAP Prevention Monograph 6 (U.S. Department of Health and Human Services, 1990), pp. 41–45.

45. Estimates of the number of regular heroin users in the United States are notoriously imprecise. One 1971 estimate placed the figure nearly 100,000 higher. See Simmons and Said, "Politics of Addiction," p. 22. Some cite a figure closer to half a million. See Musto, *American Disease*, p. 254. See also Peter Reuter, "The (Continued) Vitality of Mythical Numbers," *National Interest*, no. 75 (Spring 1984), pp. 135–47.

46. *International Narcotics Control Study Mission Report*, p. 10.

47. McAllister, "Conflicts of Interest in the International Drug Control System," p. 504.

48. Inciardi, *War on Drugs II*, p. 33.

49. Bequai, *Organized Crime*, p. 142; Robertson, *Triangle of Death*, p. 86, and *International Narcotics Control Study Mission Report*, p. 8. Mexico accounted for 15 percent of the total. Others have argued that the contribution of the Turkish opium supply to the French connection was neglible. See Joseph L. Zetner, "The 1972 Turkish Opium Ban: Needle in the Haystack Diplomacy," *World Affairs*, vol. 136 (1973), pp. 36–40.

50. Lamour and Lamberti, *International Connection*, pp. 50–53; and Simmons and Said, "Politics of Addiction," pp. 14–15.

51. Lintner, "Heroin and Highland Insurgency in the Golden Triangle," pp. 292, 295. See also Lamour and Lamberti, *International Connection*, pp. 169–70.

52. McCoy, "Heroin as a Global Commodity," p. 261; and Lamour and Lamberti, *International Connection*, p. 139.

53. *International Narcotics Control Study Mission Report*, p. 48; Scott B. MacDonald, *Mountain High, White Avalanche: Cocaine and Power in the Andean States and Panama* (Praeger, 1989), p. 19; Scott B. MacDonald, "The Southern Cone," in MacDonald and Zagaris, eds., *International Handbook on Drug Control*, p. 233; and Kelly, *Organized Crime*, p. 6.

54. For an exhaustive account of the internationalization of U.S. law enforcement, see Ethan A. Nadelmann, *Cops across Borders: The Internationalization of U.S. Criminal Law Enforcement* (Pennsylvania State University Press, 1993), p. 133.

55. Lamour and Lamberti, *International Connection*, pp. 60, 75.

56. Elaine Shannon, *Desperados: Latin Drug Lords: U.S. Lawmen and the War America Can't Win* (Viking, 1988), p. 53; and Inciardi, *War on Drugs II*, pp. 42–43.

57. This prohibition was rescinded in the following year, albeit with stringent controls applied to the licit opium cultivation. See Peter Reuter, "Eternal Hope:

America's Quest for Narcotics Control," *Public Interest*, no. 79 (Spring 1985), p. 90.

58. Robertson, *Triangle of Death*, pp. 88–90.

59. For more details on the events leading up to the 1971 convention, see Bruun and others, *Gentlemen's Club*, pp. 243–68. See also McAllister, "Conflicts of Interest in the International Drug Control System," pp. 505–13.

60. Inciardi, *War on Drugs II*, pp. 39, 41–42. See also Bureau of Justice Statistics, *Drugs, Crime, and the Justice System*, p. 84.

61. McCoy, "Heroin as a Global Commodity," p. 263.

62. Martin Booth, *The Triads: The Growing Global Threat from the Chinese Criminal Societies* (St. Martin's, 1990), pp. 112–16; and Fenton Bresler, *The Chinese Mafia* (New York: Stein and Day, 1980), pp. 13, 134–35.

63. INTERPOL, *The Balkan Route: New Challenges* (Lyons, France: INTERPOL General Secretariat, Drugs Sub-Division, 1993).

64. Peter Reuter and David Ronfeldt, "Quest for Integrity: The Mexican-U.S. Drug Issue in the 1980s," RAND Note N-3266-USDP (Santa Monica, Calif.: RAND Corp., 1991), p. 4. Some argue that the proportion was higher in 1975; see McCoy, "Heroin as a Global Commodity," p. 263.

65. Shannon, *Desperados*, p. 61.

66. See Miguel Ruiz-Cabanas I., "Mexico's Permanent Campaign: Costs, Benefits, Implications," in Smith, ed., *Drug Policy in the Americas*, p. 155; and Reuter and Ronfeldt, "Quest for Integrity," p. 19.

67. Ruiz-Cabanas I., "Mexico's Permanent Campaign," p. 155; and Shannon, *Desperados*, p. 72.

68. *International Narcotics Control Study Mission Report*, pp. 70, 103.

69. Shannon, *Desperados*, p. 67.

70. Reuter and Ronfeldt, "Quest for Integrity," p. 20.

71. Walker, *Drug Control in the Americas*, pp. 195, 71–73; and *International Narcotics Control Study Mission Report*, pp. 102–03.

72. Inciardi, *War on Drugs II*, pp. 44–45.

73. Paul Eddy, Hugo Sabogal, and Sara Walden, *The Illegal Cocaine Wars* (Norton, 1988), p. 45.

74. Inciardi, *War on Drugs II*, p. 82.

75. In 1970, 103 kilograms were seized, representing a thirty-five-year high. By 1982 the total annual seizure was 5,697 kilos. See *International Narcotics Control Study Mission Report*, p. 19.

76. The following discussion draws on Eddy and others, *Illegal Cocaine Wars*, pp. 44–45; Shannon, *Desperados*, pp. 75–76; Francisco E. Thoumi, "Why the Illegal Psychoactive Drugs Industry Grew in Colombia," *Journal of Interamerican Studies and World Affairs*, vol. 34 (Fall 1992), pp. 37–63; R. T. Naylor, *Hot Money and the Politics of Debt* (Linden Press of Simon and Schuster, 1987), p. 173; and MacDonald, *Mountain High, White Avalanche*, pp. 19–20.

77. Shannon, *Desperados*, ρ. 75.

78. See Thoumi, "Why the Illegal Psychoactive Drugs Industry Grew in Colombia," pp. 47–52.

79. For a brief overview of the economic factors encouraging coca cultivation in Peru and Bolivia, see Office of Technology Assessment, *Alternative Coca Reduction Strategies in the Andean Region*, OTA-F-556 (July 1993), pp. 51–61.

80. *International Narcotics Control Study Mission Report*, p. 21.

81. For a more detailed description of the rise of Bolivia's involvement in the cocaine trade, see Eddy and others, *Illegal Cocaine Wars*, pp. 49–53; Jaime Malamud-Goti, "Reinforcing Poverty: The Bolivian War on Cocaine," in McCoy and Block, eds., *War on Drugs*, pp. 69–75; and OTA, *Alternative Coca Reduction Strategies*, pp. 51–52.

82. *International Narcotics Control Study Mission Report*, p. 3.

83. OTA, *Alternative Coca Reduction Strategies*, pp. 50–55.

84. Ibid., p. 59.

85. See Eddy and others, *Illegal Cocaine Wars*, pp. 51–52; MacDonald, *Mountain High, White Avalanche*, pp. 72–76; and Walker, *Drug Control in the Americas*, p. 200.

86. In Bolivia, the light aircraft owned by Robert Suarez, the leading coca base trafficker, had originally been accumulated for the purpose of shipping beef from his remote cattle ranches. See Kevin Jack Riley, "Snow Job? The Efficacy of Source Country Cocaine Policies," Ph.D. dissertation, RAND Graduate School, 1993, p. 49.

87. MacDonald, *Mountain High, White Avalanche*, p. 102; and Shannon, *Desperados*, pp. 101–02.

88. See Guy Gugliotta, "The Colombian Cartels and How to Stop Them," in Smith, ed., *Drug Policy in the Americas*, p. 111.

89. See Patricia McRae and David J. Ackerman, "The Illegal Narcotics Trade (INT) as a TNC: Implications for the TNC/Government Interface," paper prepared for the 1993 annual meeting of the American Political Science Association, pp. 12–14.

90. A critical event appears to have been the kidnapping of Marta Nieves Ochoa, the daughter of Jorge Ochoa, in November 1981. See Peter A. Lupsha, "From Leaf to Nose: An Analysis of Trends and Directions in the Cocaine Industry," in *Strategic Organizational Drug Intelligence Symposium Compendium* (National Drug Intelligence Center and Ridgeway Center for International Security Studies, March 16, 1995), p. 13.

91. See Drug Enforcement Administration, *The Cali Cartel: The New Kings of Cocaine*, DEA-94086 (U.S. Department of Justice, November 1994), p. 1.

92. Its full title was the South Florida Task Force of the National Narcotic Border Interdiction System. Vice President George Bush chaired it.

93. See Peter Reuter, "After the Borders Are Sealed: Can Domestic Sources Substitute for Imported Drugs?" and Bruce M. Bagley, "Myths of Militarization: Enlisting Armed Forces in the War on Drugs," both in Smith, ed., *Drug Policy in the Americas*, pp. 172–73, 135. It has also been suggested that the South Florida Task Force may even have encouraged the Colombians to expand to other U.S. cities. See Robert E. Powis, *The Money Launderers: Lessons from the Drug Wars—How Billions of Illegal Drugs Are Washed through Banks and Businesses* (Chicago: Probus, 1992), p. 34.

94. Bureau of Justice Statistics, *Drugs, Crime, and the Justice System.*

95. See Bagley, "Myths of Militarization," pp. 134–38.

96. See Steve Coll and Douglas Farah, "Panama Still a Conduit for Cocaine Profits," *Washington Post*, September 20, 1993, p. A1.

97. "CIA Report on Heroin in Pakistan: Sowing the Wind," *Strategic Digest*, vol. 22 (October 1993), p. 1596.

98. Mary H. Cooper, *The Business of Drugs* (Washington: Congressional Quarterly Press, 1990), p. 52.

99. "CIA Report on Heroin in Pakistan," p. 1596.

100. David Kline, "Asia's 'Golden Crescent' Heroin Floods the West," *Christian Science Monitor*, November 9, 1982, p. 1; and Mark S. Steinitz, "Insurgents, Terrorists, and the Drug Trade," *Washington Quarterly*, vol. 8 (Fall 1985), pp. 147–48.

101. See Lawrence Lifschultz, "Pakistan: The Empire of Heroin," in McCoy and Block, eds., *War on Drugs*, pp. 319–58; and John Ward Anderson and Molly Moore, "Pervasive Heroin Traffic Putting Pakistan at Risk," *Washington Post*, April 29, 1993, p. A1. The Soviet-backed regime is alleged to have also benefited from the heroin trade and may even have deliberately encouraged it. See Cooper, *Business of Drugs*, p. 50.

102. See Terence White, "The Drug-Abuse Epidemic Coursing through Pakistan," *Far Eastern Economic Review*, June 13, 1985, pp. 97–99. More recent figures are contained in Doris Buddenberg, "The Opiate Industry of Pakistan," report prepared for the United Nations International Drug Control Program, January 1994; and "Drug Abuse Seen at 'Alarming Rate,'" *Pakistan Times*, May 19, 1993, p. 6, in JPRS, *Narcotics*, July 13, 1993, p. 29.

103. See Caryle Murphy, "Islamic Iran Wages War on Drug Abuse," *Washington Post*, March 3, 1993, p. A19.

104. See Bureau of International Narcotics Matters, *International Narcotics Control Strategy Report*, Publication 10145 (U.S. Department of State, April 1994), p. 234. (Hereafter *1994 INCSR.*)

105. Jon A. Wiant, "Narcotics in the Golden Triangle," *Washington Quarterly*, vol. 8 (Fall 1985), p. 129; and INTERPOL, *Balkan Route*, p. 1.

106. See Peter Reuter, Mathea Falco, and Robert MacCoun, *Comparing Western European and North American Drug Policies: An International Conference Report* (Santa Monica, Calif.: RAND Corp., 1993), p. 5. For more detailed information, see H. Klingemann and others, "European Summary on Drug Abuse: First Report (1985–1990)," EUR/ICP/ADA 527/A (Copenhagen: World Health Organization, Regional Office for Europe, 1992); and Richard Hartnoll, "Drug Misuse Trends in Thirteen European Cities: Synthesis of Individual City Reports," Pompidou Group, Strasbourg, France, June 1993.

107. One example of this was the famous "pizza connection." See Cooper, *Business of Drugs*, pp. 68–69. See also Lupsha, "La Cosa Nostra in Drug Trafficking," p. 31; and Catanzaro, *Men of Respect*, p. 195.

108. See Wiant, "Narcotics in the Golden Triangle," pp. 131–37; and Lintner, "Heroin and Highland Insurgency," p. 309.

109. Cooper, *Business of Drugs*, pp. 48–49; and Reuter and Ronfeldt, "Quest for Integrity," p. 5.

110. E. A. Wayne, "Militias Cooperate on Drug Trade to Pay for War—Against Each Other," *Christian Science Monitor*, March 9, 1988, pp. 1, 32; Nick B. Williams Jr., "Syrians Cash In on Drug Trade in Lebanon's Notorious Bekaa Valley," *Los Angeles Times*, January 26, 1992, p. A18; Cooper, *Business of Drugs*, p. 54; and Dory G. Hachem and Jall-Eddib, "Illicit Drug Use in Beirut and Lebanon," in National Institute on Drug Abuse, *Epidemiologic Trends in Drug Abuse*, vol. 2: *Proceedings* (U.S. Department of Health and Human Services, June 1994), p. 335.

111. Jack Donnelly, "The United Nations and the Global Drug Control Regime," in Smith, ed., *Drug Policy in the Americas*, pp. 288–91.

112. Bureau of Justice Statistics, *Drugs, Crime, and the Justice System*, p. 102.

113. Cited in Reuter and others, *Comparing Western European and North American Drug Policies*, pp. 6–7.

114. For discussion of these trends, see Dean R. Gerstein and Lawrence W. Green, eds., *Preventing Drug Abuse: What Do We Know?* (Washington: National Academy Press, 1993), pp. 20–37; and Denise B. Kandel, "The Social Demography of Drug Use," in Ronald Bayer and Gerald M. Oppenheimer, eds., *Confronting Drug Policy: Illicit Drugs in a Free Society* (Cambridge University Press, 1992), pp. 44–52.

115. See Mark H. Moore, "Drugs, the Criminal Law, and the Administration of Justice," in Bayer and Oppenheimer, eds., *Confronting Drug Policy*, pp. 243–45; and personal communication with John Coleman, former deputy administrator, Drug Enforcement Administration.

116. See Susan S. Everingham and C. Peter Rydell, *Modeling the Demand for Cocaine*, RAND/MR-332-ONDCP/A/DPRC (Santa Monica, Calif.: RAND Corp., 1993), pp. 13–18; and Rydell and Everingham, *Controlling Cocaine: Supply versus Demand Programs*, RAND/MR-331-ONDCP/A/DPRC (Santa Monica, Calif.: RAND Corp., 1994), pp. 1–3.

117. Drug Enforcement Administration, *U.S. Drug Threat Assessment: 1993*, DEA-93042 (U.S. Department of Justice, September 1993).

118. *1995 INCSR*, p. 27.

119. Mathea Falco, "Foreign Drugs, Foreign Wars," *Daedalus*, vol. 121 (Summer 1992), p. 5.

120. Bagley, "Myths of Militarization," p. 138; and Bureau of Justice Statistics, *Drugs, Crime, and the Justice System*, p. 103. Two "drug summits" with Latin American leaders aimed at improving cooperation were also held at Cartagena, Colombia, in February 1990 and San Antonio, Texas, in February 1992.

121. For a brief overview of Colombian violence in this period, see OTA, *Alternative Coca Reduction Strategies*, pp. 65–67. See also Riley, "Snow Job?," pp. 75–136; Malamud-Goti, "Reinforcing Poverty," p. 75; and Peter H. Smith, "The Political Economy of Drugs: Conceptual Issues and Policy Options," in Smith, ed., *Drug Policy in the Americas*, p. 13.

122. The campaign against the Medellin cartel was helped by informants working for the Cali cartel. See "Colombia: Cali in the Post-Escobar Era," *Geo-*

political Drug Dispatch, no. 28 (February 1994), pp. 1, 3; and Santa Fe de Bogota Inravision Television Canal 4 Network, October 12, 1994, in JPRS, *Narcotics*, October 12, 1994, p. 12. See also Drug Enforcement Administration, *The Cocaine Threat to the United States*, DEA-95016 (U.S. Department of Justice, March 1995), p. 4; DEA, *The Cali Cartel*; and Douglas Farah, "Colombian Drug Flow Unabated," *Washington Post*, March 9, 1993, p. A14.

123. For information on the Cali cartel, see DEA, *The Cali Cartel*; and *Overview of Core-Level Colombian/South American Trafficking Enterprises* (Washington: FBI Intelligence Unit, May 1993). For information on the various Peruvian groups, see *Expresso* (Lima), September 1993, p. A4, in JPRS, *Narcotics*, September 27, 1993, p. 21. One example of a group that the Cali cartel contracts out to is the "North Coast cartel," made up of the Lucas Cotes Sanchez, Mengual Alarcon, Nasser David, and Alexander Paz organizations. Another is a non-cartel-affiliated group led by Jaime Garcia. See *Overview of Core-Level Colombian/South American Trafficking Enterprises*, pp. 23–35.

124. The Jorge Reyes Torres and Jairo Echeverria organizations are considered the core groups in Ecuador and Venezuela, respectively. See *Overview of Core-Level Colombian/South American Trafficking Enterprises*. In Mexico there are believed to be seven main trafficking organizations that also are often referred to as "cartels," not all of which may be involved in cocaine smuggling. For information, see "Mexican Cartels Flourish," *Geopolitical Drug Dispatch*, no. 25 (November 1993), pp. 3–5; and "Mexico: Narcos at the Heart of the State," *Geopolitical Drug Dispatch*, no. 43 (May 1995), pp. 1, 3–4. See also Tim Golden, "Violently, Drug Trafficking in Mexico Rebounds," *New York Times*, March 8, 1993, p. A3.

125. This discussion draws on Drug Enforcement Administration, *Worldwide Cocaine Situation*, DEA-93048 (U.S. Department of Justice, October 1993), pp. 4–7. See also Douglas Farah and Tod Robberson, "Drug Traffickers Build a New Central American Route to U.S.," *Washington Post*, March 28, 1993, p. A1.

126. For more information on the workings of these "cells," see Joseph B. Treaster, "38 Arrested in Drug Raids over 2 Weeks," *New York Times*, December 7, 1991, pp. A25–26; Stephen Flynn, "Worldwide Drug Scourge: The Expanding Trade in Illicit Drugs," *Brookings Review*, vol. 11 (Winter 1993), pp. 9–10; and Rensselaer W. Lee III, "Colombia's Cocaine Syndicates," in McCoy and Block, eds., *War on Drugs*, p. 95.

127. See *Structure of International Drug Trafficking Organizations*, Hearings before the Senate Committee on Governmental Affairs, 101 Cong. 1 sess. (GPO, 1989), p. 169; INTERPOL, *Cocaine Scene in Europe (1993): South American Cartels Search for New Market* (Lyons, France: General Secretariat, Drugs Sub-Division, 1994); and Drug Enforcement Administration, *Cocaine Situation in Europe*, DEA–92055 (U.S. Department of Justice, November 1992). See also Andrew Hill, "Cocaine Seizures Soar in Europe," *Financial Times*, October 8, 1993, p. 3.

128. DEA, *Cocaine Situation in Europe*, p. 1; and INTERPOL, *Cocaine Scene in Europe*, pp. 2–3. See also Michael Elliott and others, "Global Mafia," *News-*

week, December 13, 1993, p. 19; Raymond Bonner, "Poland Becomes a Major Conduit for Drug Traffic," *New York Times*, December 30, 1993, p. A3; "Poland," *Geopolitical Drug Dispatch*, no. 32 (June 1994), p. 2; and "Russia: New Trafficking Trends," *Geopolitical Drug Dispatch*, no. 38 (December 1994), pp. 6–7.

129. See *El Spectador*, December 19, 1992, p. 16A, in JPRS, *Narcotics*, January 12, 1993, pp. 3–4; and Solange Duarte, "Rio Becomes Center for Italian Mafia," *O Globo*, April 10, 1993, p. 20, in JPRS, *Narcotics*, May 18, 1993, p. 5. See also Alison Jamieson, "Drug Trafficking after 1992: A Special Report," *Conflict Studies 250* (London: Research Institute for the Study of Conflict and Terrorism, April 1992), p. 4.

130. DEA, *Worldwide Cocaine Situation Report*, p. 71; and "Japan: Land of Snow," *Geopolitical Drug Dispatch*, no. 29 (March 1994), pp. 2–3.

131. See *The Guardian*, August 18, 1994, p. 9, in JPRS, *Narcotics*, September 15, 1995, pp. 55–56; and *1994 INCSR*, pp. 345–46, 373–75. The disparity between rising cocaine seizures and little or no evidence of widespread cocaine consumption may be explained by the fact that its use in Europe has been confined, much as it was in the 1970s in America, to middle-class professionals. See Reuter and others, *Comparing Western European and North American Drug Policies*, p. 6.

132. See Drug Enforcement Administration, *Cocaine in Japan*, DEA-94055 (U.S. Department of Justice, December 1994); "Japan: Land of Snow," p. 3; *Kyodo*, August 5, 1993, in JPRS, *Narcotics*, August 9, 1993, p. 15; and Robert Delfs, "Cocaine Surge," *Far Eastern Economic Review*, November 21, 1991, p. 35.

133. See Maria Elena Medina-Mora and Maria del Carmen Marino, "Drug Abuse in Latin America," in Smith, ed., *Drug Policy in the Americas*, p. 52. See also Fabricio Marques, "Case Studies in Drug Use Cessation Discussed," *Veja*, November 11, 1992, pp. 78–83, in JPRS, *Narcotics*, December 15, 1992, p. 7; Hernan Cisternas Arellano, "Study Shows Increased Drug Use in Valparaiso Area," *El Mercurio*, August 1, 1993, p. C8, in JPRS, *Narcotics*, September 27, 1993, p. 8; and Don Podesta, "Argentina Becomes Conduit for Drug Traffic," *Washington Post*, November 2, 1993, p. A16. For the most part, however, marijuana and volatile solvents have remained the most commonly consumed illicit drugs in the region, particularly among children.

134. This discussion draws on U.S. Department of Justice, *Colombian Heroin—A Baseline Assessment*, National Drug Intelligence Center Report (Johnstown, Pa., April 1994); Drug Enforcement Administration, *South American Heroin Trafficking in the United States*, DEA-94022 (U.S. Department of Justice, January 1994); and General Accounting Office, *The Drug War: Colombia Is Implementing Antidrug Efforts, But Impact Is Uncertain*, NSIAD-93-158 (August 1993), pp. 25–26. See also Steven Ambrus, "Poppies Pop Up Again," *Los Angeles Times*, Washington ed., April 26, 1994, p. C2; and Joseph B. Treaster, "Colombia's Drug Lords Add New Line: Heroin for the U.S.," *New York Times*, January 14, 1992, p. A1.

135. The assessment that the Cali cartel directs the Colombian heroin trade is contradicted somewhat by National Narcotics Intelligence Consumers Committee, *The NNICC Report, 1993: The Supply of Illicit Drugs to the United States*, DEA-94066 (U.S. Department of Justice, August 1994), p. 53. (Hereafter *NNICC Report, 1993*.) The use of Colombian heroin couriers is reflected in steadily rising arrests (ibid., p. 40).

136. See *1995 INCSR*, p. 244.

137. See Rodney Tasker, "Chasing the Red Dragon," *Far Eastern Economic Review*, August 13, 1987, pp. 28-31. Similar efforts against cannabis cultivation also displaced it into Laos.

138. *1994 INCSR*, p. 255. See also Drug Enforcement Administration, *Worldwide Heroin Situation 1991*, DEA-92031 (U.S. Department of Justice, September 1992), p. 4; and Wichit Tantrasukon, "Khun Sa's Operations Discussed," *Daily News* (Bangkok), March 22, 1993, p. 5, in JPRS, *Narcotics*, May 25, 1993, p. 27.

139. Keith B. Richburg, "New Trafficking Routes Boost SE Asian Heroin Threat," *Washington Post*, July 10, 1995, p. A13.

140. See *Thai Rat*, June 14, 1994, p. 19, in JPRS, *Narcotics*, August 17, 1994, p. 54; and *Matichon*, July 4, 1994, pp. 17, 28, in JPRS, *Narcotics*, August 17, 1994, pp. 57-58. In addition to heroin, volatile solvent use has also reportedly increased in Thailand, particularly among children. See *The Nation* (Bangkok), June 23, 1993, p. A3, in JPRS, *Narcotics*, June 25, 1993, p. 15.

141. For information on recent developments in China, see Dali L. Yang, "Illegal Drugs, Policy Change and State Power: The Case of Contemporary China," *Journal of Contemporary China*, no. 4 (Fall 1993), pp. 15-19; Shao Qin, "Brief Discussion of China's Narcotics Ban Problems in Recent Years," *Shehuixue Yanjiu [Sociological Studies]*, no. 5 (September 1994), pp. 113-16, in JPRS, *Narcotics*, December 27, 1994, pp. 53-57; Bruce Gilley, "Number of Drug Addicts Continues to Rise," *Eastern Express*, December 10, 1994, p. 8, in JPRS, *Narcotics*, December 27, 1994, pp. 52-53; Hong Yang, "China Makes Progress in Drug Control," *Beijing Review*, January 2-8, 1995, in JPRS, *Narcotics*, February, 10, 1995, pp. 36-38; and Nicholas D. Kristof, "Heroin Spreads among Young in China," *New York Times*, March 21, 1991, p. A1.

142. See *NNICC Report, 1993*, p. 42; and INTERPOL, "Southeast Asian Heroin: Developments in Source Countries and Patterns in Drug Trafficking to North America and Europe, 1987-1989" (Lyons, France: Drugs Sub-Division, n.d.), pp. 2-6. See also Customs Cooperation Council, *Customs and Drugs, 1992: A Perspective on the Role of Customs Worldwide in Fighting the Illicit Drug Trade*, Document 38-230 (Brussels, May 1993), p. 17; and Yang, "Illegal Drugs, Policy Change and State Power," p. 20. Although no estimates have ever been made public about the amount of opium produced in China, in 1992 law enforcement authorities reported the detection of opium cultivation in twenty-seven of China's thirty provinces, with the largest plots in the remote areas of Yunnan and Inner Mongolia. See Yang, "Illegal Drugs, Policy Change and State Power," pp. 15-17. The U.S. State Department believes that the opium produced is essentially for domestic consumption. See *1994 INCSR*, p. 262.

143. Chen Donghao, "Even the World behind the Iron Bars Invaded by Heroin: An Investigation into Taiwan's Ever More Serious Drug Problem," *Hsin Hsin Wen [The Journalist]*, June 4, 1994, pp. 71–72, 75, in JPRS, *Narcotics*, August 17, 1994, pp. 48–51; "Government Combats Increasingly Serious Narcotics Problem," *CNA* (Taipei), May 28, 1993, in JPRS, *Narcotics*, June 7, 1993, p. 17; and William Branigin, "Vietnam Sees Dramatic Rise in Drug Abuse," *Washington Post*, November 22, 1992, p. A31.

144. The most heavily involved are reportedly the Sun Yee On, 14K, Wo Hop To, Wo Sing Wo, and Big Circle Boy groups. For more information on the Chinese Triad organizations, see National Drug Intelligence Center, "Triads, Tongs and Street Gangs: A Baseline Assessment of Asian Organized Crime" (U.S. Department of Justice, March 1994); and Unified Intelligence Division of New York, "Chinese Criminal Groups in New York," July 1992.

145. See DEA, *U.S. Drug Threat Assessment: 1993*, pp. 38, 51; and National Drug Intelligence Center, "Triads, Tongs and Street Gangs," p. 14.

146. *1994 INCSR*, p. 20; Phil Jones, "Parties, Politics, and Poppies," in *Southwest Asia and the Narcotics Trade*, Conference Summary Report, Joint Conference of U.S. Department of State and Central Intelligence Agency, June 26, 1992, pp. 9–12; and United Nations International Drug Control Program, "Report of the Major Donors Meeting on the Operational Activities of the UNDCP" (Vienna, October 1993), p. 5.

147. For information on heroin production and processing in the region, see Buddenberg, "Opiate Industry in Pakistan," pp. 1, 2. The most comprehensive description of the Pakistani trafficking organizations is contained in "CIA Report on Heroin in Pakistan," pp. 1593–1631. In its annual intelligence assessment, the DEA places particular responsibility on the trafficking organizations based in Quetta, the capital of Pakistan's Baluchistan province. See *NNICC Report, 1993*, p. 46.

148. This is transported in nearly all directions from the principal processing centers: westward overland across the Afghan-Iranian and Pakistan-Iranian borders and then to Turkey for onward distribution; eastward across the Pakistan-Indian border to New Delhi, Dacca, and Bombay, where some is reexported to Europe by commercial shipping and airlines; south to Karachi and the Makran Coast and again by air or sea on to the Middle East, Europe, and North America. Iranian and Turkish trafficking organizations are also involved in the refinement of morphine base. According to DEA analysis, Southwest Asian heroin has made increasing inroads into the U.S. market, now accounting for as much as a third of it. See *NNICC Report, 1993*, p. 47; and DEA, *U.S. Drug Threat Assessment: 1993*, p. 38. In Canada, approximately 60 percent of the heroin supply is judged to come from Southwest Asia. See Unified Intelligence Division of New York, "Heroin from Southwest Asia," May 1993, p. 16.

149. And also in trafficking cocaine to Europe from South America via West Africa. The fact that many Nigerians lived in Brazil and traveled back and forth made this a useful and less obvious route. See Drug Enforcement Administration, *Cocaine Trafficking to Europe by Nigerians*, DEA-94068 (U.S. Department of Justice, August 1994).

150. See National Drug Intelligence Center, "Nigeria: A Country Overview" (Johnstown, Pa., March 17, 1994), p. 5. One press report states that half the heroin seized in the United States is being carried by Nigerians and other West African nationals. See Scott Kraft, "Nigeria: A Gaping Gateway for Drugs," *Los Angeles Times*, February 17, 1994, p. A1.

151. See Alan Cowell, "Heroin Pouring through Porous European Borders," *New York Times*, February 9, 1993, p. A3. The most common method for smuggling heroin into Europe is via Transport International Routier trucks that are typically registered to Turkish companies, although more west European–registered trucks, buses, and cars are being used as a result of the heightened scrutiny by customs officials. See INTERPOL, *Heroin Traffic Targets Europe: New Corridors to the West, 1993* (Lyons, France: Drugs Sub-Division, February 1994), p. 3; and Customs Cooperation Council, *Customs and Drugs, 1992*, p. 29.

152. INTERPOL, *Heroin Traffic Targets Europe*, pp. 3–7; and Customs Co-operation Council, *Customs and Drugs*, p. 29. See also William Drozdiak, "Balkan War Victor: Heroin," *Washington Post*, November 6, 1993, p. A1. The war in Yugoslavia deflected the Balkan route in a southerly way, too, by ferry from the Aegean and Mediterranean ports of Turkey and Greece into southern Italy. See also *NNICC Report, 1993*, pp. 48–49.

153. The burgeoning number of commercial air connections through Russia and the Baltic states have likewise become a target for the drug traffickers. For more information see Unified Intelligence Division of New York, "Heroin from Southwest Asia," p. 9; and INTERPOL, *Heroin Scene in Europe: 1992*.

154. See Rensselaer W. Lee III and Scott B. MacDonald, "Drugs in the East," *Foreign Policy*, no. 90 (Spring 1993), p. 97; Kimberly Neuhauser, "The Market for Illicit Drugs in the CIS [Commonwealth of Independent States]," paper prepared for U.S. State Department Conference on Narcotics in the CIS Region, September 11, 1992; Klingemann and others, "European Summary on Drug Abuse"; and International Narcotics Control Board, *Report of the International Narcotics Control Board for 1992* (United Nations, 1992), p. 34. Although there is no evidence to contradict these reports, there is nevertheless every reason to treat them with considerable caution. For most if not all of the countries in this category, there has been no systematic attempt to monitor prevalence of drug use. More often than not, assessments of national trends rely on statistics for the number of "addicts" that have registered for treatment, which could understate the true level considerably. In other cases, reports appear to be based more on anecdotal information or personal impressions than hard evidence. Furthermore, since drug use in many if not all communist countries was either deliberately downplayed or not acknowledged at all, it is also difficult to judge to what extent drug use has grown or merely become more recognized in recent years.

155. See Mathias Rueb, "A Sad Step toward Rapprochement with the West: More 'Stuff' Is Getting Hung Up in Hungary," *Frankfurter Allgemeine*, January 20, 1995, p. 3, in JPRS, *Narcotics*, April 21, 1995, pp. 51–52; Timea Spitkova, "Cut Rate Heroin Floods the Streets," *Prague Post*, February 28, 1995, p. 1, in JPRS, *Narcotics*, May 2, 1995, p. 44; Cees Zoon, "Mafia Exploits East European

Drugs Market," *De Volksrant*, January 22, 1994, p. 4, in JPRS, *Narcotics*, February 1, 1994, pp. 37–38: "Drug Abuse Seen as 'Major Social Problem,'" in JPRS, *Narcotics*, October 28, 1994, p. 71; "Press Data Document 'Frightening' Growth of Drug Addiction," in JPRS, *Narcotics*, October 28, 1994, p. 73; Marie Sustrova, "Drugs, Prevention, and the Campaign," *Lidove Noviny*, August 13, 1994, p. 5, in JPRS, *Narcotics*, September 23, 1994, p. 24; and "More People Have Begun Using Heroin," *Mlada Fronta Dnes*, July 21, 1994, p. 1, in JPRS, *Narcotics*, August 17, 1994, p. 72.

156. See Drug Enforcement Administration, *The Newly Independent States: A Special Assessment and Country Briefs* (U.S. Department of Justice, November 1994); Lee and MacDonald, "Drugs in the East"; Graham Turbiville, Jr., "Narcotics Trafficking in Central Asia: A New 'Colombia' in the World Drug Trade?" paper prepared for State Department Conference on Narcotics in the CIS Region, September 11, 1992; United Nations International Drug Control Program, *Special UNDCP Fact-Finding Mission in Seven Republics of the Commonwealth of Independent States* (Vienna, May 1992).

157. See Customs Cooperation Council, *Customs and Drugs, 1992*, p. 54; John Thor-Dalhburg, "Tracking the Russian Connection," *Los Angeles Times*, June 6, 1993, p. A1; and "Lithuania," *Geopolitical Drug Dispatch*, no. 31 (May 1994), p. 2.

158. See "Russia: Doping Moscow," *Geopolitical Drug Dispatch*, no. 17 (March 1993), p. 1.

159. A more potent hallucinogen known as phencyclidine (PCP) is also becoming more popular again in some inner-city areas of America after being in abeyance since the end of the 1980s. See Drug Enforcement Administration, *PCP*, DEA-94081 (U.S. Department of Justice, September 1994).

160. See Drug Enforcement Administration, *Mexican Methamphetamine Traffickers: A Growing Domestic Threat*, DEA-95026 (U.S. Department of Justice, March 1995); and Sam Dillon, "Mexican Drug Dealer Pushes Speed, Helping Set Off an Epidemic in U.S.," *New York Times*, December 27, 1995, p. A10.

161. National Drug Intelligence Center, *Methcathinone (CAT)—A Baseline Assessment* (U.S. Department of Justice, March 1994).

162. Drug Enforcement Administration, *Drug Trafficking in Africa: A Briefing Book* (U.S. Department of Justice, September 1994), pp. 27–28; and "The Philippines: High Level Scandal," and "South Africa: Another Headache for Mandela," both in *Geopolitical Drug Dispatch*, no. 36 (October 1994), pp. 4, 7.

163. Wild fluctuations in the U.S. estimates of Mexico's marijuana production in recent years cast more than usual doubt on its place in the global market. These estimates of Mexico's output were dramatically revised upward in 1989 due to the introduction of new counting rules, thereby bringing into question the previous year's totals. Since then, estimates of output have declined just as suddenly, allegedly the result of an unusually effective eradication program.

164. Drug Enforcement Administration, *Colombian Marijuana: A Resurgent Drug Threat*, DEA-95028 (U.S. Department of Justice, March 1995); and *NNICC Report, 1993*, pp. 60–61, 65.

165. Domestic U.S. cannabis production was estimated to be around 6,000 to 6,500 metric tons in 1992, which, if true, would make it second only to Mexico in total output. Of this, 3,405 metric tons were considered to have been eradicated. See DEA, *U.S. Drug Threat Assessment: 1993*, p. 70.

166. United Nations Economic and Social Council, Commission on Narcotic Drugs, "Illicit Drug Traffic and Supply, Including Reports from Subsidiary Bodies and Evaluation of their Activities," E/CN.7/1995/7, February 10, 1995, p. 20.

167. This information comes from Home Office, "Report of the TREVI Working Group III: Drug Trafficking Routes and Trends" (London, March 1993).

168. Michael Griffin, "Moroccan Hashish Thrives behind 'Political Smoke-screen,'" *Financial Times*, August 8, 1995, p. 17.

169. UNDCP, "Report of the Major Donors Meeting," p. 1; "The Gambia: The Cannabis Islands," *Geopolitical Drug Dispatch*, no. 32 (June 1994), p. 6; "Ivory Coast: Chocolate-Covered Marijuana," *Geopolitical Drug Dispatch*, no. 31 (May 1994), p. 7; "Chad: Wages of War," *Geopolitical Drug Dispatch*, no. 29 (March 1994), pp. 6–7; and "Niger: International Aid Irrigates Cannabis Crops," *Geopolitical Drug Dispatch*, no. 22 (August 1993), pp. 6–7.

170. UNDCP, *Special UNDCP Fact-Finding Mission*, pp. 3–4. One report says, however, that this wild hemp is used to produce hashish rather than marijuana. See Sergey Kozlov, "There Is No Marijuana in Kazakhstan: But There Is Very Much Hashish," *Nezavisimaya Gazeta*, January 28, 1993, p. 6, in JPRS, *Narcotics*, February 16, 1993, p. 27. Another report states that a total of 1 million hectares of wild hemp grow in the Russian Far East, Siberia, Tuva, Buryatiya, and Khakasiya. See "Our Narcostan: Will the CIS Become the Commonwealth of Narcotics-Producing Countries?" *Komsomolskaya Pravda*, April 24, 1993, p. 2, in JPRS, *Narcotics*, May 11, 1993, p. 79.

171. Some believe it is already being exploited. See Sergey Skorokhodov and Vladimir Tyurkin, "Down the Chu Road to Heaven and Hell," *Rossiyskaya Gazeta*, May 29, 1993, p. 6, in JPRS, *Narcotics*, June 14, 1993, p. 44.

172. See General Accounting Office, *Illicit Narcotics: Recent Efforts to Control Chemical Diversion and Money Laundering*, NSIAD-94-34 (December 1993), pp. 25–26, 14–15.

173. See Office of National Drug Control Policy, *National Drug Control Strategy: Reclaiming Our Communities from Drugs and Violence* (The White House, February 1994). For an analysis of the Clinton administration's policy, see Raphael F. Perl, "Clinton's Foreign Drug Policy," *Journal of Interamerican Studies and World Affairs*, vol. 35 (Winter 1993–94), pp. 143–51; and Perl, "United States International Drug Policy: Background, Assumptions, Recent Developments, and Emerging Trends," paper prepared for the University of Miami's North-South Center's Drug Task Force roundtable meeting on "International Drug Control Policies in the Americas: Current Trends and Future Directions," 1994.

174. Cited by Jack Donnelly, "The United Nations and the Global Drug Control Regime," in Smith, ed., *Drug Policy in the Americas*, p. 285.

Chapter Three

1. See Steven Witsotsky, *Beyond the War on Drugs: Overcoming a Failed Public Policy* (Buffalo: Prometheus Books, 1990), pp. 31–36; and Mark A. R. Kleiman, *Against Excess: Drug Policy for Results* (Basic Books, 1992), pp. 104–26. Kleiman describes the added price as a "wedge" between "the price (in money and non-money terms) the consumer pays and the price (net of enforcement risk) the producer receives," which includes the added costs of producing and distributing illicit items, evading law enforcement, including bribes and intimidation, and ultimately the penalties imposed when caught (fines, seizures, and imprisonment). See also Sam Stanley, *Drug Policy and the Decline of American Cities* (New Brunswick, N.J.: Transaction, 1992), pp. 163–72.

2. See Sid Zabludoff, "Colombian Narcotics Organizations as Business Enterprises," in *Economics of the Narcotics Industry*, report of conference sponsored by U.S. Department of State, Bureau of Intelligence and Research, and Central Intelligence Agency, November 21–22, 1994; and Phil Williams, "Organizational Risk Assessment and Management," in *Strategic Organizational Drug Intelligence Symposium Compendium* (National Drug Intelligence Center and Ridgeway Center for International Security Studies, March 16, 1995), pp. 28–32.

3. This important point was made by Francisco E. Thoumi, *Political Economy and Illegal Drugs in Colombia* (Boulder, Colo.: Lynne Rienner, 1995).

4. Williams, "Organizational Risk Assessment and Management," p. 28.

5. Phil Williams, "Transnational Criminal Organizations: Strategic Alliances," *Washington Quarterly*, vol. 18 (Winter 1995), pp. 57–72.

6. This basic argument is cited in Raphael Perl, "United States International Drug Policy: Background, Assumptions, Recent Developments and Emerging Trends," paper prepared for the University of Miami's North-South Center's Drug Task Force roundtable meeting on "International Drug Control Policies in the Americas: Current Trends and Future Directions," 1994, p. 3.

7. This framework was inspired by the presentation of Phil Williams on the key environmental factors in the emergence of transnational criminal organizations at the Brookings Institution Workshop on "The International Implications of the Transnational Drug Phenomenon," University of Pennsylvania, April 18–19, 1994. This was subsequently published in Phil Williams and Carl Florez, "Transnational Criminal Organizations and Drug Trafficking," *Bulletin on Narcotics*, vol. 46, no. 2 (1994), p. 13. I have adapted the framework for the illicit drug market. The boundaries between the different factors and the different components of the drug market are in reality more blurred than represented here. Thus incentives cannot not be easily separated from opportunities, nor can opportunities be separated from resources. Similarly, production and trafficking are not always discrete activities. Traffickers are often involved in the production phase and can also be consumers.

8. United Nations Industrial Development Organization, *Industry and Development: Global Report 1993/94* (Vienna, 1993), pp. A-16, 84, 114, 119.

9. Unless otherwise indicated, the following discussion draws on Bureau of Justice Statistics, *Drugs, Crime, and the Justice System*, N/CJ-133652 (U.S. De-

partment of Justice, December 1992), pp. 42–43; and Drug Enforcement Administration, *Coca Cultivation and Cocaine Processing: An Overview* (U.S. Department of Justice, February 1991).

10. *1994 INCSR*, p. 451.

11. UNIDO, *Industry and Development: Global Report 1993/94*, pp. 22, 180; and *1994 INCSR*, p. 456. See also Sanjoy Hazarika, "Indian Heroin Smugglers Turn to New Cargo," *New York Times*, February 21, 1993, p. A11. On the general fragmentation of the chemical industry worldwide, see UNIDO, *Industry and Development: Global Report 1993/94*, p. 125.

12. Mark S. Steinitz, "Insurgents, Terrorists, and the Drug Trade," *Washington Quarterly*, vol. 8 (Fall 1985), pp. 141–56.

13. Drug Enforcement Administration, *Source to the Street*, DEA-93036 (U.S. Department of Justice, 1993). For a more detailed breakdown of retail prices in select U.S. cities, see National Institute on Drug Abuse, *Epidemiologic Trends in Drug Abuse*, vol. 1: *Highlights and Executive Summary* (U.S. Department of Health and Human Services, June 1994).

14. Richard Hartnoll, "Drug Misuse Trends in Thirteen European Cities: Synthesis of Individual City Reports," Pompidou Group, Strasbourg, France, June 1993.

15. Sid Zabludoff, "Economics and Narcotics: A Perspective," and Zabludoff, "Colombian Narcotics Organizations as Business Enterprises," in *Economics of the Narcotics Industry*.

16. The Mexican Gulf cartel is calculated to clear $500 million to $800 million annually. See Peter A. Lupsha, "Narco Investment in Domestic Economies: Mexico: An Example of Narco Democracy?" in *Economics of the Narcotics Industry*.

17. Zabludoff, "Economics and Narcotics."

18. *1995 INCSR*, pp. 472, 474. See also H. Richard Friman, "International Pressure and Domestic Bargains: Regulating Money Laundering in Japan," *Crime, Law and Social Change*, vol. 21, no. 3 (1994), p. 255.

19. See Figen Aksit, "Terror's Main Artery: Narcotics," *Tempo*, January 18, 1995, pp. 20–23, in JPRS, *Narcotics*, March 29, 1995, pp. 46–47; "Junkies Paying for Guerrilla Struggle," *Focus*, October 24, 1994, p. 13, in JPRS, *Narcotics*, November 10, 1994, p. 52; "Army Said to Uncover Drug Labs in PKK Camps in North Iraq," *FBIS Editorial Report*, in JPRS, *Narcotics*, April 28, 1995, p. 54; Peter Scherer, "Turks Control Heroin Trade," *Die Welt*, June 4, 1994, p. 2, in JPRS, *Narcotics*, June 13, 1994, pp. 36–37; Alain Lallemand, "Turkish Extreme Right, Ankara's Objective Ally," *Le Soir*, June 4, 1994, p. 13, in JPRS, *Narcotics*, January 19, 1994, pp. 31–32; Veronica Guerin, "Top Provo Men 'in UK Drug Rackets,'" *Sunday Independent*, May 1, 1994, p. 3, in JPRS, *Narcotics*, July 26, 1994, pp. 63–64; "Germany: A Mosaic of Criminal Organizations," and "Algeria," *Geopolitical Drug Dispatch*, no. 41 (March 1995), pp. 1–4; and "France: The Specter of Algerian Fundamentalist Networks," *Geopolitical Drug Dispatch*, no. 26 (December 1993), pp. 1, 3–4. For other examples, see Rensselaer W. Lee III, "Drugs in Communist and Post-Communist Countries," in *Strategic Organizational Drug Intelligence Symposium Compendium*, p. 9.

20. "Somalia: Legitimate Trade, Qat and Heroin," *Geopolitical Drug Dispatch*, no. 21 (July 1993), pp. 4–6; "Liberia: Trafficking in a Forgotten War," *Geopolitical Drug Dispatch*, no. 28 (February 1994), pp. 6–7; "Mexico: The Chiapas Route," *Geopolitical Drug Dispatch*, no. 28 (February 1994), pp. 5–6; "Kashmir Insurgency Described as 'Camouflage' for Drug Smuggling," *Hindustan Times*, January 15, 1994, p. 24, in JPRS, *Narcotics*, January 26, 1994, p. 23; Mumin Shakirov and Zigmund Dzientsiolovskiy, "Opium for the Peoples of Europe: The Drug Trade—Profit and Survival?" *Literaturnaya Gazeta*, no. 4, January 25, 1995, p. 12, in JPRS, *Narcotics*, March 8, 1995, pp. 50–51; and "Macedonia: Guns and Ammo for 'Greater Albania,'" *Geopolitical Drug Dispatch*, no. 32 (June 1994), pp. 1, 3–5.

21. See reports by INTERPOL and the Customs Cooperation Council for a truly astounding array of concealment methods.

22. See Scott Kraft, "Nigeria: A Gaping Gateway for Drugs," *Los Angeles Times*, February 17, 1994, p. A1. See also Alison Jamieson, "Drug Trafficking after 1992: A Special Report," *Conflict Studies 250* (London: Research Institute for the Study of Conflict and Terrorism, April 1992), pp. 5–6.

23. Marcia Macleod, "New Markets in the Old World," *Air Cargo World* (July 1992), pp. 20–27.

24. See *NNICC Report, 1993*, p. 53; and Drug Enforcement Administration, *Southern Cone Situation Report*, DEA–94079 (U.S. Department of Justice, November 1994), pp. 1–2.

25. Unless otherwise indicated, this discussion draws on *Latin America and the Caribbean: A Decade after the Debt Crisis* (World Bank, September 1993), pp. 89–90.

26. *NNICC Report, 1993*, p. 21.

27. Michael Elliott, "Global Mafia: A New and Dangerous Criminal Threat," *Newsweek*, December 13, 1993, pp. 12–18.

28. Although money laundering has in general received more attention, the process of underwriting drug operations is just as important. After all, farmers must be paid, local officials bribed, chemicals and refining materials purchased, and the pilots, sea captains, and couriers rewarded for transporting the drugs. Likewise, at the wholesale level, safe houses need to be rented, cars hired, communications equipment bought or leased, and weaponry obtained. Legal help may also be required if the traffickers are caught and arrested. Not all of these activities, however, require transferring money across international borders. In some cases those involved can also be rewarded by noncash payments, including the drugs themselves.

29. The following is adapted from Office of the Comptroller of the Currency, *Money Laundering: A Banker's Guide to Avoiding Problems* (December 1989), p. 2.

30. *1994 INCSR*, p. 468; Fredric Dannien, "Colombian Gold," *New Yorker*, August 15, 1994, p. 26; and Douglas Farah and Steve Coll, "Cocaine Dollars Flow via Unique Network," *Washington Post*, September 19, 1993, pp. A1, A26.

31. Dimitris N. Chorafas, *The Globalization of Money and Securities: The New Products, Players, and Markets* (Chicago: Probus, 1992), pp. 16–17.

32. *1994 INCSR*, p. 481. For a full list and details, see *Butterworth's Tax Havens Encyclopedia*.

33. Elliott, "Global Mafia."

34. *1994 INCSR*, p. 470.

35. Drug Enforcement Administration, *Asian Money Movement Methods*, DEA–94023 (U.S. Department of Justice, July 1994), p. 3; and Jamieson, "Drug Trafficking after 1992," pp. 32–33.

36. Farah and Coll, "Cocaine Dollars Flow via Unique Network."

37. DEA, *Asian Money Movement Methods*, pp. 14–16; and "Laundering for the Mafia," *Focus*, February 22, 1993, pp. 44–45, in JPRS, *Narcotics*, March 9, 1993, p. 47.

38. This discussion draws on *1995 INCSR*, pp. 467–73.

39. For example, Roosevelt Avenue in Queens, New York, has become what one observer describes as the "Wall Street of the drug trade, with literally hundreds of establishments that constitute a financial service industry for the money launderers." Dannien, "Colombian Gold," pp. 29–30.

40. *1994 INCSR*, p. 470.

41. Donald Im, "Colombian Economic Reform: The Impact on Drug Money Laundering within the Colombian Economy," in *Economics of the Narcotics Industry*.

42. *1995 INCSR*, p. 471.

43. *1994 INCSR*, p. 471.

44. Margaret Shapiro, "New Russia: A Country on the Take," *Washington Post*, November 13, 1994, p. A1.

45. This discussion draws heavily on the insights of Richard R. Clayton in his background paper, "Drugs versus Public Health: Assessing the Risk of a Global Drug Epidemic," prepared for the Brookings Institution Workshop on "The International Implications of the Transnational Drug Phenomenon," University of Pennsylvania, April 18–19, 1994.

46. On the taxonomy of drug consumption, see World Health Organization, Regional Office for Europe, "Sociocultural Factors in Drug Abuse," EUR/ICP/ADA 531 (Copenhagen, 1991), p. 2. An alternative taxonomy based on consequences (personal and societal) rather than frequency of use is offered in World Health Organization, Regional Office for Europe, "The Family and the Use of Illegal Drugs: The Role of the Family and Other Primary Social Groups in Treatment and Prevention in Europe," EUR/ICP/ADA 518 (Copenhagen, 1990), p. 3.

47. Clayton, "Drugs versus Public Health." See also the classic study, Norman E. Zinberg, *Drug, Set, and Setting: The Basis for Controlled Intoxicant Use* (Yale University Press, 1984), p. 5.

48. This dichotomy is similar to and may be considered an extension of the traditional medicinal and ceremonial functions of psychoactive substances. See Andrew Weil and Winifred Rosen, *From Chocolate to Morphine: Everything You Needed to Know about Mind-Altering Drugs* (Houghton Mifflin, 1993).

49. Bridging the two types is drug use that forms part of a general pattern of unconventional, antisocial, or delinquent behavior, which springs from a personality disorder.

50. See Bureau of Justice Statistics, *Drugs, Crime, and the Justice System*, pp. 20–21, for a concise description of the most popular drugs and their typical effects.

51. See Todd Gitlin, "On Drugs and Mass Media in America's Consumer Society," in Hank Resnick, ed., *Youth and Drugs: Society's Mixed Messages*, OSAP Prevention Monograph 6 (U.S. Department of Health and Human Services, 1990), p. 43. Gitlin distinguishes between "recreational," "transcendental," and "medicinal" motives for drug use.

52. See General Accounting Office, *Drug Use among Youth: No Simple Answers to Guide Prevention*, HRD–94–24 (December 1993), p. 11; and WHO, "The Family and the Use of Illegal Drugs," pp. 4–7.

53. See Bureau of Justice Statistics, *Drugs, Crime, and the Justice System*, pp. 22–23; and Hartnoll, "Drug Misuse Trends in Thirteen European Cities."

54. For a longer discussion of this phenomenon, see Kleiman, *Against Excess*, pp. 42–44.

55. See Saskia Sassen, *The Global City: New York, London, Tokyo* (Princeton University Press, 1991), p. 31; and John Naisbitt, *Global Paradox: The Bigger the World Economy, the More Powerful Its Smallest Players* (William Morrow, 1994), p. 20.

56. The United States remains the dominant source of most of the TV programs and movies being broadcast globally. American lifestyles and consumer tastes have a disproportionate impact in shaping tastes and attitudes. For example, in Europe more than 70 percent of nondocumentary TV programming is imported and more than 50 percent comes from the United States. American films dominate the world movie industry and, given the increasing number of VCRs, the world video market too. Naisbitt, *Global Paradox*, p. 32. This accounts for France's attempts to set quotas on the broadcast of non-European TV programs as well as Iran's and China's efforts to restrict satellite TV reception. See "Well, Excuse Moi! English Suffers Kick in the Derriere," *Wall Street Journal*, February 24, 1994, p. A12; Alan Riding, "The Media Business: New Curbs Reported on Foreign TV Programs in Europe," *New York Times*, March 23, 1995, p. D8; Elaine Sciolino, "Khomeini's Legacy: A Special Report," *New York Times*, May 30, 1995, p. A1; and Craig S. Smith, "Hong Kong TV Producer Chua Casts His Beam into China's Satellite Market," *Wall Street Journal*, April 5, 1994, p. A14.

57. This effect has been noted in South America with cocaine consumption. See Edmundo Morales, *Cocaine: White Gold Rush in Peru* (University of Arizona Press, 1989), p. 116.

58. Avram Goldstein and Harold Kalant, "Drug Policy: Striking the Right Balance," *Science*, September 28, 1990, p. 1515. It is important to note here that for some first-time users, who might be introduced to drugs by friends, the price is irrelevant because it is offered free of charge.

59. See Bureau of Justice Statistics, *Drugs, Crime, and the Justice System*, p. 55. See also Kleiman, *Against Excess*, pp. 70–72, for a more theoretical treatment of this subject.

60. Some economists combine the two elements under the umbrella term "effective price," which can also include in this context other factors, such as uncertainty about the quality of the drug. See Bureau of Justice Statistics, *Drugs, Crime, and the Justice System*, p. 55.

61. Kleiman, *Against Excess*, pp. 111–12.

62. Kevin Jack Riley, "Snow Job? The Efficacy of Source Country Cocaine Policies," Ph.D. dissertation, RAND Graduate School, 1993, pp. 29–30; and Felipe E. MacGregor, *Coca and Cocaine: An Andean Perspective* (Westport, Conn.: Greenwood Press, 1993), p. 136.

63. Riley, "Snow Job?," p. 35; and LaMond Tullis, *Handbook of Research on the Illicit Drug Traffic: Socioeconomic and Political Consequences* (Westport, Conn.: Greenwood Press, 1991), pp. 124–27.

64. "Standing Guard for Uncle Sam," *Economist*, January 14, 1995, p. 42.

65. For a comprehensive discussion of herbicidal spraying and other forms of biological control, see Office of Technology Assessment, *Alternative Coca Reduction Strategies in the Andean Region*, OTA-F-556 (July 1993), pp. 183–203.

66. Riley, "Snow Job?," p. 36; Rensselaer Lee and Patrick Clawson, *Crop Substitution in the Andes* (Office of National Drug Control Policy, 1993), p. 58; and Tullis, *Handbook of Research on the Illicit Drug Traffic*, pp. 126–27.

67. General Accounting Office, *Illicit Narcotics: Recent Efforts to Control Chemical Diversion and Money Laundering*, NSIAD-94-34 (December 1993), pp. 14, 15–20; and *1995 INCSR*, p. 458.

68. Samuel Salazar Nieto, "Control of Precursor Chemicals Discussed," *El Tiempo*, September 12, 1994, p. 14A, in JPRS, *Narcotics*, October 28, 1994, pp. 18–20.

69. Interview with U.S. law enforcement officer, 1994; and *1994 INCSR*, p. 456.

70. For an analysis of two major campaigns in Latin America—Operation Blast Furnace and Operation SNOWCAP—see Riley, "Snow Job?," pp. 51–55. See also Bruce M. Bagley, "The Myths of Militarization: Enlisting Armed Forces in the War on Drugs," in Peter H. Smith, ed., *Drug Policy in the Americas* (Boulder, Colo.: Westview Press, 1992), pp. 134–36.

71. Lee and Clawson, *Crop Substitution in the Andes*, pp. 43–48, 54–56, 59–60; and OTA, *Alternative Coca Reduction Strategies in the Andean Region*, especially pp. 81–98.

72. Lee and Clawson, *Crop Substitution in the Andes*, pp. 56–57.

73. See Eric Rosenquist, "Agricultural Factors in the Illicit Drug Trade: Agro-Economic Factors in Drug Cultivation," and Rensselaer W. Lee III, "Controlling Production of Opiates: The Case of Thailand," in *Economics of the Narcotics Industry*.

74. This relative attractiveness of alternative crops is also partly attributable to a decline in coca prices. See Patrick Clawson, "How Profitable for Farmers Is Cultivation of Coca Leaves?" and Ray Henkel, "Coca Crop Substitution and Alternative Development in Bolivia," in *Economics of the Narcotics Industry*.

75. General Accounting Office, *The Drug War: U.S. Programs in Peru Face Serious Obstacles*, NSIAD-92-36 (October 1991), p. 23.

76. Lee, "Drugs in Communist and Post-Communist Countries," p. 4.

77. "Iran: The Great Wall," *Geopolitical Drug Dispatch*, no. 30 (April 1994), pp. 1, 3–4. See also *Ettela'at*, August 23, 1994, p. 13, in JPRS, *Narcotics*, September 15, 1994, pp. 45–46. There is reportedly extensive bribery of border guards to let the drug caravans through the fortified areas. See *1995 INCSR*, p. 221.

78. U.S. Customs Service, Office of Public Affairs, *The Year in Review, 1994* (U.S. Department of the Treasury, 1995), p. 34; and U.S. Department of Transportation, *U.S. International Air Passenger and Freight Statistics, Calendar Year 1993*, vol. 1 (July 1994), p. 1.

79. Katherine Wanton, "Cargo Business Is Hot at Sunbelt Airports," *Air Cargo World*, vol. 82 (May 1992), pp. 31, 40; and *U.S. International Air Passenger and Freight Statistics, Calendar Year 1993*, pp. 1–2.

80. *U.S. International Air Passenger and Freight Statistics, Calendar Year 1993*, p. 2; and Naisbitt, *Global Paradox*, pp. 116, 193.

81. Institute of Shipping Economics and Logistics, "Shipping Statistics," Bremen, Germany, February 1993, p. 62; and Ernie Pereira, "Report from Hong Kong," *Pacific Shipper*, November 22, 1993, pp. 16, 28, 32.

82. *1994 INCSR*, p. 315; "Hungary: Record Seizures on the Balkan Route," *Geopolitical Drug Dispatch*, no. 35 (September 1994), pp. 5–6; and Paul Blustein, "U.S. Seeks Compromise on NAFTA Truck Rules," *Washington Post*, December 18, 1995, p. A13.

83. Along the Balkan route, it reportedly takes eight to sixteen hours to search an individual container. See "Hungary: Record Seizures on the Balkan Route," p. 5.

84. General Accounting Office, *Drug Control: Status Report on Counterdrug Technology Development*, NSIAD–93–104 (January 1993), pp. 7–8.

85. Interview conducted by Stephen Flynn with U.S. Customs inspectors at the Port of Newark, April 13, 1993.

86. U.S. Department of Justice, *Colombian Heroin—A Baseline Assessment*, National Drug Intelligence Center Report (Johnstown, Pa., April 1994), p. 17; and Blustein, "U.S. Seeks Compromise on NAFTA Truck Rules."

87. For an excellent overview of the many cases of drug-related bribery and corruption, see Tullis, *Handbook of Research on the Illicit Drug Traffic*, pp. 64–70. See also Peter R. Andreas and others, "Dead-End Drug Wars," *Foreign Policy*, no. 85 (Winter 1991–92), pp. 117–19; testimony of Rensselaer W. Lee III before the Subcommittee on Foreign Commerce and Tourism of the Senate Committee on Commerce, Science, and Transportation, 101 Cong. 2 sess. (Government Printing Office, 1990), pp. 31–32; Rensselaer Lee III, "Colombia's Cocaine Syndicates," Peter A. Lupsha, "Drug Lords and Narco-Corruption: The Players Change But the Game Continues," and Lawrence Lifschultz, "Pakistan: The Empire of Heroin," in Alfred McCoy and Alan A. Block, eds., *War on Drugs: Studies in the Failure of U.S. Narcotics Policy* (Boulder, Colo.: Westview Press,

1992), pp. 93–124, 177–96, 319–58; and Jerome H. Skolnick, "Rethinking the Drug Problem," *Daedalus*, vol. 121 (Summer 1992), p. 147.

88. For example, see Ethan A. Nadelmann, "The DEA in Latin America: Dealing with Institutionalized Corruption," *Journal of Interamerican Studies and World Affairs*, vol. 29 (Winter 1987–1988), pp. 1–39; and more generally Michael Elliott, "Corruption: How Bribes, Payoffs, and Crooked Officials Are Blocking Economic Growth," *Newsweek*, November 14, 1994, pp. 40–42.

89. Jeff Gerth, "Report Says Mercenaries Aided Colombian Cartels," *New York Times*, February 28, 1991, p. A20.

90. There has been one report of Colombian trafficking organizations' trying to lease a communications satellite to prevent U.S. eavesdropping. See Elliott, "Global Mafia," p. 14.

91. Martin Booth, *The Triads: The Growing Global Threat from the Chinese Criminal Societies* (St. Martin's, 1990), pp. 119, 123–26.

92. Various interviews with DEA officers and European law enforcement officials. See also Jamieson, "Drug Trafficking after 1992," pp. 10–17.

93. Jonathan P. Caulkins, "Evaluating the Effectiveness of Interdiction and Source Country Control," and Zabludoff, "Colombian Narcotics Organizations as Business Enterprises," in *Economics of the Narcotics Industry*. See also Riley, "Snow Job?," pp. 77–79.

94. This discussion relies heavily on *1995 INCSR*, pp. 466–70; and GAO, *Illicit Narcotics*, pp. 28–31.

95. Drug Enforcement Administration, *Drug Money Laundering in Canada*, DEA-94085 (U.S. Department of Justice, September 1994), p. 1.

96. For further information, see Thoumi, *Political Economy and Illegal Drugs in Colombia*, pp. 226–28; Guy Gugliotta, "The Colombian Cartels and How to Stop Them," in Smith, ed., *Drug Policy in the Americas*, p. 127; Rensselaer W. Lee III, "Global Reach: The Threat of International Drug Trafficking," *Current History*, vol. 94 (May 1995), pp. 210–11; Tullis, *Handbook of Research on the Illicit Drug Traffic*, p. 131; and *1994 INCSR*, p. 255.

97. Karel van Wolferen, *The Enigma of Japanese Power: People and Politics in a Stateless Nation* (Knopf, 1989), pp. 105, 107, 194.

98. Stanley, *Drug Policy and the Decline of American Cities*, pp. 247–48.

99. "G-7 Gives New Push to MOUs," *CCC News*, no. 19 (1991); and United Nations Economic and Social Council, Resolution 1993/41, July 27, 1993, and Resolution 1994/4, July 20, 1994.

100. This approach has value in other areas. See the comprehensive discussion of self-regulatory regimes in Wolfgang H. Reinicke, "Cooperative Security and the Political Economy of Nonproliferation," in Janne E. Nolan, ed., *Global Engagement: Cooperation and Security in the 21st Century* (Brookings, 1994), p. 185.

101. Many countries do not prohibit drug use per se but instead consider possession and possession with a view to use as offenses. In the European context, see Bernard Leroy, "European Legislative Systems in Relation to the Demand in 1993: Recent Developments and Comparative Study," in Georges Estievenart,

Policies and Strategies to Combat Drugs in Europe: The Treaty on European Union: Framework for a New European Strategy to Combat Drugs? (Netherlands: Martinus Nijhoff, 1995), pp. 116–19.

102. Mark H. Moore, "Drugs, the Criminal Law, and the Administration of Justice," in Ronald Bayer and Gerald M. Oppenheimer, eds., *Confronting Drug Policy: Illicit Drugs in a Free Society* (Cambridge University Press, 1993), pp. 243–44. See also Patricia G. Erickson, "The Law, Social Control, and Drug Policy: Models, Factors, and Processes," *International Journal of the Addictions*, vol. 28, no. 12 (1993), pp. 1155–76.

103. Unless otherwise indicated, this discussion draws heavily on the excellent article by Robert J. MacCoun, "Drugs and the Law: A Psychological Analysis of Drug Prohibition," *Psychological Bulletin*, vol. 113 (May 1993), pp. 497–512.

104. Zinberg, *Drug, Set, and Setting*, p. 5; Hernando Gomez Buendia, ed., *Urban Crime: Global Trends and Policies* (Tokyo: United Nations University, 1989), pp. 142–43; WHO, "The Family and the Use of Illegal Drugs," pp. 5–8; and Ronald K. Siegel, *Intoxication: Life in Pursuit of Artificial Paradise* (Dutton, 1989).

105. Denise B. Kandel, "The Social Demography of Drug Use," in Bayer and Oppenheimer, eds., *Confronting Drug Policy*, pp. 68–69.

106. Goldstein and Kalant, "Drug Policy: Striking the Right Balance," p. 1515; and Buendia, *Urban Crime*, p. 5.

107. J. Jablensky, "Characteristics of Current Substance Abuse Patterns in Countries of Central and Eastern Europe," in H. Klingemann and others, "European Summary on Drug Abuse, First Report (1985–1990)," EUR/ICP/ADA 527/A, World Health Organization, Regional Office, Copenhagen, 1992, p. 29.

108. MacCoun, "Drugs and the Law," pp. 498–502.

109. Nkechi Taifa, "Drug Laws 100 Times Harder on Blacks," *Focus*, vol. 23 (April 1995), pp. 5–6; Ann Devroy, "Clinton Retains Tough Law on Crack Cocaine," *Washington Post*, October 31, 1995, p. A1; Fox Butterfield, "More Blacks in Their 20's Have Trouble with the Law," *New York Times*, October 5, 1995, p. A18; and Dirk Johnson, "For Drug Offenders, How Tough Is Too Tough?" *New York Times*, November 8, 1993, p. A16.

110. This discussion draws on the following sources: William J. Bukoski, "A Framework for Drug Abuse Prevention," in National Institute on Drug Abuse, *Drug Use Prevention Intervention Research: Methodological Issues*, Research Monograph Series 107 (U.S. Department of Health and Human Services, 1990), pp. 14–16; Elaine Norman and Sandra Turner, "Prevention Programmes for Adolescents in the USA," *International Journal of Drug Policy*, vol. 5, no. 2 (1994), pp. 90–97; Peter Stoker, "A Rough Ride for Prevention," *International Journal on Drug Policy*, vol. 3, no. 2 (1992), pp. 66–70; and Marc Eliany and Brian Rush, *How Effective Are Alcohol and Other Drug Prevention and Treatment Programs? A Review of Evaluation Studies*, report prepared for Health and Welfare Canada (Ottawa: January 1992).

111. Zinberg, *Drug, Set, and Setting*, p. 10; and Kleiman, *Against Excess*, pp. 166–67.

112. Earl Wysong, Richard Aniskiewicz, and David Wright, "Truth and DARE: Tracking Drug Education to Graduation and Symbolic Politics," *Social Problems*, vol. 41 (August 1994), pp. 448–72.

113. Eliany and Rush, *How Effective Are Alcohol and Other Drug Prevention and Treatment Programs?*, pp. 13–15.

114. Moore, "Drugs, the Criminal Law, and the Administration of Justice," p. 243; and Daniel Romer, "Using Mass Media to Reduce Adolescent Involvement in Drug Trafficking," *Pediatrics*, vol. 93 (June 1994), p. 1074.

115. Eliany and Rush, *How Effective Are Alcohol and Other Drug Prevention and Treatment Programs?*, pp. 47–76. See also Office of Technology Assessment, *The Effectiveness of Drug Abuse Treatment: Implications for Controlling AIDS/HIV Infection*, Background Paper (September 1990), pp. 41–49.

116. Eliany and Rush, *How Effective Are Alcohol and Other Drug Prevention and Treatment Programs?*, pp. 47–76, 79–80.

117. Wallace Mandell, "The Problem of Drug Prevention and Treatment in Developing Countries," paper prepared for the Brookings Institution Workshop on "Global Responses to the Transnational Drug Challenge," July 7–8, 1994.

118. Roger L. Conner and Patrick C. Burns, "How Communities Are Eradicating Local Drug Markets," *Brookings Review*, vol. 10 (Summer 1992), pp. 26–29.

119. For a cogent and comprehensive review of the harm-reduction philosophy and its associated methods, see Ethan Nadelmann and others, "The Harm Reduction Approach to Drug Control: International Progress," Princeton University, Woodrow Wilson School of Public and International Affairs, April 1994.

120. For further details, see ibid.

121. Ibid.; General Accounting Office, *Needle Exchange Programs: Research Suggests Promise as an AIDS Prevention Strategy*, HRD 93-60 (March 1993); and "Studies Support Needle Exchanges," *Washington Post*, January 12, 1994, p. A3.

122. Nadelmann and others, "Harm Reduction Approach to Drug Control," pp. 24–31; and Eliany and Rush, *How Effective Are Alcohol and Other Drug Prevention and Treatment Programs?*, p. 50.

123. Richard Stevenson, "Harm Reduction, Rational Addiction, and the Optimal Prescribing of Illegal Drugs," *Contemporary Economic Policy*, vol. 12 (July 1994), pp. 102, 106.

124. Switzerland has since adopted an experimental heroin prescription program on a national scale. See Nadelmann and others, "Harm Reduction Approach to Drug Control."

125. Werner Schneider, "Report on the Drug Policy in the City of Frankfurt," in European Cities on Drug Policy Network, "The Frankfurt Resolution" (Frankfurt am Main, August 1993), pp. 14–18.

126. Ministry of Welfare, Health and Cultural Affairs and Ministry of Justice, "The Drug Policy in the Netherlands," December 1992, p. 5; Marlise Simons, "Maastricht Journal: Drug Floodgates Open, Inundating the Dutch," *New York Times*, April 20, 1994, p. A4; and William Drozdiak, "Dutch Tolerance for Drugs Irks Neighbors," *International Herald Tribune*, November 8, 1995, p. 2.

127. Stephen Kinzer, "German State Eases Its Policy on Drug Arrests," *New York Times*, May 18, 1994, p. A5. For an overview of individual German Lander policies, see "Whatever the Land Likes Is Permitted," *Die Tageszeitung*, May 18, 1994, p. 3, in JPRS, *Narcotics*, May 24, 1994, p. 53.

128. MacCoun, "Drugs and the Law," p. 567.

Chapter Four

1. Eduard Bos and others, *World Population Projections: Estimates and Projections with Related Demographic Statistics, 1994–95* (Johns Hopkins University Press for the World Bank, 1994), p. 78.

2. Richard R. Clayton, "Drugs versus Public Health: Assessing the Risk of a Global Drug Epidemic," paper prepared for the Brookings Institution workshop on "The International Implications of the Transnational Drug Phenomenon," University of Pennsylvania, April 18–19, 1994. I am particularly grateful for Clayton's insights in preparing this discussion. See also Laura Sessions Stepp and Richard Morin, "Fast Track to Adulthood." *Washington Post*, December 10, 1995, p. A1.

3. Bos and others, *World Population Projections*, p. 90.

4. It is interesting to note that increased levels of crime are being projected on the basis of similar calculations. See John J. DiIulio Jr., "The Next War on Drugs: Targeting the Inner Cities," *Brookings Review*, vol. 11 (Summer 1993), pp. 28–33; DiIulio, "Crime Solutions: Rescue the Young from Barbarism," *American Enterprise*, vol. 6 (May–June 1995), pp. 32–33; and Office of National Drug Control Policy, *National Drug Control Strategy: Executive Summary* (The White House, April 1995), pp. 8–14.

5. Pierre Thomas, "Teens Use More Drugs, Worry Less about Consequences," *Washington Post*, December 16, 1995, p. A1; and David F. Musto, *The American Disease: Origins of Narcotic Control*, expanded ed. (Oxford University Press, 1987), p. 251.

6. Abigail Trafford, "The Snare of Illegal Drugs," *Washington Post Health*, December 12, 1995, p. 6; Substance Abuse and Mental Health Services Administration, Office of Applied Studies, *National Household Survey on Drug Abuse: Population Estimates, 1993* (U.S. Department of Health and Human Services, October 1994); and Lloyd D. Johnston, Patrick O'Malley, and Jerald Bachman, "National Survey Results on Drug Use," in *The Monitoring the Future Study, 1975–1995*, vol. 1: *Secondary School Students* (National Institute on Drug Abuse, forthcoming).

7. Robert Reich, "America's Anxious Class," *New Perspectives Quarterly*, vol. 12 (Winter 1995), pp. 28–29. For a similar assessment, see also Paul Krugman, "Europe Jobless, America Penniless?" *Foreign Policy*, no. 95 (Summer 1994), p. 29.

8. Reich, "America's Anxious Class," p. 28.

9. Paul Kennedy, *Preparing for the Twenty-First Century* (Random House, 1993), p. 60.

10. Gene Stephens, "Drugs, Crime, and Public Policy: New Approaches for the 21st Century," in *Altered States of Mind: Current Issues in Criminal Justice,* vol. 8 (1993), p. 239.

11. United Nations Conference on Trade and Development, *Trade and Development Report, 1993* (New York: United Nations, 1993), pp. 146–47; and John Salt, *Migration and Population Change in Europe,* UNIDIR/93/23 (New York: United Nations, 1993), p. 29.

12. Rensselaer Lee and Patrick Clawson, *Crop Substitution in the Andes* (Office of National Drug Control Policy, 1993), p. 20.

13. Frances Williams, "Coca Still Vital to Bolivian Economy," *Financial Times,* March 31, 1993, p. 8. For lower estimates, see Elena Alvarez, "The Political Economy of Coca Production in Bolivia and Peru: Economic Importance and Political Implications," report prepared for the North-South Center, University of Miami, July 1993, p. 34. See also Lee and Clawson, *Crop Substitution in the Andes,* p. 20.

14. Williams, "Coca Still Vital to Bolivian Economy."

15. "Drugs Have Not Made Colombia Rich," *Cambio 16/America,* June 14, 1993, pp. 34–35, in JPRS, *Narcotics,* July 13, 1993, p. 15; and "How Much Money Is Coming In, After All?" *Semana,* April 13, 1993, in JPRS, *Narcotics,* June 14, 1993, pp. 10–14.

16. *1994 INCSR,* p. 118; and Lee and Clawson, *Crop Substitution in the Andes,* pp. 53–54.

17. Drug Enforcement Administration, *IDEC X: Annual Assessment of Accomplishments,* DEA-599 (U.S. Department of Justice, April 1993), pp. 33, 77–78; and National Narcotics Intelligence Consumers Committee, *The NNICC Report, 1992: The Supply of Illicit Drugs to the United States,* DEA-93051 (U.S. Department of Justice, September 1993), pp. 9–10.

18. Drug Enforcement Administration, *Worldwide Cocaine Situation,* DEA-93048 (U.S. Department of Justice, October 1993), pp. xi, 7; "Peru: A Budding National Cartel," *Geopolitical Drug Dispatch,* no. 25 (November 1993), p. 5; and David Schrieberg, "Birth of the Baby Cartels," *Newsweek,* August 21, 1995, p. 37.

19. Two new, more violent groups under the leadership of Juan Carlos Ortiz and Juan Carlos Ramirez are reportedly already challenging the "old guard" in Cali. See Douglas Farah, "Young Gangs Decentralize Drug Trade," *Washington Post,* June 11, 1994, p. A29; and "Colombia: One Down, More to Go," *Economist,* June 17, 1995, p. 47.

20. See Francisco Reyes, "Peru's Deadly Drug Habit," *Washington Post,* February 28, 1993, p. C4; "A Second Front," *U.S. News and World Report,* May 18, 1992, p. 18; and DEA, *Worldwide Cocaine Situation,* pp. 29, 34–35.

21. A study sponsored by the United Nations International Drug Control Program estimates that the 1994 crop will produce between 3,200 and 3,500 metric tons of opium, which not only dwarfs the official U.S. estimate of 687 tons for 1993 but is also well over three times the size of the DEA's conservative estimate of 900 metric tons for the same year. See "Afghanistan: All Records Shattered," *Geopolitical Drug Dispatch,* no. 34 (August 1994), p. 5; and *1994*

INCSR, p. 20. Other sources also suggest that Afghanistan's production is much higher than the U.S. estimate. In its annual report for 1992, the UN International Narcotics Control Board states that surveys conducted in several provinces suggest potential production greater than 900 metric tons for those areas alone. See International Narcotics Control Board, *Report of the International Narcotics Control Board for 1992* (United Nations, December 1992), p. 28; and Doris Buddenberg, "The Opiate Industry of Pakistan," report prepared for the United Nations International Drug Control Program, January 1994, p. 1.

22. Buddenberg, "Opiate Industry of Pakistan," pp. 4–5.

23. Thura Aung, "Khun Sa Compete for Drug Trade," SEASIA Internet Listserv, December 9, 1994, in JPRS, *Narcotics*, January 12, 1995, p. 59.

24. See United Nations International Drug Control Program, "Vietnam," Country Program Framework Report, September 7, 1993, pp. 1–2; and "Cambodia: The Golden Triangle Reaches Out," *Geopolitical Drug Dispatch*, no. 26 (December 1993), pp. 6–7.

25. Rensselaer W. Lee III, "Drugs in Communist and Post-Communist Countries," in *Strategic Organizational Drug Intelligence Symposium Compendium* (National Drug Intelligence Center and Ridgeway Center for International Security Studies, March 16, 1995), p. 5.

26. James Brooke, "International Business: More Open Latin Borders Mirror Region's Freer Markets," *New York Times,* July 4, 1995, p. A47. See also Nora Lustig, Barry P. Bosworth, and Robert Z. Lawrence, *North American Free Trade: Assessing the Impact* (Brookings, 1992).

27. Michael Richardson, "U.S. Presses Pacific Trade Forum on Opening Markets," *International Herald Tribune*, June 26, 1995, p. 6. See also Richardson, "ASEAN Puts Free Trade on Fast Track," *International Herald Tribune*, July 31, 1995, p. 9.

28. Craig R. Whitney, "France, Rebuffed, to Stand Alone on Border Controls," *International Herald Tribune*, June 30, 1995, p. 5; and "2 European Zones Agree to End Border Controls," *International Herald Tribune*, June 17–18, 1995, p. 2.

29. Alison Jamieson, "Drug Trafficking after 1992: A Special Report," Conflict Studies 250 (London: Research Institute for the Study of Conflict and Terrorism, April 1992), p. 9. As this excellent study goes on to state: "The northern Community seas are dotted with myriads of archipelagos and natural harbours which could afford cover to traffickers; likewise, the southern Mediterranean may become extremely attractive for drug smuggling vessels, particularly in the guise of cruise or pleasure boats."

30. Bos and others, *World Population Projections*, pp. 9–10.

31. Stephens, "Drugs, Crime, and Public Policy," p. 232.

32. Bos and others, *World Population Projections*, pp. 3–4, 9; and George D. Moffett, *Critical Masses: The Global Population Challenge* (Viking Press, 1994), p. 15. See also Kennedy, *Preparing for the Twenty-First Century.*

33. In some countries the distribution will be even more skewed; 75 percent of Brazil's population, for example, is already living in cities. United Nations Development Program, *Human Development Report, 1990* (New York: Oxford

University Press, 1990), pp. 160, 170; and Department of Economic and Social Information and Policy Analysis, *World Urbanization Prospects: The 1992 Revision* (New York: United Nations, 1993), p. 3.

34. Kennedy, *Preparing for the Twenty-First Century*, pp. 26–27.

35. Department of Economic and Social Information and Policy Analysis, *World Urbanization Prospects*, p. 15.

36. See World Bank, *Global Economic Prospects and the Developing Countries, 1995* (Washington, 1995), pp. 1–6.

37. United Nations International Drug Control Program, "The Social and Economic Impact of Drug Abuse and Control," position paper, United Nations System, June 29, 1994, p. 32. See also Stanley Meisler, "Unemployment Ravages Nations on Global Scale," *Los Angeles Times*, February 19, 1994.

38. Moffett, *Critical Masses*, p. 19; and Kennedy, *Preparing for the Twenty-First Century*, p. 27. See also Uner Kirdar, "Issues and Questions," in Uner Kirdar, ed., *Change: Threat or Opportunity for Human Development*, vol. 4: *Changes in the Human Dimension of Development, Ethics and Values* (New York: United Nations, 1992), p. 4.

39. UNCTAD, *Trade and Development Report, 1993*, p. 94.

40. UNDCP, "Social and Economic Impact of Drug Abuse and Control," p. 32.

41. Paul Kennedy, "The Threat of Modernization," *New Perspectives Quarterly*, vol. 12 (Winter 1995), p. 33.

42. United Nations International Drug Control Program, "Drugs and Development," discussion paper prepared for World Summit on Social Development, June 1994, p. 13.

43. UNCTAD, *Trade and Development Report, 1993*, pp. vi, 93.

44. See World Bank, *Global Economic Prospects*, pp. 18–19.

45. Ibid., p. 19.

46. UNCTAD, *Trade and Development Report, 1993*, p. 29.

47. Kennedy, *Preparing for the Twenty-First Century*, pp. 69, 80.

48. See Lally Weymouth, "Mitch McConnell's World View," *Washington Post*, January 8, 1995, p. C7; and "EU Splits on Aid to Ex-Colonies," *International Herald Tribune*, February 7, 1995, p. 8.

49. See Peter Pauly, "Transfers, Real Interest Rates and Regional Development: International Economic Implications of Financial Support for the Economies in Transition," in United Nations Conference on Trade and Development, *International Monetary and Financial Issues for the 1990s*, vol. 1 (New York: United Nations, 1992), pp. 55–78; and Rob Vos, "Prospects of Financial Flows to Developing Countries in the 1990s: The Global Macroeconomic Trade-Offs," in United Nations Conference on Trade and Development, *International Monetary and Financial Issues for the 1990s*, vol. 2 (New York: United Nations, 1993), pp. 1–56.

50. UNCTAD, *Trade and Development Report, 1993*, p. 102. In this context it is interesting to note that nine of twenty-one U.S. foreign aid missions in Africa are to be closed by 1997. See Robert D. Kaplan, "The Coming Anarchy," *Atlantic Monthly* (February 1994), p. 54.

51. Erik Ipsen, "East Europe's Failure to 'Emerge,'" *International Herald Tribune*, February 4–5, 1995, p. 7.

52. World Bank, *Global Economic Prospects*, p. 2.

53. Ismail Serageldin, *Nurturing Development: Aid and Cooperation in Today's Changing World* (Washington: World Bank, 1995), pp. 8–9, 114.

54. Kaplan, "The Coming Anarchy," p. 60. Paul Kennedy makes the same point when he argues that "just as the gap between the upper one-fifth and lower four-fifths of global society has increased, so also, though less drastically, has the upper one-fifth in American society detached itself from the rest." *Preparing for the Twenty-First Century*, p. 60.

55. UNDCP, "Drugs and Development," p. 3.

56. See ibid., p. 13.

57. One expert has calculated that about 700,000 hectares of Peru have been deforested either directly or indirectly as a consequence of coca cultivation. If true, this would represent 10 percent of the total area deforested in the Peruvian Amazon in the twentieth century. See Elena Alvarez, "Coca Production in Peru," in Peter H. Smith, ed., *Drug Policy in the Americas* (Boulder, Colo.: Westview Press, 1992), pp. 82–83. Some areas have suffered severe soil erosion and even the extinction of species. Coca cultivation is believed to have blighted a broadly similar swath of territory in Bolivia. See UNDCP, "Social and Economic Impact of Drug Abuse and Control," p. 37. For an assessment of the effect of opium poppy cultivation on Colombia, see Ignacio G. Gomez, "Opium Poppies in the Prairies and in Streets," *El Espectador*, May 27, 1993, p. 9A, in JPRS, *Narcotics*, July 6, 1993, pp. 16–17. These areas have all become polluted by the combined effect of improperly used pesticides and fertilizers and the disposal of chemicals used for drug processing and refinement. In Colombia, each year "more than 20 million liters of ethyl ether, acetone, ammonia, sulfuric acid . . . are dumped into streams and tributaries that lead to the Amazon and Orinoco Rivers. In Peru, an estimated 30,000 tons of sulfuric acid, 2,000 tons of calcium carbonate, and 50 million liters of kerosene are used annually to produce coca paste." UNDCP, "Drugs and Development," pp. 6–7.

58. Rensselaer W. Lee III, "Trends in the Evolution of Narcotics Industries: Problems of Influence and Legitimacy," in *Economics of the Narcotics Industry*, report of conference sponsored by U.S. Department of State, Bureau of Intelligence and Research, and Central Intelligence Agency, November 21–22, 1994.

59. Robert Filippone, "The Medellin Cartel: Why We Can't Win the Drug War," *Studies in Conflict and Terrorism*, vol. 17, no. 3 (1994), p. 337.

60. Francisco E. Thoumi, "The Economic Impact of the Illegal Drugs Industry in Bolivia, Colombia and Peru," in *Economics of the Narcotics Industry*.

61. Robert Munro, "Macro-Economic Regional Perspectives," in *Economics of the Narcotics Industry*.

62. Francisco E. Thoumi, "Some Implications of the Growth of the Underground Economy in Colombia," *Journal of Interamerican Studies and World Affairs*, vol. 29 (Summer 1987), p. 46.

63. Donald Im, "Colombian Economic Reform: The Impact on Drug Money Laundering within the Colombian Economy," in *Economics of the Narcotics Industry.*

64. "Drugs Have Not Made Colombia Rich," p. 16.

65. Rensselaer W. Lee III, "Global Reach: The Threat of International Drug Trafficking," *Current History*, vol. 94 (May 1995), p. 208; and Buddenberg, "Opiate Industry of Pakistan," p. 6.

66. Lee, "Trends in the Evolution of Narcotics Industries."

67. This description of events draws heavily on Thoumi, "Some Implications of the Growth of the Underground Economy in Colombia," pp. 45–48. See also LaMond Tullis, *Handbook of Research on the Illicit Drug Traffic: Socioeconomic and Political Consequences* (Westport, Conn.: Greenwood Press, 1991), pp. 55–72.

68. "Rio—Gunsmoke and Fear Win Out," *International Herald Tribune*, October 28, 1994, pp. 1, 5. See also "Out of Control," *Jornal Do Brasil*, January 17, 1994, p. 10, in JPRS, *Narcotics*, February 23, 1994, pp. 12–13; and Fabio Lau, "Rio Drug Traffickers Reportedly Employ 5,000 Minors," *O Globo*, January 23, 1994, p. 12, in JPRS, *Narcotics*, March 21, 1994, pp. 12–14.

69. "Military Sweeps into Rio's Drug Slums," *International Herald Tribune*, November 21, 1994, p. 3; and "Troops Quit Rio Drug Slums after Weekend of Searches," *International Herald Tribune*, November 22, 1994, p. 3.

70. "Crime Wave," *Economist*, October 29, 1994, p. 48; John F. Burns, "Heroin Scourges Million Pakistanis," *New York Times*, April 5, 1995, p. A12; "Asia's Answer to Beirut," *Economist*, July 1, 1995, p. 30; "Nigeria: Heroin Turns into Cassava," *Geopolitical Drug Dispatch*, no. 37 (November 1994), p. 7; Axel Klein, "Trapped in Traffick: Growing Problems of Drug Consumption in Lagos," *Journal of Modern African Studies*, vol. 32, no. 4 (1994), pp. 657–77; and Hernando Gomez Buendia, ed., *Urban Crime: Global Trends and Policies* (Tokyo: United Nations University, 1989), p. 160.

71. Im, "Colombian Economic Reform." The former finance minister, Rudolf Hommes, has also stated that foreign investment in Colombia would be 25 percent higher if it were not for drug-related violence and kidnapping.

72. This discussion draws on Phil Williams, "Organizational Risk Assessment and Management," in *Strategic Organizational Drug Symposium Compendium*, pp. 30–31; and Ethan A. Nadelmann, *Cops across Borders: The Internationalization of U.S. Criminal Law Enforcement* (Pennsylvania State University Press, 1993), pp. 251–312.

73. *1994 INCSR*, p. 103; "Peru: Soldiers against the Army," *Geopolitical Drug Dispatch*, no. 39 (January 1995), pp. 1, 3–4; "Peru: The Military on the Grill," *Geopolitical Drug Dispatch*, no. 33 (July 1994), pp. 6–7; and Rosario Mayorga, "Army Involvement in Drug Trafficking Viewed," *La Republica*, November 27, 1994, pp. 23–25, in JPRS, *Narcotics*, January 12, 1995, pp. 42–45. It has also been alleged that Colombian Air Force aircraft were used to ship coca paste from Peru to Colombia. See Oscar Vargas Romero, "Former DEA 'Agent' Links Generals to Drug Traffickers," *La Republica*, February 7, 1994, pp. 16, 17, in JPRS, *Narcotics*, February 23, 1994, pp. 28–30.

74. *1995 INCSR*, p. 83.

75. Richard Cole, "U.S. Is Probing Drugs in Haiti," *Philadelphia Inquirer*, May 22, 1994, p. 1.

76. "Nigeria: Bad Cops Persevere," *Geopolitical Drug Dispatch*, no. 38 (December 1994), p. 8; and "Nigeria: Explosive Revelations," *Geopolitical Drug Dispatch*, no. 25 (November 1993), p. 7.

77. "Manila 'Drug Police' Claim," *Financial Times*, April 7, 1994.

78. Williams, "Organizational Risk Assessment and Management," p. 30.

79. "Ten Opposition Deputies Linked to Narcotics Trade," *Bangkok Post*, May 18, 1994, pp. 1, 3, in JPRS, *Narcotics*, May 24, 1994, p. 28; "Thailand: The Geopolitics of Narco-Corruption," *Geopolitical Drug Dispatch*, no. 32 (June 1994), p. 7; "Turkey: Drugs in a Dirty War," *Geopolitical Drug Dispatch*, no. 40 (February 1995), pp. 1, 3; "The Philippines: High-Level Scandal," *Geopolitical Drug Dispatch*, no. 36 (October 1994), p. 4; "Taiwan: The Democratization of Crime," *Geopolitical Drug Dispatch*, no. 41 (March 1995), p. 6; "Morocco," *Geopolitical Drug Dispatch*, no. 40 (February 1995), p. 2; "Pakistan: Black List," *Geopolitical Drug Dispatch*, no. 23 (September 1993), pp. 1, 3; "Pakistan: The Politics of Drug Seizures," *Geopolitical Drug Dispatch*, no. 35 (September 1994), p. 7; and "Pakistan," *Geopolitical Drug Dispatch*, no. 43 (May 1995), p. 2.

80. Stanley A. Weiss, "The United States Has to Move against the Drug Trade in Mexico," *International Herald Tribune*, July 1–2, 1995, p. 8.

81. Rensselaer W. Lee III, "The Global Narcotics Trade: Economic Patterns and Implications," in *Economics of the Drug Industry*; and "Colombia: Towards a Narco-Democracy," *Geopolitical Drug Dispatch*, no. 31 (May 1994), pp. 4–5. The latter report states that 3 million hectares represents 30 percent of the total.

82. Im, "Colombian Economic Reform."

83. Antonio Urdinola, "The Wealth of the Colombian Mafia," *El Tiempo*, December 12, 1993, p. 2C, in JPRS, *Narcotics*, February 1, 1994, p. 11.

84. "Drugsgate, Bogota," *Economist*, August 5, 1995, p. 39; Tracy Wilkinson, "Image vs. Reality in Colombia," *Los Angeles Times*, July 8, 1994, p. A1; and Luis Javier Garrido, "The Narco System," *La Jornada*, June 11, 1993, p. 10, in JPRS, *Narcotics*, July 6, 1993, p. 20.

85. Past experience is not encouraging. Even while imprisoned, traffickers have continued to run their operations. See Schrieberg, "Birth of the Baby Cartels," p. 37.

86. Peter A. Lupsha, "Narco Investment in Domestic Economies: Mexico: An Example of Narco-Democracy?" in *Economics of the Narcotics Industry*.

87. See Tim Golden, "Agents of Graft—A Special Report," *New York Times*, April 19, 1995, p. A1; Tod Robberson, "Mexican Held in U.S. Linked to Drug Cartel," *Washington Post*, March 9, 1995, p. A1; and Tod Robberson and Douglas Farah, "Mexico's Spreading Drug Stain," *Washington Post*, March 12, 1995, p. A1. See also three-part article by Rodolfo Rojas-Zea, "The Owl's Song," *El Financiero*, September 6, 1994, p. 33, in JPRS, *Narcotics*, September 15, 1995, pp. 20–25.

88. Lupsha, "Narco Investment in Domestic Economies."

89. Ibid.

90. Robberson and Farah, "Mexican Held in U.S. Linked to Drug Cartel"; Edmundo Dominguez Aragones, "'Narco-Dollar' Seen as Factor in Financial Crisis," *Excelsior*, February 4, 1995, p. 7A, 16A, in JPRS, *Narcotics*, March 29, 1995, p. 25; and Martin Feldstein, "Too Little, Not Too Much," *Economist*, June 24, 1995, pp. 72–73.

91. "Venezuela and Colombia: And Guerrillas," *Economist*, March 25, 1995, p. 58.

92. Douglas Farah, "A Free-Trade Zone in the Traffic of Humans," *Washington Post*, October 23, 1995, p. A1; "The New Trade in Humans," *Economist*, August 5, 1995, pp. 45–46; and William Drozdiak, "The Balkan Heroin Connection," *National Times*, April–May 1994, pp. 19–20.

93. See Jim Leitzel, Clifford Gaddy, and Michael Alexeev, "Mafiosi and Matrioshki: Organized Crime and Russian Reform," *Brookings Review*, vol. 13 (Winter 1995), pp. 26–29; Rensselaer W. Lee III, "Foreign Policy Implications of Post-Soviet Organized Crime," testimony before Subcommittee on International Security, International Organization and Human Rights of House Committee on Foreign Affairs, November 4, 1993; Louise I. Shelley, "Post-Soviet Organized Crime: Implications for Economic, Social, and Political Development," *Demokratizatsiya*, vol. 2 (Summer 1994), pp. 351–58; and Claire Sterling, "Redfellas," *New Republic*, April 11, 1994, pp. 19–22.

94. Michael Specter, "A Caravan of Drugs Crosses Wilds of Central Asia," *International Herald Tribune*, May 3, 1995, p. 2.

95. Paul A. Goble, "Nationalities and Narcotics: A Combustible Mix in the Post-Soviet Successor States," paper prepared for Meridian House conference on "Drugs in the Post-Communist World," 1993, p. 5.

96. These indirect costs are drawn from Bureau of Justice Statistics, *Drugs, Crime, and the Justice System*, NCJ-133652 (U.S. Department of Justice, December 1992), pp. 2–19; and UNDCP, "Social and Economic Impact of Drug Abuse and Control."

97. Gina Kolata, "Drug Abuse and AIDS Increasingly Linked," *International Herald Tribune*, March 2, 1995, p. 10. In Thailand, Brazil, Poland, and parts of the former Yugoslavia, intravenous drug use is reportedly already a major factor in the spread of HIV.

98. Don Oldenburg, "The Other U.S. Budget," *Washington Post*, November 24, 1995, p. D5.

99. Ibid. See also "Legalization: Panacea or Pandora's Box," White Paper 1, Center on Addiction and Substance Abuse at Columbia University, September 1995, pp. 20–26, 34–35; and Dana Priest, "Smoking-Related Medical Care in '93 Estimated at $50 Billion," *Washington Post*, July 8, 1994, p. A2. When lost productivity was added, the total cost was estimated to have reached $65 billion by 1985.

100. See "Fighting and Switching," *Newsweek*, March 21, 1994, pp. 52–53; and Richard Tomkins, "Showdown in the Last Gasp Saloon," *Financial Times*, April 21, 1994, p. 21. In this context it is also interesting to repeat the analysis of one tobacco industry observer: "As poor countries get richer, they

smoke more American cigarettes. That doesn't change until they get rich enough to worry about their health."

101. Richard G. A. Feacham and others, *The Health of Adults in the Developing World* (Washington: World Bank, 1993), p. 25. Officials from China's Ministry of Health estimate that 1.2 million people die each year from smoking-related illnesses. See Steven Mufson, "Power Puff: World's Biggest Cigarette Market Lights Up," *International Herald Tribune*, July 3, 1995, p. 4.

102. James A. Cercone, "Alcohol-Related Problems as an Obstacle to the Development of Human Capital," World Bank Technical Paper 219 (1993), pp. 13–19.

Chapter Five

1. To be fair, some have argued that even a relatively brief disruption in supply might be worthwhile, especially if combined with other demand-reduction measures, in curbing short-term consumption and therefore long-term addiction. Whether the effort and resources expended would be worth the potential gain, however, requires further analysis. See Kevin Jack Riley, "Snow Job? The Efficacy of Source Country Cocaine Policies," Ph.D. dissertation, RAND Graduate School, 1993, pp. 137–52. Similar arguments have also been made with respect to interdiction, that the number of potential experimenters could be lowered by raising retail prices. See John J. DiIulio Jr., "Cracking Down," *New Republic*, May 10, 1993, p. 55. Other arguments have been made about the political desirability of supporting source-country control efforts. See Rensselaer Lee and Patrick Clawson, *Crop Substitution in the Andes* (Office of National Drug Control Policy, 1993), p. 3.

2. Some have been more specific than others, however. For example, see Theodore R. Vallance, *Prohibition's Second Failure: The Quest for a Rational and Humane Drug Policy* (Praeger, 1993), pp. 117–19; and Ethan A. Nadelmann, "Thinking Seriously about Alternatives to Drug Prohibition," *Daedalus*, vol. 121 (Summer 1992), pp. 85–132.

3. See, for example, Sam Stanley, *Drug Policy and the Decline of American Cities* (New Brunswick, N.J.: Transaction, 1992), p. 219. *Decriminalization* usually refers to the removal of criminal sanctions for possessing small quantities of drugs for personal use. See Vallance, *Prohibition's Second Failure*, p. 95.

4. This point is argued most persuasively by Mark A. R. Kleiman, *Against Excess: Drug Policy for Results* (Basic Books, 1992), p. 101; and Nadelmann, "Thinking Seriously about Alternatives to Drug Prohibition," p. 95.

5. Avram Goldstein and Harold Kalant, "Drug Policy: Striking the Right Balance," *Science*, September 28, 1990, pp. 1515–16; and David T. Courtwright, "Should We Legalize Drugs? History Answers: No," *American Heritage*, vol. 44 (February–March 1993), p. 50.

6. Tom Morganthau with others, "Should Drugs Be Legal," *Newsweek*, May 30, 1988, pp. 37–38; Morton M. Kondracke, "Don't Legalize Drugs: The Costs

Are Still Too High," *New Republic*, June 27, 1988, p. 17; Taylor Branch, "Let Koop Do It," *New Republic*, October 24, 1988, p. 26; and A. M. Rosenthal, "Stacking the Deck," *New York Times*, April 14, 1995, p. A15.

7. For the best discussion of this, see Nadelmann, "Thinking Seriously about Alternatives to Drug Prohibition," pp. 114–17.

8. Ethan A. Nadelmann, "Should We Legalize Drugs? History Answers: Yes," *American Heritage*, vol. 44 (February–March 1993), pp. 42–48; Nadelmann, "Drug Prohibition in the United States: Cost, Consequences, and the Alternatives," *Science*, September 1, 1989, p. 945; and "Bring Drugs within the Law," *Economist*, May 15, 1993, pp. 13–14.

9. For more on the problem of comparing case studies, see Robert J. Mac-Coun and others, "Drug Policies and Problems: The Promise and Pitfalls of Cross-National Comparison," in Nick Heather and others, eds., *Psychoactive Drugs and Harm Reduction: From Faith to Science* (London: Whurr Publishers, 1993), pp. 103–17.

10. Courtwright, "Should We Legalize Drugs," pp. 52–56.

11. Ibid., p. 50.

12. Nadelmann, "Thinking Seriously about Alternatives to Drug Prohibition," pp. 114–17.

13. This problem is discussed in Peter Reuter, "The Legalization Debate: A Brief Survey," EUI Colloquium Papers DOC.IUE 381/93 (col. 52), European University Institute, Florence, December 1993; and Ethan A. Nadelmann, "Beyond Drug Prohibition: Evaluating the Alternatives," in Melvyn B. Krauss and Edward P. Lazear, eds., *Searching for Alternatives: Drug-Control Policy in the United States* (Stanford: Hoover Institution Press, 1991), pp. 241–50.

14. The negative reaction that the former U.S. surgeon general, Joycelyn Elders, received after she suggested in 1993 that legalization should be studied is one example of this. Her remarks eventually contributed to her later resignation.

15. See Reuter, "The Legalization Debate: A Brief Survey," pp. 13–14.

16. It is encouraging that the Clinton administration has begun to accept the logic of this approach. See Raphael F. Perl, "United States International Drug Policy: Background, Assumptions, Recent Developments, and Emerging Trends," paper prepared for the University of Miami's North-South Center's Drug Task Force roundtable meeting on "International Drug Control Policies in the Americas: Current Trends and Future Directions," 1994, p. 5.

17. Nicholas Dorn, "Clarifying Policy Options on Drug Trafficking: Harm Minimization Is Distinct from Legalization," in Patrick O'Hare and others, eds., *The Reduction of Drug-Related Harm* (London: Routledge, 1992), pp. 108–21.

18. Council Regulation (EEC) No. 302/93 of February 8, 1993, on the establishment of a European Monitoring Centre for Drugs and Drug Addiction, in *Official Journal of the European Communities*, L 36/1-8, February 12, 1993; and Commission of the European Communities, *Communication from the Commission to the Council and the European Parliament on a European Union Action Plan to Combat Drugs (1995–1999)*, Com (94) 234 final, Brussels, June 23, 1994.

19. National Institute on Drug Abuse, Community Epidemiology Work Group, *Epidemiologic Trends in Drug Abuse*, vol. 1: *Highlights and Summary* (U.S. Department of Health and Human Services, June 1994).

20. Similar contradictions exist in public attitudes toward prescription drugs. Although the consumption of illicit drugs to relieve such conditions as anxiety, depression, pain, and grief is routinely and openly condemned, self-medication with prescribed antidepressants and painkillers, which can lead to similar kinds of dependency, remains largely beyond reproach—if it is acknowledged at all.

21. Similar suggestions have been made before. See Peter Stoker, "A Rough Ride for Prevention," *International Journal on Drug Policy*, vol. 3, no. 2 (1992), p. 69.

22. Although the situation is reportedly improving as the proportion of the developing world's children enrolled in primary school has risen by two-thirds in thirty years (from 48 percent in 1960 to 78 percent in 1990), there are many street children who never receive a formal education or who drop out very quickly. See United Nations International Drug Control Program, "Drugs and Development," discussion paper prepared for the World Summit on Social Development, June 1994, p. 14.

23. The latter entails agreeing to swap a specific portion of the outstanding debt into a local currency fund that could be used to underwrite specific drug prevention programs. The general idea is laid out in "The Role of International Financial Institutions (IFIs) in Drug Abuse Control and the Ability of Those Institutions to Promote Economic Stability and Undermine the Drug Industry," UNDCP discussion note prepared for meeting of the ACC Sub-Committee on Coordination in Matters of International Drug Abuse Control, September 6–8, 1993.

24. The idea of moving toward "interoperable criminal justice systems" was proposed by Phil Williams at the Brookings Institution Workshop on "Global Responses to the Transnational Drug Challenge," July 7–8, 1994.

25. For a thorough description of the treaty on European Union and its relevance to the drug issue, see Georges Estievenart, "The European Community and the Global Drug Phenomenon," in Estievenart, ed., *Policies and Strategies to Combat Drugs in Europe: The Treaty on European Union: Framework for a New European Strategy to Combat Drugs?* (Netherlands: Martinus Nijhoff, 1995), pp. 83–90.

26. *Ministerial Agreement on the Establishment of the Europol Drugs Unit*, Copenhagen, June 2, 1993.

27. Since the mid-1980s the European Community customs authorities have been exchanging drug liaison officers, some of whom have been posted to key transit and producer countries. In 1989 the Mutual Assistance Group, established originally by the Naples convention, was reinvigorated under an initiative known as MAG92 to develop compatible plans for customs controls in a single market. For a more detailed description of these various initiatives, see Commission of the European Communities, *Communication from the Commission to the Council and the European Parliament on a European Action Plan*, especially Annex 1, pp.

35–43. See also General Accounting Office, *Drugs: International Efforts to Attack a Global Problem*, NSIAD-93-165 (June 1993).

28. Some of these initiatives are discussed in General Accounting Office, *Drug Control: Status Report on Counterdrug Technology Development*, NSIAD-93-104 (January 1993).

29. Rupert Bruce, "Offshore Financial Centers Move to Shake Stigma of Shadiness," *International Herald Tribune*, February 11–12, 1995, p. 13; and David A. Andelman, "The Drug Money Maze," *Foreign Affairs*, vol. 73 (July–August 1994), pp. 94–108.

30. Andelman, "Drug Money Maze," p. 107. I am also very grateful for suggestions made by Martin Meyer and Wolfgang Reinicke at the Brookings Institution Workshop on "Global Responses to the Transnational Drug Challenge," July 7–8, 1994.

Index

GL🌐BAL HABIT

By all indications the market for illicit drugs is expanding inexorably around the world. More kinds of drugs are becoming more available in more places than ever before. In the process, the drug trade has ceased to be a marginal area of criminal activity and has now become a major global enterprise. With retail sales believed to be between $180 billion and $300 billion a year, the international drug trade is one of the biggest commercial activities in the world.

In this book, Paul Stares presents a compelling portrait of the rise of the global drug market and the powerful forces that are driving and aiding its expansion. The immense profits from selling drugs not only provide strong incentives to enlarge the market, but also give the principal trafficking organizations formidable power to corrupt and intimidate public officials and institutions, especially in areas where government authority is weak. As the ability of nations to control what comes across their borders and what takes place within them has diminished because of declining trade barriers, economic deregulation, and revolutionary advances in communications technology, it has become easier to traffic drugs and launder the proceeds. And with the end of the cold war, new areas of the world have opened up for the drug trade.

As Stares argues, the push-and-pull factors propelling the global drug market show no sign of abating and could intensify in coming years. In many countries of the developing and post-communist world, new drug markets are already emerging that could grow significantly, with ominous implications for these countries' economic development and political stability — to say nothing of the health of their citizens.

What can be done about this growing problem? One commonly proposed option is legalization, but Stares contends that its implementation would be problematic and its benefits uncertain. He argues instead for a fundamental shift away from the current emphasis on negative sanctions to deter and deny drug production, trafficking, and consumption to more positive control